D1445978

7/15

WORKINGMAN'S WIFE

Her Personality, World and Life Style

BY

LEE RAINWATER
RICHARD P. COLEMAN
GERALD HANDEL

preface by

W. LLOYD WARNER
UNIVERSITY OF CHICAGO

introduction by

BURLEIGH B. GARDNER
SOCIAL RESEARCH, INC.

OCEANA PUBLICATIONS, INC.
New York

CONTENTS

Acknowledgments   IV

Preface   V

Introduction   IX

PART I
THE PSYCHOSOCIAL WORLD OF THE
WORKINGMAN'S WIFE

   I. The Working Class in America   15

  II. Day In, Day Out   26

 III. Inner Life and the Outer World   42

 IV. The Man in Her Life   67

  V. Nature's Law: Motherhood   88

 VI. Friendly Relations   103

VII. Not All Americans Are Joiners   114

VIII. Morality and Hope: The Case of *True Story*   126

PART II
CONSUMER BEHAVIOR

 IX. Dollar Decisions   145

  X. Priorities and Preferences   168

 XI. Blue Collar Aesthetics   184

PART III
STRATEGY IN MARKETING AND ADVERTISING

XII. Reaching the Workingman's Wife   205

    Bibliography   217

    Methodological Appendix   219

    Index   237

ACKNOWLEDGMENTS

This book reports on observations made of the working class house-wives in a variety of socio-psychological studies conducted at Social Research, Inc. over a period of twelve years. We wish to acknowledge all of our colleagues at Social Research, Inc. who have contributed in the way of ideas and research effort.

We are particularly indebted to two of them, Harriett Bruce Moore and Sidney J. Levy for their stimulation and encouragement, and for their perception in understanding the psyche and world of housewives of all social classes. Dr. Levy was also kind enough to analyze a set of figure drawings useful in understanding the personality of the working class wife.

W. Lloyd Warner has, over the years, both as teacher and consult-ant on these studies, given us much help, as has William E. Henry in some of the earlier stage of our investigations. Martin B. Loeb, as a consultant in the initial stage of the study which forms the core of our analysis, was particularly helpful in clarifying some of the issues of the working class style of life.

Mrs. Leone W. Phillips, Social Research's Field Director, supervised many complex sets of interviews, and gave us the kind of data we needed to work with. We also owe a large measure of thanks to the many interviewers and the many respondents who, through their con-versations, produced the data used in this study.

Macfadden Publications, Inc. has sponsored a number of studies concerned particularly with the working class housewife, and provided us with the necessary support to organize and collate many of the find-ings reported here. Everett R. Smith, their Director of Research, has been both client and stimulating critic. We wish to thank him for his continuing interest in full socio-psychological investigation of this group of women. Others at Macfadden Publications have also given stimulus to a kind of research which provides business with usable knowledge about the wage earner group: Irving S. Manheimer, Lee Andrews, Gene Waggaman and Helen Smith.

Finally, we wish to thank Charles B. McCann for his editorial as-sistance, and Mrs. Frances C. Strauss for making the preparation of the manuscript as easy as it could possibly be.

PREFACE

The present study of the wives of American working men is a notable advance in the development of our knowledge about the lives of the ordinary Americans who compose most of our population and whose beliefs and values play a significant part in our culture and its future. In my opinion it also has moved ahead methodologically. The research successfully combines the several disciplines of the social and psychological sciences in an effort to learn about the broad sweep of American life and to study in depth the intimate lives and the private worlds of the individuals who are the wives and mothers of working men and their families. These statements need further elaboration. To see the present work in its proper perspective, we must examine the background of earlier research on social class in America which led to the present investigation of one of the largest, most important, and least known American groups.

For some twenty years the study of social class in the United States has greatly contributed to our understanding of American behavior and has equipped us with valuable tools to use in applying social science to the practical affairs of everyday life. During this time the social and psychological sciences have investigated the subcultures which compose the several layers of class in American communities. They have also examined the child training methods of the different strata, isolating the social processes that produce children with personalities predisposed to remain at their own levels or those ready to climb to higher positions. From these researches we have learned how the class order is maintained through the generations as an open system where men and their families may move upward or remain at the station to which they were born.

Other investigations have studied the effect of social class on the intellectual and social performances of children in our public and private schools. They have learned how our schools, although with a deserved reputation for democratic principles, have helped reinforce the earlier pre-school training of the infant and child in his family. In fact many aspects of our society, from income and occupation to political behavior, have been subjected to the social class analyst's scrutiny and most have yielded results showing that the status position of a man and his family is a potent determiner of what they feel, think and do.

It is not strange, it must be added, that Americans at the several levels, so conditioned, respond differently to the several symbol systems of our national life, particularly the media of the masses. The print of newspapers and magazines, the pictures and sounds of TV and radio, and the advertising appeals and meanings of the products that are thus communicated are likely to have different significances for the several class levels. To those of us who have done research on markets, media, and class behavior it does not surprise that the same ideas, the same human dilemmas, in fact at times the same plots which fail to excite the interest of the mass audience when presented in the symbolic format of classical theatre over TV, may rate in the top ten for mass appeal when shown within the outward form of a horse opera. These studies, of which the present one is an excellent example, have given us many subtle insights into the relations of social class, symbolic behavior, and human motivation.

Until recently, despite the many excellent researches, the investigation of social class on a nationwide basis, particularly the analysis of it in great metropolitan agglomerations, as well as the study of its manifestations at the working class levels, had not been undertaken. Instead we make do with the often misleading status indices of amount of rent paid, or income and occupation. We conveniently forgot that the values of a family and the motivations of its members to buy or sell, do or not do something, care or not care about the things in the world around them, may have little relation to such rough market measurements of status. The present study of social class behavior is reliably placed on a national basis; it does examine metropolitan areas with class procedures; it does study the least known of all Americans, the wives of working class men; and it does successfully make use of social and psychological disciplines. Hence its substantive and methodological importance.

I wish now to examine and interpret one of the book's significant findings, the pervasive anxiety among those women studied. To do so, I wish to place the results in a somewhat different framework.

The American society in which these women live is an emergent one; change is structured into the nature of its being. What it is now and will be tomorrow can be understood only in terms of the paradoxical fact that to be what it is now it must perforce be on the way toward being something different than it is today. Consequently, all individuals, men and women, in our culture cannot, on reaching maturity, as they do in most cultures, stop learning. To maintain their adaptation to the real world around them (and in them, for that matter) they must forever be learning to relate themselves to a reality that is continually becoming something new. To be more specific and concrete, our scientific technology has research and change built into it and not only change but accumulated and accelerating change. Moreover, while the common core-values of our culture constantly remold and tame the new developments in family life, in economic life, in labor and leisure, as well as in politics and even in our conceptions of the nature of Deity, emergent change is an integral part of them all. These new developments are not so much additions as something which emerges as a natural product of the immediate past.

While such change may be exciting for some and provide opportunity for mental and physical adventure and wholesome achievement for many, there are few Americans who will not feel anxious about what takes place as part of this cultural process. The wives of working men, being less well equipped educationally than their sisters in the upper middle class, experience these developments not only as rewards with increased incomes, leisure and other valued experiences, but also (I suspect from this study) with a sense of inadequacy and feel an inability to cope with the new conditions that surround them and invade the privacies of their inner lives.

Moreover, they do not live in a "closed" social class system where there is no mobility and each stays within the security of his own place; they are in an open class order where there is a high degree of fluidity. Given these circumstances—the flux of time, the fluidity of status and position, and the flow of people from city to city and region to region—it would be maladaptive for them to be anything else than anxious about the changing realities about them.

If one is fitted into a tight little social system where each knows, and everyone around him knows, what his or her place is and the society rigidly holds to its traditional past, the thinking about oneself or about what one must think and do are less important mental commodities for adaptation and survival. Or, to say it more positively, individual autonomy with individual choice making are necessary equipment for people living in a fluid world. Given a world which is constantly in change and does not go on being what it was, anxiety is these women's natural lot.

The authors of this book, I believe, have examined the most conservative members of our society. Within the women are imbedded the deep and enduring values of our culture. They carry the central and largest core of our conscious and unconscious life. Unlike those above them, they are trained to be women who are not the life time competitors of men in the job market, but to grow as daughters into wives and mothers and then to train once again those of the new generation who in their turn will be like them. Their roles are highly restricted, the principles and precepts that guide their thought and often rule their conduct are rooted in the early beginnings and foundations of American culture. Compared with women of the upper middle classes who are professionally conscious and taught to have the second thoughts of the college educated, they are more conservative and traditionally oriented. Yet when compared with the same kind of women one or two generations ago they are far more independent and necessarily more autonomous. The rapidly changing outside world has not only revolutionized the physical arena where they act out their lives, but drastically re-ordered the traditional sanctuaries of their immediate families and invaded the innermost recesses of their personalities, their unconscious privacies. They too must themselves be adaptive, flexible, emergent beings. There's no hiding place down here. The meaning of life for them is largely class bound and traditional. But within them the fluid world of today is too rapidly being invaded by tomorrow for emotional comfort.

Whatever may be their destiny they share their anxieties with all of us. They cannot know whether their world is hell bent for heaven or hell bent for hell. But, for that matter, neither can anyone else. The price they and other Americans pay for progress must necessarily include anxiety—anxiety about the real world about them and about the necessarily unresolved internal problems of personalities that have come into being in such a world.

W. LLOYD WARNER
University of Chicago

INTRODUCTION

An increasingly important, and economically substantial segment of our society—the working class—has, in the past, received only glancing attention from most of the writers reporting on the American class system. Recently, however, the economic importance of this class is beginning to be recognized. The fact is that the members of the working class in America form a group of major importance to every company which seeks a mass market for its products or services. This group is of vital concern to every advertiser who uses the mass media, and it is the target of most of the advertising communications prepared by American advertising agencies. Unfortunately, many of the businesses which, to operate profitably, must sell to or communicate with this class, fail to recognize its importance or its existence. These businesses do not recognize either the economic power of the group, or the differences inherent in it, which make communicating with it a special kind of problem. It is the purpose of this book to set forth in some detail the life style of the working class family, and to provide some clues regarding how best to reach these people with advertising and sales messages.

Since 1940, we have seen a steady growth in the income and consumption level of the working class family. As consumers they are no longer restricted to the basic needs of food, clothing, and shelter. They need no longer limit themselves to the cheapest possible products. Now, in fact, they have become a tremendous market, and often the major market, for a fantastic range of products.

No producer of consumer goods can expect to join the ranks of the "Billion Dollar" corporations unless it produces and sells with an eye on the working class consumer. Some indication of the power of this market is shown by the growth of certain corporations or businesses which took as a goal service and sales to the working class. Sears, Roebuck and Co. is an outstanding example. From the time that Sears moved into retail operations, it has deliberately catered to the tastes and desires of the masses of America. In 1940, when the working class was just recovering from the Great Depression, Sears' volume was $700,000,000. Today, the company's annual sales are over $3,000,000,000. It was during this period—the years 1940 to the present —that the working class was expanding its level of consumption at an unprecedented rate.

Even in the financial field, in the business of lending and saving, the power of the blue collar worker has been felt. The savings and loan associations, which cater heavily to the working class, have enjoyed spectacular growth. Their combined assets have jumped from $5.7 billion in 1940 to $52.7 billion today.[1] While there is no specific data regarding the share of this growth attributable to the working class, it is evident that blue collar families constitute the majority of depositors.

Concurrent with the great expansion of working class savings, members of the class have also greatly increased their use of borrowed money. During the period under consideration, the personal finance companies have enjoyed a fabulous growth. With high wages and stable jobs, the factory workers have become excellent credit risks and companies, such as Household Finance Corp., have not hesitated to advance money. In fact, this one company has increased its lending from $159,000,000 in 1940 to $833,000,000 today.

Members of the working class are also avid users of consumer credit through installment buying. Here again, Sears, Roebuck and Co. is a case in point. In 1940, 31% of its sales were made on credit. In 1957, that figure was up to 46%.

Evidence of the numbers and strength of this segment of the population continues to pile up.

A report by Macfadden Publications, Inc. tells us that 73% of all families in the $3,000 to $5,000 income group are working class families. In addition, working class families comprise 52% of all families with income in excess of $5,000 per year.[2] This is not merely a mass market. It is a massive market.

Furthermore, this group has been increasing in buying power faster than any other group in the society. President Griswold of Yale University pointed out in a recent speech that "The buying power in the past sixteen years has increased 64% for industrial workers as compared to 29% for lawyers and 12% for college teachers." And Arno H. Johnson vice president and senior economist of J. Walter Thompson Company, in a speech given September 8, 1958,[3] said:

> Prewar, our economy was typified by the $25 a week family—average weekly earnings for production workers in manufacturing, in 1940, were $25.20. The "middle income" family, for example, fell in the $1,000 to $1,500 income group. Now the "middle income" family is in the $4,000 to $6,000 income group. Weekly earnings in manufacturing, by July 1958 had grown to $83.50 or $3\frac{1}{3}$ times the 1940 level. Even after correction for inflation that is an increase of over 60% in *real* wages.

It is clear that the working class is a group whose economic status has undergone dramatic improvement. Given the steadily increasing industrialization and urbanization of American society, the implications are clear that the group will continue to have tremendous importance in the economy of the nation.

Although today's wage earners do have tremendous buying and consuming power, they are still consumers with a set of rather special characteristics. *They are not just like everyone else* now that they have money to spend. Not everyone recognizes this, however, As Pierre Martineau points out:

> It seems that many an economist overlooks the possibility of any psychological differences between individuals resulting from different class membership. It is assumed that a rich man is simply a poor man with more money and that, given the same income, the poor man would behave exactly like the rich man. The *Chicago Tribune* studies crystallize a wealth of evidence from other sources that this is just not so, and that the Lower-Status person is profoundly different in his mode of thinking and his way of handling the world from the Middle-Class individual. Where he buys and what he buys will differ not only by economics but in symbolic value.[5]

Arno Johnson added his note to this comment when he pointed out that the

> Mass millions are climbing the income ladder—into areas of high consumption potential,

but

> As these families move up from one income class to the next, they could represent substantially increased markets for goods, services, and investments if only they were to take on the habits and desires of the income group into which they move. This is true even though taxes and the cost of living have increased.

> But there are reasons why they don't take on these new habits automatically. Their whole previous lifetime training, in most cases, was built around a different concept of how to live. There is a major job for advertising and selling to change these concepts and educate our population to desire and work for the better standard of living their increased productive ability justifies—a change in line with the changes in income now available as *discretionary* spending power. Shortening the "Habit Lag" can make possible a rapid resumption of growth in our economy.[6]

And further, as Martineau pointed out, "Even in their fantasies, people are governed by class membership. In his day-dreaming and wishful thinking, the Lower-Status individual will aspire in different patterns from the Middle-Class individual."[7] With all these class differences, it is also easy to see why the saving and spending habits of the working class differ sharply from those of the upper middle class.

These class differences have important implications for the manufacturer or merchant. Here is a vast group of consumers who have their own special dreams and desires, their own value systems, their own way of reacting to products, to advertising, or to sales messages. The advertiser who wants to talk meaningfully to these people must understand the symbols and messages which will have the most meaning to them. He must, in short, understand *how* to talk to them.

Unfortunately, the working class group seems to be poorly understood by both social scientists and business men. Frequently, the executive comes from the world of the white collar family or the executive or professional group. Thus, his whole life experience has been in a world strikingly different from that of a working class person living "on the wrong side of the tracks" and associating with people of modest attainments and even modest expectations.

This lack of understanding or even sensitivity toward the working class is often strikingly clear in mass communications. Over the years, Social Research, Inc. has studied countless advertisements which were in many subtle ways talking only to the higher status groups. The reactions of wage earners to such advertisements, we have found, ranges from indifference and apathy to downright hostility.

A striking example of some of the problems of communication between upper middle class advertising people and the working class readers was shown in studies conducted by Dr. Rudolph Flesch for Macfadden Women's Group.[8] Dr. Flesch, author of the well known, *The Art of Plain Talk*,[9] devised a rating system to determine whether writing would be hard or easy to read. When he applied this system to a group of advertisements which had already been studied by Starch, he found that the ads with the highest "read most" scores were also the easiest to read based on his rating system. On the other hand, ads with the lowest Starch rating were difficult to read based on the Flesch system.

This lack of understanding between middle class people (who are usually the creative people and decision makers) and members of the working class is illustrated again by media judgments. Generally, the executives with their higher levels of education and their more sophisticated tastes, look down on many of the mass communications which, we find, are so important to the working class. Thus the behavior magazines or soap operas, which are strong media in the working class, are intensely disliked by the majority of upper middle class people. They fail to recognize that such media, despite their own likes and dislikes, are clear channels of communication to the working class.

From all indications, the blue collar class will continue, as a consuming group, to increase in importance. With the urban expansion, and the rise of the "belt cities" extending across the country, there will be new and tremendous aggregations of working class people. Furthermore, one of the effects of all efforts to stabilize the economy will be to increase the stability of this class as a major group of consumers.

Although social scientific studies of the working class have had a long history, most of the early work in the field dealt with a class of people who were economically depressed and socially deprived. For example, E. Wight Bakke of Yale University contributed a classic to the field with his study of the unemployed worker during the Great Depression.[10] In 1929, Professor W. Lloyd Warner started his studies of modern communities. It was during the course of these studies that the American social class system was delineated and the various social class groups were examined in detail.[11]

Recent research, dealing with a more economically privileged working class, is revealing more and more about the modern working class and its customs, habits and life style under the changed economic conditions. Social Research, Inc., for example, has been almost constantly engaged in studies of this class—studies of its buying habits, of its reactions to media and advertising, and of its understanding of sales communications presumably directed to it. In short, we have attempted to learn how to talk most effectively to the members of the blue collar class.

Over the past ten years, Social Research has worked closely with Macfadden Publications on a number of specific studies of the working class group.[12] In addition, through its consumer panel and through other studies, Macfadden has accumulated a vast body of information on many aspects of the working class woman: her way of life, her consuming habits, her attitudes and opinions. This book, therefore, represents a drawing together of much that has been learned in a wide variety of studies. The studies for Macfadden have been combined with information derived from many sources, to provide a better understanding of the working class. We believe that all who must deal with mass communications and mass markets will find in its pages significant insights and information. And we are firmly convinced that effective communication to these women requires understanding of them and their lives.

BURLEIGH B. GARDNER

Chicago, 1959

INTRODUCTION

FOOTNOTES TO INTRODUCTION

1. United States Saving and Loan League. *Savings and Loan Fact Book,* 1958.
2. True Story Women's Group. *The New America.* New York: Macfadden Publications, 1957, p. 13.
3. Johnson, Arno H. "The Economic Outlet"—an address given before the Ebasco Client Companies, Sales and Public Relations Work Shop, New York, September, 1958.
5. Martineau, Pierre. "Social Classes and Spending Behavior," *The Journal of Marketing,* Vol. 23, No. 2, October, 1958.
6. Johnson, *op. cit.*
7. Martineau, *op. cit.,* p. 129.
8. Rudolph Flesch. *A Study of What Makes it Hard or Easy to Read.*
9. Flesch, Rudolph. *The Art of Plain Talk.* New York: Harper and Bros., 1946.
10. Bakke, E. Wight. *Citizen Without Work: A Study of the Effects of Unemployment upon the Workers' Social Relations and Practices.* New Haven: Yale University Press, 1940. Also: *The Unemployed Worker: A Study of the Task of Making a Living Without a Job.* New Haven: Yale University Press, 1940.
11. Warner, W. Lloyd, *The Yankee City Series.* New Haven: Yale University Press. Vol. I. (with Paul S. Lunt), *The Social Life of a Modern Community,* 1941. Vol. II. (with Paul S. Lunt), *The Status Systems of a Modern Community,* 1942. Vol. III. (with Leo Srole), *Social Systems of American Ethnic Groups,* 1945. Vol. IV. (with J. O. Low), *The Social System of the Modern Factory,* 1947. Vol. V. *The Living and the Dead,* (in press; to be published Spring, 1959).
12. Report on Center City, 1949; The Meaning and Function of *True Story* for Its Readers, 1955; Personal and Social Characteristics of *True Story* Readers and the Meaning of *True Story* to Them, 1955; The Family Behavior Group House-Wife Market, 1957, 1958 and continuing.

Part I

THE PSYCHOSOCIAL WORLD OF THE WORKINGMAN'S WIFE

CHAPTER I

THE WORKING CLASS IN AMERICA

The working class is the largest social class in our society, yet it is the one which most businessmen, professionals, and even social scientists know least about. This is not surprising since most of them grew up in families which had some pride in not being of that group, families which bent their efforts to being and staying part of the middle class of white collar workers, businessmen and professionals. The chances are that even those who have been socially mobile, who grew up in a working class family but have moved on in adult life, no longer have a clear understanding of what a working class life is like; the mobile person must "unlearn" much of what his background has taught him if he is to be successful in his ambition to get ahead in the world. In retrospect, he may romanticize or damn or perhaps just ignore what life was like in the working class milieu he knew as a child.

Yet, the significant events in our society are heavily dependent on what goes on in this group. Before we discuss this point, however, a preliminary definition of what the working class is will be helpful. By working class we mean that social level in our society which used to be characterized as "poor, but honest." As we shall see, the first part of the statement must be modified; the working class family is no longer accurately described as poor, even though it may not be as financially well off as a middle class family. Perhaps the most general way in which people divide society into working and middle class in by using the "collar-color" criterion. We Americans generally make a distinction between "blue collar" workers and "white collar." We generally group together those families in which the main breadwinner works with his hands at some manual task, or in which he performs what is traditionally a relatively menial service. Such people are usually rated lower socially than those who work primarily with their "heads," and those who work through relationships with other people—like the salesman. Such criteria are not absolute, however. Certain highly skilled manual workers, like tool-and-die makers, will generally rank higher socially than such white collar workers as the clerk in a dime store. Almost coinciding with the collar-color criterion is the form of a man's income. The salary earner and the profit taker are generally ranked higher socially than the wage earner. This, too, is an imperfect division; the profit-taking pushcart operator will not be accorded the prestige of the railroad engineer.

In short, social class is not the result of any one criterion, but rather represents a constellation of things about a man and his family, including most critically their way of living and of earning that living. It is important to note that social class is not primarily a matter of income. An individual's placement by others in his community will depend much more on *how* he gets his income, and *how* he spends it, than it will on the absolute amount. Thus, the $9,000 a year gasoline truck driver will be accorded a lower social status than the $5,000 a year college instructor. On the average, of course, the higher the income, the higher the social status, but this has become decreasingly true with each rise in the unionized bargaining power of the working class.

The working class, whose housewives are the subject of this book, must, then, be complexly defined. It is composed of families in which the head of the household is usually a blue collar worker, and they usually live in neighborhoods populated mainly by other wage earning blue collar families. The white collar, lower middle class individual and the business or professional upper middle class person regard themselves as socially a step or two above such working class people. The latter recognize the social reality of this distinction even if they do not thereby feel that they must hang their heads in shame.

Social class in a democratic society is always a subject of some ambivalence, since we believe that people should be equal, but know that in day to day life they are not always treated as equals. Our solution is generally to believe that all people are essentially "good" even though their experience in life give them higher or lower social prestige, and greater or lesser amounts of the goods which the society has to offer.

Thus, we can speak of the working class which is composed of over half of the population and which, as research has recurrently shown, shapes many ways of thinking, feeling and acting. We cannot be too exact about the proportion of working class people, even non-farm families, because census-type studies do not ordinarily involve the complex criteria required to assess social status. Nevertheless, we do know that about 60% of urban families are wage earner families, and that the proportion of such families in the population has been steadily increasing during the past fifty years. We known that in those communities that have been intensively studied, by methods of social class analysis, the proportion of working class families has varied from a low of slightly less than 60% in less industrialized communities, to a high of almost three-quarters of the population in such highly industrialized communities as Gary, Indiana. We are discussing, then, a group which composes perhaps 60% to 65% of the non-farm population. (Our discussion applies only to the non-farm group since our

16

research experience with farm families is quite limited.)

The working class life in America has undergone dramatic changes in the last twenty to fifty years. While all social groups have participated in the growing prosperity of the country, it is through growing job security and in the increase of leisure time that those in the working class have experienced the greatest improvement. Frederick Lewis Allen, in his book, *The Big Change*,[1] details some of the shifts in experience and way of life since the early 1900's. In those days, the working class was primarily a poor class. It was poor both because it received a smaller share of the total income of the country, and also because that income was much smaller (even in dollars of constant purchasing power) than it is today. Even within a decade, the changes can be great. Galbraith notes, in *The Affluent Society*,[2] that from 1941 to 1950 people whose incomes were below average for the country experienced increases in purchasing power of about 40%, compared to an increase of about 20% for those with above average incomes. Changes in income and its distribution have been so dramatic that Galbraith asserts that economic inequality is no longer a really crucial issue in our society; he believes it has been relegated to the status of political rhetoric. Similarly, he points out that poverty has become, in modern America, a special problem of social or psychological pathology, and no longer is primarily an economic problem.

As with such economic issues as income and purchasing power, so with more social changes. The working class, fifty years ago, was heavily immigrant in composition. Today, most of its members are native born, and within another generation there will be few whose parents were not also born here. The Negro sector of the working class constitutes a distinctly different problem, so this research does not include working class Negro women within its realm of concern.

The difference in working class life brought about by a heavier proportion of native born is obviously great. The native born working class person feels much more at home in his society, and he feels more securely that it *is* his, even though he may have a lower social position in it. His purchasing habits will differ, not only because he has more money than his parents had, but also because his consumer goals are not even partially formed in the "old country."

The other big change in way of life has grown out of the shorter work week, with its promise of increased leisure time. Fifty years ago industrial work weeks averaged over sixty hours; today the average is less than forty hours. This is, of course, the basic week. A worker can often work overtime, or he may take a second job on a part-time basis, or operate as a part-time independent contractor, and thus supplement his income. But the choice is up to him, and he gets paid handsomely if he chooses to take on this extra work. The ten hour

17

day and the six day week meant that the working class family, *qua* family, had little time with the breadwinner, particularly since—as legend has it—the men spent more of their after work hours "drinking with the boys." It will be apparent in the discussion in later chapters that working class people do not make as varied use of their leisure time as social scientists believe they should. Even so, the greater leisure available to them has certainly meant an increased feeling of well-being, and also an increased incentive toward the purchase of all kinds of goods.

We are dealing, then, with a group which not only looms large numerically, but also with the group which has participated most dramatically in the economic and social changes this country has experienced during this century. Yet, not only do most of us know little about this group of people, but what we do think we know will often be no more than an image of the working class held over from earlier eras.

Certainly this is true in terms of a political understanding of the working class. Political parties seem remarkably resistant to the implications of the changes which the group has experienced in the last ten, or twenty, or even fifty years. Businessmen often seem to orient themselves to the working class as if it were still poor, and therefore relatively unimportant as a market, or uneducated (although the majority now graduate from high school), or totally bargain-basement-minded. Or, we go to another extreme and conclude that because the working class is prosperous and rather well educated compared to earlier years, it really exists no longer and its members are not really different from the white collar class.

Those who must deal with the group in terms of social welfare functions often do not understand them much better. Doctors and nurses often find it difficult to understand why these people do not exhibit the same sophisticated attitudes toward medical care that middle class people show. School teachers and administrators are perplexed by the lower interest in school which many working class parents and children display, even when the child is encouraged to stick it out until high school graduation. Home economics and consumer experts worry because the group does not share the standards of quality and appropriateness of goods which these professionals feel they should.

Yet, solutions to many pressing economic, political and social problems require a better understanding of what working class people are like, and why they act as they do. Advertising and merchandising to such a large group clearly profit from a better understanding of how these people think about consuming, and why they show the purchasing patterns they do. The group becomes increasingly dominant in the market, and no really mass market product or brand can succeed without attracting a large share of the working class. The shift, for example, from 35% to 65% penetration of a new appliance depends primarily on making that appliance an imagined necessity to the working class housewives described in the following chapters.

Various pressing social problems require a better appreciation of working class life and personality. Juvenile delinquency has always been concentrated in this group, and in recent years seems to have increased in prevalence among that very group of working class families who have experienced the greatest relative increase in prosperity; that is, among the children of semi-skilled industrial workers. Hollingshead and Redlich describe, in their recent book, *Social Class and Mental Illness*,[3] a relationship between social class and mental disease, generally, as well as in its seriousness. Consequently, working class families contribute significantly more patients than do middle class families (although it should be noted that this is most dramatically true of the lowest fourth of the working class). Although many a business executive likes to think of his ulcer as the wound-stripe of success and responsibility, actually the prevalence of psychosomatic disease in all its forms is greater among the working class than in the middle class.

The subject of this book, however, is not the whole of the working class. Our particular concern is the working class wife and mother, the housewife who keeps the household and family going while the husband earns their keep (and sometimes she helps with that, too, although her major definition of herself is almost always as wife and mother, not as worker). Further, we shall be concerned with the relatively young working class housewife, rather than with the older woman whose chidren have grown up. Because we wish to concentrate our attention on the social class factor, we have not tried to discuss variation in style of life or personality or consumer behavior in terms of age, but have taken as our group those housewives who have children and are still in the child-bearing age. We know that this is the period of greatest significance to the woman. Before she becomes a wife, and then a mother, she regards herself as getting ready for that role decreed by society and nature; as her children grow up the working class woman is inclined to feel that her life is "over." It is in the child-bearing and mothering years, then, that we find the working class woman most fully engaged with life.

It should be apparent that it is in this period that the working class woman is of greatest interest to those whose work involves her as a customer, a client, or a "case." As a wife and mother, she occupies a central place in the family and in the destinies of her children. It is she on whom the brunt of child-rearing falls, and whose behavior counts most in determining what kind of people her children will grow up to be, what problems they will have, and how they will act as citizens, consumers, and parents of another generation. (Our society is so "mother" conscious, that it is perhaps needless to labor this point.)

In terms of consumer behavior, the working class housewife is of particular importance. As will be shown, she usually controls the family finances, and she certainly does most of the shopping. In this area, her duties involve the purchase of those products which take up the lion's share of the family budget: food, household maintenance products and furnishings, cosmetics and toiletries, clothing, appliances (which are primarily for her use). If selling to the working class is the prerequisite to building a mass market product and brand, then selling to the housewife in that class is the key to such success.

The individual, or organization, which offers products or services to the working class housewife profits from an understanding of what she is like and why she acts as she does. (And this is true whether the primary motive for offering those products and services is profit, or her own welfare. Many educational and social welfare functionaries behave as if their clients require no understanding because the service offered is for their own good.)

But any understanding of why she acts as she does in some area of practical significance cannot come from studying those acts alone. Rather, we need to know some of the basic facts about the working class housewife's personality and life style, about the pressures which bear in on her, and the satisfactions she seeks, before we can understand her or predict her behavior or influence it through counselling or education, or persuasion, or advertising.

Such understanding must ultimately come from a careful study of the woman in her own environment and on her own terms. That is, we must learn something of her personality and its development, about the world in which she must live, and how she sees it. In looking at her world and how she lives in it, we will need to examine her relationships to her husband and her children; the way in which she handles her duties as housewife and housekeeper; the way she relates to those outside the immediate family, to relatives and friends, and to more formal organizations such as clubs, churches, and schools. Such is the goal of the first half of this book.

These socio-psychological characteristics determine the way the working class housewife acts as consumer. These actions and the attitudes, feelings and motives which lie behind them are examined in the second part of the book. We will be concerned with these women's orientation to consuming, with their predispositions to buy and use things, and to buy and use them in particular ways. These predispositions we call her *consuming style*. This consuming style, in turn, strongly conditions and guides her more concrete actions in the day-to-day purchase and consumption of particular products and brands and her pre-purchase response to the advertising for these.

These, then, are the topics which will concern us in the following chapters. As mentioned in Burleigh B. Gardner's introduction, the conclusions offered here about the working class housewife stem both from the results of a wide range of researches over the years at Social Research, Inc., and in universities, and from a particular study conducted for Macfadden Publications, Inc. which investigated the personalities, life style and consumer behavior of a particular group of young working class housewives. These are women who read one of the four Family Behavior Group magazines.

Research experience with working class housewives in Social Research, Inc's motivation research ranges from such topics as sickness and disease, doctors and dentists, to money management and borrowing; from such products as the telephone to sanitary napkins; from such institutions as the department store to big business. Behind such applied research lies a range of studies involving social class and various aspects of human development and behavior, much of it stemming from the basic work of social anthropologist W. Lloyd Warner and his colleagues.[4]

Throughout the book, we will draw upon the study done for Macfadden Publications for examples of the various points made, and we will quote extensively from interview and projective material collected from the young working class housewives and a "contrast" sample of middle class women during that study. (Whenever specific reference is made to numerical sample results from that study, the phrase "our study sample" is used.) This study has provided us with an opportunity to address our attention intensively to the personality, life style and consumer behavior of the working class housewife. We wish, however, to stress that the generalizations made in the following chapters about this group stem not only from our study sample, but are further informed by a range of research done by ourselves and other social scientists.

Our study sample consisted of 420 working class housewives in four cities: Chicago, Louisville, Tacoma, and Trenton. In addition, and in order to provide contrasting material, we interviewed 120 middle class women who were similarly occupied as mothers and wives. The interviews conducted with these women covered the range of topics discussed in the book. Not all the respondents were interviewed with the same questionnaire. The amount of information needed for our analyses was too great for any one woman to supply in a reasonable length of time. The interviews collected averaged an hour and one-half.

Therefore, after preliminary work, three main interview guides were designed.

The first of these probed widely in all three areas studied: personality, social world, and consumption. The second concentrated on personality and the social world, and the third on consumption and family relations. The interviews were primarily qualitative in nature.

Working class respondents and contrast respondents were asked the same questions, and in the same order. The emphasis was on open-ended, conversational interviewing, in which the respondent was encouraged to talk freely and discuss what seemed relevant to her after a topic had been raised by the interviewer. In addition, the interviews involved the use of various standard and specially designed projective techniques, multiple choice objective questions, and directed interviewing about amounts of money involved in the family's budget.

Specifically, the interviews provided the following kinds of information relevant to the working class wife's social and consumer-behavior:

1. Detailed material on present socio-economic status, and background of the wives and their husbands. (We concerned ourselves with such things as occupation, education, housing, neighborhood, association membership, etc.)

2. Material on the housewife's daily routine, and the family's manner of living through the week, the seasons and at holidays. (We found out what she did on normal days and not-so-normal ones, and sought to relate this to the kind of family she had.)

3. Material on her relations with her husband; the kinds of activities she shares with him; the ways they divide the responsibility of running a household; her knowledge of her husband's job; and her hopes and expectations of how he relates to her.

4. Similar material on her relationship with her children; what she wants from them; and how she deals with them; the kind of image she has of children, and their overall importance in her way of life.

5. Detailed information on her informal social relations—her friends, her preferred social activities, the value she puts on friendship, and the types of people she prefers to be with.

6. Several kinds of data on her participation in voluntary associations and particularly in the church; the extent of her participation; the kinds of organizations to which she belongs, her feelings about religion and club life, and her hopes in these areas.

7. Her attitudes and behavior toward some of the more formal social institutions: government and politics, education, the neighborhood community, and the economic order and her place in it.

8. The present pattern of family possessions; ways in which the family's income is spent and managed; feelings about money management, shopping and purchase decisions.

9. Aspirations for the future in terms of products and services; interest in different kinds of products; ways in which planning is made for future purchases; and goals sought through these purchases.

10. Patterns of taste and aesthetics in connection with furnishings, appliances and clothing. Sensitivity to taste and style changes, and importance of aesthetic considerations in buying and use.

On all these points, data were collected through our open-ended conversational interviews. The interviewer simply raised a topic (for example: "Tell me about what your normal daily routine is like?") and then would carry on probing until that area had been adequately covered. In a later phase of the field work, we constructed a series of multiple choice questions, based on the way women talked in the first 200 interviews, to pin down some of the dominant patterns in various areas, such as the husband, the children, friendships, religion, politics, etc. These quantitative instruments provided us with a simple index of some of the more complicated patterns which emerged from the open-ended interviewing.

Most of the material collected and assessed as having primary relevance to the social world, proved to be important in the personality analysis. When a woman tells about a *thing*, she also tells quite a bit about *herself*. The material on family relations was particularly revelant to the personality analysis. However, we used additional techniques designed specifically to get at aspects of the personality.

The main instrument used in the personality analysis was the Thematic Apperception Test. This test involves the analysis of stories which people tell to pictures. The pictures are selected to represent various life situations and problems. The respondent tells a story to each picture and projects her point of view in the story. Analysis of each story reveals the teller's basic orientation and her typical ways of feeling, and of dealing with problems. It provides evidence of the way the personality is organized, probing both the more conscious and the unconscious levels of personality. The test has been widely used in studies of normal personality for both basic and applied research purposes.[5]

In all, we collected stories to twenty-four TAT-type pictures. Some of the pictures used were from the original Harvard series, some from the University of Michigan series, some from the Tavistock Institute series, and some from two unpublished series. We used several special projective questions to get more specifically at particular aspects of the

23

personality. For example, we set up a situation in which two women were talking, and we specified that they were discussing the problems one of the women was having with her husband. The stories to this stimulus then were useful in analysing the respondent's conception of a husband-wife relationship under stress. They also revealed the kinds of solutions proposed for such problems. These techniques, while not providing information essentially different from that elicited by the TAT, often sharpened interpretations, and helped to illustrate the findings.

We also had a small group of working class respondents and contrast cases do the Draw-A-Person task, in which the individual is asked to draw a person, and then to draw a companion, of the opposite sex, to the first drawn. This material was analyzed independently, thus providing some check on the analysis carried out by the research team.

This type of research, emphasizing qualitative data, interpretation based on the several social or behavioral sciences, and a somewhat technical vocabulary of analysis—much of which is unfamiliar to those not trained in the social sciences—makes certain demands on the authors. We have tried throughout to introduce as few technical terms as possible and to explain as fully as possible, without interrupting the flow of reporting, those terms which are used, and the specialized methods (like projective techniques) which helped produce the findings.

We believe that this report represents one of the most fully documented motivation researches to date. We have given many excerpts from interviews and projective test protocols to illustrate the data from which we form our conclusions. We have presented, from time to time, fairly detailed examples of our interpretive reasoning. We hope that we have provided enough material for the informed and interested reader to follow the interpretive process. We also are hopeful that the many interview quotes and projective test responses given will prove interesting in and of themselves. They illustrate how these women actually think, and feel and behave, and as such should be of interest to people whose work involves these women as a "market."

One further point concerning the nature of the findings. It is unfortunately true that the language of the social sciences (and not only of clinical psychology, as is sometimes believed) tends to have a rather negative sound to the layman. We speak of "anxiety," of "low status," of "emotional volatility" and the like. Whenever we delve deeply into the dynamics of a personality, whether that of a business executive or of a working class housewife, we are inclined to talk about aspects of the personality in a way which does not conform to everyday optimistic views of people. Therefore, when we look at the personalities of these women, we are likely to say things that, at a quick glance, might seem derogatory. However, it must be remembered that this would be true of a psychological analysis of almost any group of people,[6] and that in the technical language of the social sciences, these words do not carry the same positive or negative loadings that they do in everyday language.

Further, in order to objectively appraise these women, the reader must keep in mind his or her own social class placement. The reader's present life (and family background) are probably far removed from the world in which working class wives and their families live their daily lives. Much of their outlook and many of their values and attitudes are quite different from his own. Yet, from the point of view of the social scientist, both working class and middle class ways of life represent people's constructive or not-so-constructive efforts to accommodate to their environments. The working class woman would have a great deal of difficulty understanding the upper middle class world of values and behavior, but the reader of this report is equally apt to misunderstand the working class world of values and behavior. Yet, the businessman and professional must learn how to deal with the realities of this working class world if he is to do the best possible job of dealing with these people and increasing the vitality of the American business system.

FOOTNOTES TO CHAPTER I

1. Frederick Lewis Allen, *The Big Change*. New York: Harper & Bros., 1952.
2. John K. Galbraith, *The Affluent Society*. Boston: Houghton Mifflin Co., 1958.
3. August B. Hollingshead and Frederick C. Redlich, *Social Class and Mental Illness*. New York: John Wiley and Sons, 1958.
4. Among the more significant works for our study are: W. Lloyd Warner, et al. *Democracy in Jonesville*. N. Y.: Harper & Bros., 1949; W. Lloyd Warner, Robert J. Havighurst, Martin Loeb, *Who Shall Be Educated?* New York: Harper & Bros., 1944; Warner, *American Life-Dream and Reality*. Chicago: University of Chicago Press, 1953; Alison Davis and Robert J. Havighurst, *Father of the Man*. Boston: Houghton, Mifflin Co., 1947; Alison Davis, *Social Class and Influences Upon Learning*. Cambridge: Harvard University Press, 1948; Jergen B. Rausch and Martin Loeb, *Chronic Disease and Psychological Invalidism*. Berkeley, Calif.: University of California Press, 1951; W. Lloyd Warner and William E. Henry, "The Radio Daytime Serial: A Symbolic Analysis," *Genetic Psychology Monographs*, Vol. 37 (1948), 3-71; August B. Hollingshead, *Elmtown's Youth*. New York: John Wiley & Sons, 1949; Hollingshead and Redlich, *op. cit*; Leonard Schatzman and Anselm L. Strauss, "Social Class and Modes of Commonication, *Am. J. Soc.*, Vol. LX, No. 4 (Jan., 1955); Lee Rainwater, "A Study of Personality Differences Between Middle and Lower Class Adolescents: The Szondi Test in Culture-Personality Research," *Genetic Psych. Monographs*, Vol. 4, 1956.
5. See, William E. Henry, *The Analysis of Fantasy: The Thematic Apperception Technique in Study of Personality*. New York: John Wiley and Sons, 1956.
6. The doubting reader might look at W. Lloyd Warner and J. Abegglen, *Big Business Leaders in America*. New York: Harper & Bros., 1955.

CHAPTER II

DAY IN, DAY OUT

We have discussed briefly the social position in the American social hierarchy which is called "working class," and have noted that the women whose lives are being described belong to this class by virtue of their husbands' blue collar jobs, their own and their husbands' modest educational attainments (mostly high school graduation, sometimes less) and their similarly modest housing and residential acquisitions. In this chapter we shall concern ourselves with the way in which these women live their daily lives within such a social context. In our research, we have asked working class women to tell us what their day-to-day activities are and how they feel about these by asking: "What is a typical day like?", "How does the week go?", "How are the weekends different from weekdays?", "What happens at vacation time?", "Which holidays are celebrated?", and "How does winter differ from summer, or spring from fall?".

The way working class and middle class women talk in response to such questions provides us with insight into the variety of activities in which they engage, and indicates the hierarchy or importance of time consumption for them. We learn about the "daily rhythm" in these women's lives and come to some understanding of the "annual round of life"—the adjustments made to the changing seasons and the ways holidays and vacations interrupt the normal routine. Finally, we gain insight into their emotional response to the content of their daily lives.

The working class wife's daily life is centered upon the tasks of homemaking, child-rearing, and husband-servicing. When these women describe a "typical day" they devote most of their reportorial attention to three aspects of the day: their housework, their children, and their husbands. The attention devoted to their children is only partially affected by the age of these children—the mothers of very young children quite naturally believe their "typical days" are consumed by both nurturant and policeman-like attention to these children; however, the mothers of older children seem to be equally wrapped up in the activities of these not-so-necessarily-dependent children. The working class women whose lives seem to contain any other important foci are those who hold jobs. In the following description we occasionally differentiate between the "working women" and the "homemakers only." And, of course, we also find it useful to separate the mothers of older children from those of very young children. However, it is this latter group which we have taken as our main model.

We will let some of these women speak for themselves about their days. These samples are rather typical in the range and kind of daily activity mentioned even though these particular women are more articulate than many in the richness of detail they provide. The first description was given by a 24-year old woman from Trenton, New Jersey. She lives in one of Levittown's modest new houses:

Well, naturally, I get up first, make breakfast for my husband and put a load of clothes in my washer while breakfast cooks. Then I wake him up, give him his breakfast and he's off to work. Then I make breakfast for the children. After the children eat I dress them and they go out to play. Then I hang the clothes up and clean lightly through the house. In between times I do the dishes—that's understood, of course. Then I make lunch for the children and myself and I bring them in, clean them up, and they eat. I send them out to play when they're done and I do the dishes, bring the clothes in, and iron them. When I'm done ironing it's usually time to make supper, or at least start preparing it. Sometimes I have time to watch a TV story for half an hour or so. Then my husband comes home and we have our meals. Then I do the dishes again. Then he goes out to work again—he has a part-time job—at his uncle's beverage company. Well, he does that two or three nights a week. If he stays home he watches TV and in the meantime I get the kids ready for bed. He and I have a light snack, watch TV awhile and then go to bed.

A 22-year old housewife from Tacoma tells much the same story: Ye Gods—what do I do. Well, I get up and out of bed at 6 A.M. I get my son dressed and then get breakfast. After breakfast I wash dishes then bathe and feed my baby. She's 3 months old. Then I start the procedure of house cleaning. I make beds—dust, mop, sweep, vacuum. Then I do my baby's wash. Then I get lunch for the three of us. Then I put my baby to bed, and the little boy to bed for his nap. Then I usually sew or mend or wash windows or iron and do the things I can't possibly get done before noon. Then I cook supper for my family. After supper my husband usually watches TV while I wash dishes. I get the kids to bed. Then—if I'm lucky—I'm able to sit down, watch TV or read a magazine. Then I set my hair and go to bed.

Here is a story of harassment told by a 23-year old Louisville mother of two young children:

Well, I fight with the children to eat for one thing. They don't want to eat. The little girl—she's 4—is hungry and then she won't eat. They usually go on outside after breakfast. I feed the baby and

27

give him a bath and then I put him on the floor. Then I make the bed up, dust the floors and dust the furniture and by that time it's time for dinner. Then I fix dinner and do the dishes. In between time I have to feed him and give him a bath and put him to bed. Then it's time to fix supper and Daddy comes home. After supper we just sit here and watch TV or I visit one of the neighbors. We very seldom go out during the week because he works. My husband may wash the car or something like that. Other than that he just watches TV or goes to sleep. He putters around the yard or reads maybe. He is usually too tired after he comes home from work. The children just spend the whole day playing and getting messed up. Then they watch TV after supper with me. Then they get washed and go to bed about 9 o'clock.

And finally, we have a daily-tale told by a 29-year old Trenton women in which a mode of relaxation other than TV is mentioned:

I get up and do the dishes and make the beds and sweep the floors. I scrub the kitchen once a day, wash and iron, and then towards evening I get dinner. I do just what most everybody does. In the afternoons—well, my husband works nights—so I get his meal about 2 o'clock, and clean up after him. Then I usually have a couple of hours I spend at the neighbors yaking. This backyard takes a lot of work too because we are going to seed it over. This place was a mess when we moved in here a year ago. I usually go to the store once a day and my little boy takes a nap too. Usually I sit and sew half the evening and read the rest of the evening.

These four accounts of "my day" illustrate quite clearly how extremely busy the woman is with her housework. She fixes breakfast, washes clothes, dresses children, cleans the house, does the dishes, makes lunch, irons the clothes, makes supper, makes light snacks, makes beds, dusts, mops, sweeps, mends old clothes, washes windows, scrubs the kitchen, works out in the yard, shops for groceries, and sews on new clothes or curtains. She has no maid to help her with any of these tasks. Her children are too young to be of assistance. Her husband often has an extra income job or has his own responsibilities (such as washing the car or seeding the yard), so that he cannot be counted on to help her.

It is no wonder that with all these homemaking activities to perform, she is sometimes tempted to describe her daily life as one in which:

I wash or iron or clean up the house or sew and that just about covers my days. I haven't ever caught up with myself since the twins were born four years ago.

or where,

> By the time I get breakfast and dishes done my morning's gone and by the time the canning I'm doing this summer is over the whole day's gone. And it's been just housework all day long.

She also views her children as a source of considerable concern in her daily life. She must feed them, clothe them, bathe them, and put them to bed, and she must keep a continual weather-eye out for them, even when she is not immediately ministering to their habitual wants and needs, lest "I spend half of my day kissing all their little hurts and bruises." Or, as another said, "What with hunting for the kids I'm running in and out most of the day."

These women frequently find that "life around little children" is one perpetual battle—either with them, or between them. When they are asked how the children spend their time—and hers, many chorused: "The children—they fight," or "The kids get up in the morning and they don't do anything but fuss all day," or "In between fights, the children play and eat and sleep." And sometimes, "They don't want to eat," so that the mother must "fight with the children to get them to eat."

Time and again working class women express the feeling that their responsibilities toward their children preclude many expeditions into the outside world of clubs or parties or travels. To these women the presence of small children in a home is an automatic definition for the busy woman: "I have three boys so you can imagine I'm busy all right."

In these descriptions of daily routines, the husbands seem to come in a poor third in the attention they get. The wives serve them breakfast, sometimes fix their lunch, prepare their suppers, wash and mend their clothes—but don't "waste" nearly as many words on them, as on the house and children. Perhaps this is because the presence of the husband is only a part-time phenomenon, while the children are a "full-time nuisance."

The principal effect of the husband's activities on these daily routines seems to be in setting the hour for breakfast, supper, and bedtime. If a husband does not work the standard eight-hour day (between 8:00 and 5:00), the working class woman regards this as upsetting her time schedule. She may have to fix her big meal at 2:00 in the afternoon, instead of at noon or in the early evening. If the husband has an extra job in the evening or on the weekends, this enlarges the amount of home and yard responsibilities she must undertake. If the husband drives the car to work, she finds herself isolated in her own immediate neighborhood while he's gone.

By the time she fulfills the tasks which arise from these three important roles as homemaker, child-rearer, and husband-servicer, she finds herself with little time for, or interest in, any other kind of activity. She rarely attends a club meeting or goes to a party—at least she doesn't mention this as being a part of her typical day. She may get time for reading, "while the children are napping," or "before going to bed." She almost never mentions playing games, such as bridge or canasta, or spending time at sports, such as bowling or swimming.

The "daily routine" of a working class wife typically includes only two activities beyond the big three of house, children, and husband. These "other two" activities are TV watching and neighbor or relative visiting. However, "casual visiting" as a daily activity is not mentioned by a majority of these women. Television, in contrast, ranks very high in their devotion: well over a majority of working class women consider their television sessions important enough aspects of their days to be included in their descriptions. Very few of these women, however, work in any TV time until the evening when they are able to sit down in front of the set with either their husbands or children. Occasionally a young housewife mentions that her family takes daily car rides in the evening, or that she chauffeurs the children to a nearby swimming pool in the summer. But such adventures beyond the realm of homemaking or TV watching are distinct exceptions.

The only "adventurers" among these young housewives are those with jobs which take them out of their homes every day. This kind of "adventure" however does not change their daily life much, except to confine it to a quadrangle instead of a triangle: the job becomes a fourth point of energy output. They do not use their jobs as an avenue toward additional adventure. Perhaps this report of "her day" from a 39-year old Chicago working wife will illustrate the typical effect of a job upon the daily routine.

> I just run from one day to the next. I get up at six, eat breakfast and fix lunch for myself and my husband. We get up at the same time, but he leaves a half-hour before me. He takes the bus to work and then later on at five I pick him up in the car and we drive home. I drive if he is tired, or else he does the driving. You see, we both work near each other—it's really only a few blocks away. I let mother keep care of my youngest daughter, and then I send Carol, who is 3, to nursery school. In the evenings I just get the supper and then do the dishes, plus maybe some ironing or cleaning. There's always enough to do: too much in fact. Mostly we just watch TV in the evening, or if it's hot like yesterday we go out and sit on the lawn. But mostly we're both tired. Our jobs just knock us out and in the evenings we just plop down.

Where the wife has no children around her house—because she is still a "young bride," or has become a "deserted mother," or was never anything other than a "childless wife," a slight increase is noted in the extent of her "visiting" or "movie going." However, the evidence leans in the direction of indicating a relatively "empty" existence for these women rather than one of equal "busyness" directed elsewhere. When asked how their days went, these women were singularly non-verbal, as if their days were not as full of meaningful activity.

A young bride related the events of her typical day in the following fashion:

> We get up at 5:45. I make my husband's breakfast and pack his lunch. I have coffee and straighten up the house, then I go to work at 8:45. Both my husband and I work all day long. My husband gets home at 4. I get home an hour later and I start supper. Afterwards, I clean the dishes. We spend our evenings either visiting or going to movies. We watch television when we get home and then retire at 10 or 11.

And a deserted mother describes her "deserted day" with these comments:

> I get up at 5:30 in the morning and make breakfast. I get my husband off to work by 6:30. He comes home about 4 o'clock and I make dinner. In between times I do some household chores and look at television maybe an hour or so. In the evening we visit friends for several hours in the neighborhood and then go to bed about 11 o'clock.

One suspects that her television set is left on for more than "an hour or so," and that she has not reported the amount of time she spends in magazine reading.

At the other extreme from the daily boredom implied by this woman's report of her day, is that given us by a "school-age mother" who is trying to expand her mental and social horizons.

> First of all I fix breakfast for everybody—We have six people in the house—then I start the wash—when there is enough to bother with. That's about three times a week. Then right away I fix my husband's lunch to take to work. I get up at 5:45 in order to get everything done. After breakfast I get the wash out and put it in the dryer, clean the dishes and fix lunch for myself and my children. They have come home from school, and I keep them home for a full hour so they will rest. Then I send them back at 1 o'clock. After lunch I straighten things up around the home and do some sewing —you see I make my own dresses and a lot of other things. I'm not a TV watcher like some people. I'd rather sew or read. By 5:45 it's time to start supper so we can all eat around 6:00. In the evenings

31

I just read or sew or I visit with the neighbors. A lot of the time I show them how to sew. I have classes, sort of—I taught it to myself, you know. I'm not a professional dressmaker—what I want to do now is to take some evening course so that I'll learn to sew without a pattern like a real professional.

This woman is an exception: as a rule, working class housewives whose children are of school age do not get out of the house much more than the younger mothers. A minority of them, mostly upper working class mothers in new suburbs, mention some PTA activity or work in the scouting movements or attendance at Little League games.

THE WORKING CLASS WIFE CLASSIFIES HER DAILY ROUTINE AS "DULL, NORMAL"

She characterizes her daily life as "busy," "crowded," "a mess," "humdrum," "dull, just dull." But she feels that this is the lot of most housewives, except, perhaps, "those society leaders you read about in the papers." The general tenor of her attitude toward what a day in her life is like is indicated by the following comments:

Crowded, just crowded—that's what every day is like. They're all busy. They're just dull too. We just don't do much except work. They're all dull compared to those you read about in the newspapers of people who run around all the time.

Oh, it's housework all day long. We really don't do very much —I would like to get out more if I weren't so isolated out here. My husband has the car all day long, so I'm sort of stuck here.

All I ever seem to do is mess around. I get up at 8—I make breakfast, so I do the dishes, have lunch, do some more dishes ,and then some more work in the afternoon. Then it's supper dishes and I get to sit down for a few minutes before the children have to be sent to bed. That's it—that's all there is to my day.

My day's just like any other wife's. It's just routine. Humdrum. It's really just what every other housewife does.

We don't do much of anything special. I imagine my day is spent doing what any housewife does. Just cooking and cleaning, washing the dishes and mending clothes. Then the biggest part of the time I am chasing kids.

If she feels that her own life is one of monotony or is a "humdrum" existence, she is consoled by her belief that this does not make her different from most of the other women she knows.

She usually does not know many middle class women. Since middle class women and working class women tend to live in different sections of the city, the latter are not sufficiently acquainted with the middle class mode of life to draw comparisons of self or life styles. Even if the working class woman were able to make such comparisons, she might not see her own life as so very different. After all, the "young mothers" among the middle class also spend a considerable amount of time in infant care; they also wash dishes and clothes; they also fix three meals a day for their families (as a rule). Where the middle class woman is really different is not so much in what she does (though this is different in noticeable ways, as will be described shortly), but in her reaction to her life circumstances.

The middle class woman does not see her daily life as "dull, normal." To her one day is not "just like the next." Life is not "routine," or "humdrum"—if anything, it sometimes seems not quite "routine" enough. When middle class women were asked to describe a typical day they reacted with statements such as:

> Are there any typical days? Every day there's something new! How can I possibly describe a typical day?

or,

> Each day is different. I do try to accomplish certain things each day—but my schedule usually gets upset.

or,

> Every day is different when you have two little ones around. I have a teenager and then this little child, and I can assure you that with them coming up with something new, there are no two days alike. You can't even plan very well.

Where the working class wife finds her children "fighting every day," the middle class woman sees her children "coming up with something new." Undoubtedly both groups of children do their share of squabbling and "coming up with something new." But the working class mother is more conscious of the fights and their wearing effect upon her patience, while the middle class woman is more conscious of the "new", and this engenders pride and wonderment at her children. The difference in these women's days seems as much a matter of viewpoint as behavior.

Middle class women do not believe they have "typical days." The variety which they impute to their "days" is not solely a product of different viewpoint, however. They frequently schedule the days in the week so each has its function. The weekend is assigned its importance as a time when the whole "family can get together and do something as a unit." It is a time specifically laid aside for relaxation. The various seasons are thought of as providing opportunities for exploration of different facets of life: winter is for social pleasures, and summer is for the personal pleasures of swimming or boating or working in the garden. This is the way the middle class woman thinks of her year. When, therefore, she is asked to describe a typical day, her first thought is to ask: "Do you mean a weekday, or a Sunday?"; "Do you mean in summer or winter—we've got a different pattern, you know."

The middle class woman, despite her knowledge that it might not work out as she intends, usually assigns a function to each of her days:

> Monday is laundry; Tuesday, I shop for groceries; Wednesday, the cleaning woman comes; Thursday, I buy the meats for the weekend; and Friday, I go to the beauty parlor.

> Monday is washing and ironing; Tuesday is club meeting; Wednesday is mending and shopping; Thursday is downstairs day, and Friday is upstairs day.

She obviously homemakes just as does the working class wife. However, she does not appear to be hell-bent on doing everything every single day. Thereby she apparently makes more efficient use of her housekeeping time.

The middle class woman also child-rears and husband-tends. She fixes their meals, sews their clothes frequently, and makes sure they get to work or school on time. But that is not all she does.

> I get up at 6:45 A.M. and get every one off—my husband to work, and my daughter to school. Then I get my younger two children dressed for outside so they can play while I do up my dishes and my general housework. In the afternoons I do a lot of sewing—making things for the girls and myself. I have a lot of organizations I belong to and sometimes I attend those if I can find someone to take care of the children. Then my husband comes home—and we have a fairly late dinner, usually, unless he has to run out to attend a couple of his meetings. If he doesn't, he may work around the house, while I read or sew—and then again, we may just watch TV. Right now we're getting ready to have an open house this weekend—so my husband will probably help me get the place in ship-shape.

The middle class woman experiences more variety in her life, and less monotony, because she has a much greater number of personal, avocational and outside interests than does the working class wife. Most middle class women have a "meeting" to go to at least twice a month. And they report that every now and then one of their "typical" days might include:

Going out for dinner and a dance,
Getting together with another couple to play mahjongg,
Having an open house for 40 or 50 people,
Going to a tea today—we'll probably play bridge also,
Doing voluntary work for the Red Cross,
Playing volleyball down at the club with a bunch of the girls,
Doing some backstage work at the Little Theater.

Both groups of women report with fairly considerable frequency that a typical day might include some "visiting." But when the middle class woman speaks of visiting, she is usually referring to the talking she does at one of these meetings or parties, while the working class woman usually refers to visits with a "neighbor," "relatives and in-laws," or "a girl friend" whom she's known since her childhood. Thus, even the visiting a working class wife does during a day might seem monotonous to her (as compared with that done by the middle class woman), inasmuch as she's doing it with the "same old people" she has always known.

Let us conclude this comparison of the "typical" day by noting that time and again the middle class women refused to describe a "typical day." They combined elements from several of their days into their description of one. Perhaps they were afraid a "typical day" would not really do justice to the variety of interests which occupy them during a month. Perhaps they did not want to appear to lead as dull a life as a single day, taken at random, might indicate. On the other hand, the working class women did not seem to mind describing a "typical day," though they were mindful and conscious of how routinely similar the days are.

The Weekend Routine Is Also Dull, Normal

Weekends are "not too much different from the rest of the week" for the working class wives. When these women are asked: "How are the weekends different from the rest of the week?" they are apt to curtly reply, "They're not." They may issue this judgment in a variety of ways: the chorus is different, but the tune is essentially the same.

Nothing different about them. They're much the same except that I may go for a swim.
There's really not too much to do around this town so they're pretty much the same.
The only thing different about them is that my husband has a different job—he works right through Saturday and Sunday.
The weekend is just the same as the week except the children

35

sometimes go to Sunday School. We're pretty much the home-bodies—we really lead quite dull lives.

Oh well, there's hardly any difference. My husband has to work part of Saturday and Sunday, too.

They are just about the same, except I refuse to do housework on weekends. They're really just like any other day. A day's a day to me.

I'm a lot busier, that's what. I do the same things as I do the rest of the week, but with everybody home, I have less time to do them in.

Let it be noted that "weekend days" are not always the same: the housewife refuses to work, or else she's busier. The children may go to Sunday school, the husband may have a different job, the wife may go for a swim. But these differences seem less significant to them than the similarities. They seem surprisingly ready to believe that "every day is like every other." Perhaps the worst indictment of the weekend was rendered by a woman who reported:

Saturday is different from Sunday because my husband brings home all his work clothes and I wash them.

In fact, it is far from true that "the weekends are no different from the rest of the week" for the majority of these women. There is one custom practiced by a great many (on either Saturday or Sunday) which is not paid such regular heed during the week. This is a visit to the relatives. Many echo the statement made by the 32-year old housewife from Tacoma:

On Sunday we always get the family together; that's just automatic.

For some families, this weekend visit is Sunday dinner at either the mother's home or the mother-in-law's; for others it requires a drive into the country or to a nearby town to visit "the folks" or perhaps a brother and sister-in-law who still live in the "old home-town."

Other activities, which various working class women report as characteristic of their weekends (in contrast to their weekdays), are "taking a ride out into the country," "going to the shore," "my husband goes fishing or hunting," "taking in a movie," or "going out to eat." For many families there is a division between Saturday and Sunday: Saturday is for yard work and shopping, while Sunday is for church and relaxation. However, less than half of the women in our study sample go to church as often as twice a month. They are not church-going women for the most part, just as they are not club members.

Working class women do not actually experience a weekend as it is known by most "white collar" Americans. Many of the husbands have "extra income jobs" on Saturday or Sunday (or perhaps in the evenings during the week). Another large portion of the husbands, particularly those in the transportation industries or in public service as policemen or firemen, are required by the nature of their employment, to serve the public during the weekend as well as on weekdays.

In direct contrast, middle class women think of their weekends as entirely different from the weekdays. The weekend theme is "doing things as a family" and "relaxing from the ardors of mid-week." Middle class women describe their weekends in a strikingly different tone.

The difference is that I try to do things with my family more than some housework. Sometimes I prepare a lunch or dinner out on the lawn in summertime—and we do a little extra entertaining in the winter.

Sunday is the day we do things together—the whole family goes to church and then we may go visiting. We want to do it all together if we can.

We never have a set routine for the weekend. We do whatever we feel like on the spur of the moment. I don't worry about the work as much. I spend more time with my family—and we just enjoy loafing around the house and get more relaxation out of it. We may have some extra-good things to eat.

We break out of the weekday grind. Our meals are at different times. Sunday, we go to church, and maybe we will shop on Saturday, or my husband will play golf, or sometimes we all go bowling. During the week, when the children are in school, I'm more or less my own boss. I do as I please—but on the weekends my family is around and we do a lot together.

We belong to a club of couples—we play cards about once a month. My husband is a Mason and we go to the Shrine Club on Saturday nights quite often. Sometimes we take the children, sometimes we don't. Sunday, after church, it's just 'mess-around.' We may go swimming or out to the beach in the afternoon during the summer. We do just what we want to do and when we want to do it. There is no really set pattern for anything.

Occasionally they visit relatives on the weekend, but most of the instances cited involved a relative who had a "beach cottage" or perhaps a horse farm where the "children can learn how to handle animals." In short, when middle class women say they do "things as a family" during the weekend, they are usually referring to the immediate family circle of their children and husband; whereas, the working class women who say that "getting the whole family together

37

is automatic" every weekend, are talking about the extended clan of in-laws, brothers, and perhaps aunts, uncles or grandparents.

SUMMER IS DULL, NORMAL, JUST LIKE WINTER

Working class women, generally, believe that their lives are very little influenced by the changing seasons. The biggest change they envision is the invitation from summer weather to stay outside in their yards more often, while winter forbiddingly keeps them "holed up in their houses."

As with their reaction to the "weekend" or the "weekday," working class women are more conscious of the overall similarities in daily events than they are of whatever diversity and variety may be present.

> We're outside more in the summer and inside more in the winter, that's all. My husband remodelled the inside of the house this past winter. He'll paint the outside next summer.
>
> We stay inside more at night in winter. We usually sit outside in the summer time. I wouldn't really say that the time of the year makes any difference in what we do—when you have three children you've got to stay home a lot the whole year round.
>
> It's about the same in summer or winter. I'm still sewing. All we do is work no matter what month of the year it is.
>
> One thing that's different is that summer is cheaper for us. We can eat outdoors quite often, and it doesn't cost us so much. It doesn't use up so much electric power. We're confined to the inside during the winter and we watch TV all the time. (She also said: "The TV relaxes me and gives me a change from reading so many short stories," presumably Macfadden's.)

Working class husbands seem to be more affected by the changing of season, thereby eliciting varying reactions from their wives. At times it leaves the wives somewhat less than happy, as when:

> My husband fishes in summer and hunts up in the mountains in winter—but in either case I stay home.

On the other hand, the change in seasons can be a blessing when:

> My husband doesn't fish in the wintertime, so he stays home and I get to enjoy his company.

or,

> He doesn't go off playing sandlot ball in the winter.

But then, there is the woman who wishes the seasons did make a difference in her husband's life, because:

> There's no difference at all in the wintertime—my husband still makes his model cars, boats, and airplanes.

These bleak references to the lack of any difference between the seasons fortunately are not the whole picture. Though a good many of these women take this view, for others the winter is a time when they can go ice-skating, attend church more often, play cards every now and then, go bowling, take part in some of the children's school activities, or spend more time on home improvement projects. And the summer is a time when they can take more drives out into "nature," when they can garden, go on barbecues, swim, take in a baseball game every now and then, go berry picking or clam digging, watch their son's Little League games, or do some outdoor cooking.

Middle class women report many of the same differences between their summertime lives and their winter days. They also view winter as the time for indoor life and summer as the season for outdoor living. However, above and beyond these changes in the details of life, middle class women see the different seasons as having essentially different functions. Winter is the "social season," and summer is "for more purely personal pleasures":

> We do more entertaining in the winter evenings than during the summer. In the summertime so many friends are vacationing at any one time and are out of town that it's simpler to get the group together in the winter than during the summer.
>
> We have all these social activities in the winter—parties and dances, school affairs, or civic things like Community Chest drives, and then there's football games most every Saturday in the fall, and plays or concerts all through the winter. But in summer, we have our lake cottage, and we go out there more and get away from people. We just swim and relax. By the time summer is over, we're ready to pitch into our winter schedule once again.

If winter is highly active for the middle class families, then the summer's function is recuperative.

Working class wives do not usually have vacations which they can devote to travel. What they do with their vacation time is strictly influenced by the wife's age or child-rearing status. Many of the young mothers" scoff at the idea of a "vacation". As one said: "Vacations, what are those? You don't ever get one when you have three little kids around." Most "older mothers" are able to report trips of one kind or another, even if their only purpose is to visit a relative in a nearby city.

The "young" working class wife is unlikely to take a vacation either, because her husband is not established enough in his occupation:

> My husband hasn't always worked long enough or steady

enough for a vacation—but we plan the first one he gets to go to the beach or camping and fishing.

We don't have vacation time—my husband never gets a paid vacation. We're going to plan on it for next year though.

My husband isn't going to get a vacation this year. Last year he got one—but it wasn't exactly a vacation. He went out to visit his sick mother. Sometime I'd like to leave the children behind and go to Mexico or Hawaii or Paris and do a lot of sightseeing.

or because her brood of children would be "too much trouble carting around the country."

We visited my relatives in Iowa last year—but it was a nightmare taking two children along. I certainly didn't think I'd had any vacation. I'm waiting till they get a little older before I try that again.

Babies are such a mess to bother with—they don't enjoy it and neither do you.

Or else, she and her husband choose to spend any vacation time on home projects:

Last year we spent it building the house.

We just stay around the house—he paints the outside of the house, and I try to keep the kids out of his way.

or perhaps on extra jobs which will eventually provide a better "home in the suburbs."

Middle class women in this same age group are also quite frequently inclined to "pass up real vacations while the kids are young." However, instead of letting the tender age of these children interfere with their own vacations, many manage to persuade forbearing grandparents to "take over the kids for a week or two." They say, in justification of their behavior, "That makes everybody happy: we get away from the kids, they get away from us . . . and then the grandparents are tickled to have them for a while, and for the kids it's a great treat too."

For many working class women the celebration of one of the big holidays (Christmas or Easter or Thanksgiving) is the nearest thing to a vacation. These holidays are usually celebrated in family-clan fashion at the grandparents' home. This, again, is somewhat different and in contrast with the middle class pattern of spending such holidays with the immediate family or with adult friends of long standing.

Overall, it appears that the lives of working class wives are relatively more constricted to the triangle of the home, children, and husband than is the case with the middle class families. Many satisfactions are found within this triangle, which often expands to include the whole circle of relatives and the family clan. However, they also respond to the life lived within this triangle by feeling it does not provide them with as much variety or relief from monotony as they might like. They see themselves as "hard working" women. They feel "tied down to the house" by their small children. They are solaced in their sometimes unhappy reaction by the recognition that their "dull" lot in life is shared by many American housewives, including most of the women they know.

The satisfactions which they do find are vested primarily in the people with whom they live so closely, and in the daily occupation of their lives as wives and mothers. We will see later the strong effect this has on their attitudes and motivations as consumers.

CHAPTER III

INNER LIFE AND THE OUTER WORLD

DIMENSIONS OF PERSONALITY

Before embarking on a discussion of the personality characteristics of the working class wife, it will be useful to sketch briefly what is included in the concept of personality. This will provide a perspective that will facilitate understanding the particular nature of the group we are describing.

The origin of personality is found in the situation of the child at birth. The infant is helpless, dependent upon others, especially the mother, for care. The quality of that care can range from extreme neglect, threatening survival (as we sometimes learn from newspaper accounts), to extreme pampering and over-indulgence. The child's personality begins to form in that initial *interaction*. From it the child develops his fundamental *outlook upon the world—feelings* about the dependability of others, *assurance or anxiety* over how adequately his needs will be met. In this interaction that goes on through the first few years of life, the child forms fundamental *conceptions of the parents,* and these become the groundwork on which are built more general *definitions of what men and women in general are like.*

From the way others, i.e., the parents at first, react to him, and in connection with his own inner states of tension (such as hunger, fatigue, anger or frustration if the parents do not minister soon enough or in a fully satisfying way) the child begins to develop *a sense of himself.* He learns something of *his importance to others*—for example, whether his parents show pleasure at his gurgling or pay little attention. He learns, too, something of *his own powers.* From parental reaction, he learns that he is capable (or not) of providing pleasure to them.

When he begins to walk, to ask questions, and to do things for himself, he gains *self-confidence* in finding that his manipulation of things is encouraged and that his questions are answered. If these activities are treated by the parents as a nuisance, if they are punished or at least discouraged, the child abandons them because they have not proven rewarding. In the course of his basic learning experiences, the child also develops basic *interests, concerns,* and perhaps *preoccupations.* Pleasing others, being a success, being good, gaining pleasure for oneself—any one or several of these and other aims may become central and underlie many later activities. Similarly, *standards* and *beliefs* are established, providing ways for dealing with issues of morality, as well as questions of *taste and preference.*

Sometimes a child becomes confused, because the parents who have shown pleasure in him during infancy, reverse their attitudes when the child becomes active, getting into things that disrupt adults. Thus, at different periods in development, the child may have experiences that seem inconsistent with what has gone before.

This poses the problem of how to cope with such inconsistency. We call this *the problem of integrating experience into the personality.* The child may become convinced that it is impossible to predict what may heppen next. Derived from this may be the intention to get as much pleasure for himself as he can. Or, the child may feel that disappointment is alawys bound to come. A third possibility is a determination to believe the best and disbelieve in any trouble; one consequence of this determination is a diminished *ability to deal in realistic ways with difficulties that do arise.* All three of these ways of coping with experience may co-exist in the same person.

Indeed, not only inconsistency, but *all new experience must be integrated into the individual's personal organization as it exists up to then.* Crossing the street for the first time, starting school, going out with a person of the opposite sex for the first time, beginning the first job—all of these give rise to emotions and call upon the person to summon his skills and resources to deal with the situation. They may be met with ease or with anxiety. If the latter, the anxiety may persist or may be overcome.

As a result of childhood experience, a person enters adulthood with a set of relatively enduring attitudes, emotions, personal resources and skills, and apprehensions. These constitute the equipment —complex or simple—with which reality is appraised and action taken. While these may develop, or be altered with further experience, it is rare for marked reorganization of personality to occur. Essential continuity or personality is maintained throughout adult life. (Only very recently has research attention been turned to the problem of what kind of personality changes, if any, take place in the course of adult life.)

With this necessarily brief sketch of the concept of personality as background, we turn now to a discussion of the personality of the working class wife. The statements describing the personality of the working class woman should be regarded as statements of central tendency. Each and every working class wife does not match perfectly with each and every characteristic here set forth. Still, the picture presented here *typifies the group as a whole.*

THE WORKING CLASS WOMAN'S PERCEPTION OF
HERSELF IN THE WORLD

Specific actions and feelings in any area of life are in one way or another related to the basic guidelines of personality. These refer to *the way in which the person places himself in relation to the world*. The aggressive businessman, for example, often sees the world in terms of the possibilities it offers for expanding and improving his operations. For him, the world consists of resources that he can bring together into a combination that suits his aims and through which he can exert an impact. He sees the external world as amenable to his manipulation. He can see that through his efforts he can change some segment of reality. To take another example, the painter or poet is likely to be more interested in developing and perfecting his perception and understanding of the external world than in manipulating it. For him the external world consists of interesting things to observe, to think about, and portray artistically. For both the businessman and the artist, their own aims and intentions are of at least as much weight and significance as the properties of the world around them.

A central characteristic of the working class wife is her underlying conviction that most significant action originates from the world external to herself rather than from within herself. For her, the world is largely unchangable, a kind of massive, immovable apparatus that is simply there. When some feature of it approaches her she responds to it. While not all of these women think of themselves self-consciously as "little" people, a great many of them do and say so. This is well illustrated in the statements which many made in response to the question: "Are you a member of any clubs or other organization?" Some of them say:

> I'm not in any clubs because I don't know anyone who belongs to introduce me.
> I haven't been asked to join any club.
> I'm just not the type to get out and meet people easily.
> I'm not very social myself. I'm too shy and reserved.
> I'm the backward type and I don't like to mix a lot.
> I don't think I'd be very good at it. I'm too self-conscious.
> I've never been asked. Nobody ever talked to me about anything.
> I'd like to join, but I will wait until I'm asked. I'd like to have some place to go.
> No one has ever invited me to join. I'd like to join, but nobody up here bothers with me.
> They don't interest me at all. I'm just an ordinary person, and

44

could never take part in anything and I could never belong. People scare me, and I was always shy even when I went to school.

I'm just a common ole girl.

You have to have an interest and I'm no pusher. I like to be told what to do.

In these comments, the women express a certain internal immobility and a *reliance upon the outer world coming to them in terms that are specific, clearly defined, and readily understood.* Lacking such presented stimulation, they do not know how to go about taking suitable action in unfamiliar areas. They do not know where or how to begin. They require, indeed crave, explicit guidance. They feel grateful when it is provided in a form they can use. Without it, they feel self-conscious, painfully conspicuous, and quite uncertain.

This feeling of smallness before the world is not restricted to a specific context, but is pervasive in their outlook. The working class woman's education and upbringing have acquainted her with a relatively small segment of the world. She knows what is close to home. The rest of the world is not furnished with signs, markers, and guidelines. Consequently, whenever it impinges on her life she is likely to feel that it is at best unsettling. She does not know what governs events and people beyond her ken. With such a meager chart, *she tends to see the world beyond her doorstep and neighborhood as fairly chaotic, and potentially catastrophic.*

She feels she has little ability to influence the larger forces and events which affect her life. She cannot provide for herself an organized view that would help her orient herself in the context of larger happenings around her. In comparison with the middle class wife, *reality is, in its ordinary presentation to her, flat, unvarnished and not highly differentiated.*

She would like things to go nicely and smoothly, and her everyday life may often approach such stability, though at the same time, it often feels dull and not adequately rewarding.

A sense of dullness, as well as hope for escape from it, is communicated in these stories to a picture of a young woman who sits with her chin in her hand looking off into space.

It looks like a mother after a hard day's work. She isn't quite done and wondering what to do next. It is the story of motherhood. There is no outcome. The work just goes on.

This reminds me of a mother after a hard day with the kids. Thinking what's going to happen next, and wondering how she can make them behave better.

Probably a mother that has been working all day. Been wondering about meals, washing, ironing, and just sat down for a rest before starting in again. There is no end. Just work.

Oh, this one. A woman with a large family. Of moderate means. She's just sent her children off to school. She is probably sitting there thinking of all she has to do today. And that's the end of it. (Did she get it done?) Like most women, there's always more to do tomorrow.

Yet always lurking nearby are potential threats. *The working class wife's outlook is shaded by a fairly pervasive anxiety over possible fundamental deprivations.* She is anxious about her physical safety, stability of affection, dependable income. She sometimes lives in neighborhoods where violence is common, where physical fights between husbands and wives are not unknown, and where tavern brawls are even more frequent. Whether or not she has ever witnessed or been party to such occurrences, she knows about them and knows that they may take place close by. She knows, too, the threat of curtailed income, the loss of dependable funds for necessities through layoffs, strikes, reductions in the hours of work. These are things she knows *may* happen. They may come upon her with no advance warning, the result of larger forces which she has little ability to influence or control. None of these dire events may actually have happened to her, but they are a sufficiently close part of her environment to seem real.

The nature of her anxiety may be illustrated by presenting some stories told to a picture of a little girl sitting in the doorway of a cabin. There are no other details in the picture, so that whatever respondents add to this elementary description is contributed from their own personalities. Experience has taught us that most of the stories told to this picture will be somewhat depressed in tone, so that we do not conclude simply from that fact that the storyteller is deeply concerned. The discrminating features will be pointed out below.

Looks as though her home is not a very nice one. She looks as though nobody has anything to do with her. Trying to think what she can do to make other kids like her, and what the folks could do to help the place so folks would not think they are so poor. She will get other kids to like her and things will turn out all right.

Looks like a lonely little girl, sitting at the doorway watching for somebody. It looks as if her family have gone away and left her. Well, the somebody who cares for her is not going to show up.

From a picture of a solitary girl, these women conclude that she has been actively rejected, pushed aside, or left behind. This type of story does not appear in the stories from middle class women. To be sure, they see the girl in a forlorn situation. For example:

> A poor child all by herself. Living conditions don't seem to be too good. Left with too much time, no playmates, nothing to occupy her mind. Could lead to a great deal of trouble. Looks as if the child needs someone to love it and protect it.

This woman construes the situation negatively, as do the working class women. Her story differs, however, in at least three significant respects:

1. The working class women identify more completely with the depicted girl than does the middle class woman. Both of the working class stories are told almost entirely from the point of view of the little girl, giving her feelings and confining themselves to a description of her situation vis-a-vis those who ignore her. The middle class woman shows more distance from this situation; she steps outside the framework of the girl and gives her own comments upon this situation less in terms of personal relevance than in terms of relevance to an impersonal generalized principle, i.e., idle and solitary children often get into trouble. Thus, she can step back and see this as a meaningful human situation, yet not one which is so directly related to her own life.

2. The middle class woman does not impute an experience of active rejection, as do the working class women, suggesting that she does not construe the world in such bruising terms as do the latter.

3. Finally, the middle class woman proposes a reasonable remedy to the situation. The story of the first working class woman does indeed indicate a happy ending, but with no indication as to how it is brought about in view of the initial situation she states. It is entirely wishful.

The first working class woman does give evidence of active effort to cope with her situation. In fact, as we shall point out in greater detail below, many such women show a determination to make their world more satisfactory. However, as illustrated in this particular story, they encounter some difficulty in thinking of specific ways to achieve their resolves.

One further story, this from an upper middle class woman, will illustrate how a person relatively free from anxiety can deal with this picture of a solitary girl:

> This is a girl at a summer camp. She sees chipmunks and squirrels near the door and she is sitting real still so as not to frighten them away. If she watches long enough, they will come up and take some food from her.

Not only does she see the log cabin as part of a summer camp instead of as a deprived home (either interpretation is reasonable in view of what is actually depicted) but she is also able to see the girl

47

as being giving—feeding animals, instead of seeing her as deprivea. Furthermore, the girl is seen as entirely in control of her own behavior; she is sitting there because she wants to, is able to regulate her conduct in line with her self-chosen aim. The behavior imputed to the girl is realistic and specific in the light of her aim.

In sum, it is not necessary to respond to a picture of a solitary girl sitting in a rude cabin with a story of deprivation and rejection. Nor, if deprivation is seen, is it necessary to respond so directly and immediately as though it related to one's own life. The working class women tend overwhelmingly to respond to the picture in the latter fashion—reflecting their concerns. The middle class women tend to show much greater freedom from such concerns.* The differences between the working class women and upper middle class women are generally greater than the differences between the former and lower middle class women. This is true not only in the area of personality just discussed, but overall.

We have pointed out that the working class wife is heavily reliant on the external world as it presents itself to her, and that this means further that she is reliant upon her immediate environment. The immediate environment is the source of the stimulation she can respond to and cope with; beyond it lies what is for her an unknown and uncharted realm.

The most important elements in her world are the people in her family. (See Chapters IV and V for greater detail on this point.) This, of course, is largely true for the middle class wife as well. But the working class wife, so overwhelmingly bound up in them, with few significant connections to anything beyond, is faced with the problem of what her life would be like if anything should happen to her family. And we find that *among the working class wives loneliness is widely feared.* Though it is not necessarily in the forefront of their mind, it looms as a disquieting possibility. This insecurity regarding the stability and dependability of ties to others can be illustrated by these stories to a picture of a young woman standing with downcast head, her face covered with her right hand. Her left is stretched forward against a door.

> This looks like there might have been a quarrel between her and her husband. It looks like she's pretty depressed by it. I get the feeling of—wonder if he'll come back or is he definitely gone. Doesn't look like a case of family grief for there would be others

---

*To obviate possible misunderstanding, it should be noted that no interpretation rests only on stories presented illustratively, or, in fact, on stories only to one card. Within the compass of this report, it will not be possible always to present detailed story analyses as in this instance. The reader will be able to appraise later illustrative stories in terms of the interpretive procedure exemplified above.

around her. It's a quarrel between the two, I guess. She's waiting at the door wondering if he's coming back in, or the door is closed definitely.

Looks like a woman just got some bad news. Maybe her husband left her or died or went away. She's beside herself and heartbroken. She will just have to go on, that's all.

She's crying because her husband left her with two kids. Another woman, yeah, it's another woman. He's no good, anyway. This woman got a divorce in the end. He drank too much—too many times—too often.

That, I don't know. Unless something has happened. Maybe she lost her father. Or her mother. Or her husband. Some sorrow. I don't know how it will come out. I don't know how it will come out. You got to look—let it work out for them. That is best.

This one looks like she's been hurt or something. Some tragedy or something and she's crying. Either that or she's just had a fight with her boy-friend. She may have been out on a date and talked to some other boy and her boyfriend didn't like it. (How come out?) Oh, she'll probably make up with him and they'll get along fine until the next time. Could have been a lot of things.

Further evidence of their fear of loneliness and of their desire to remain close to people comes from a projective question in which we asked our respondents to tell us what they would most and least like to be turned into if a magician were to change them into something other than a human being. The most common type of working class response was along these lines:

> A dog, because it is so faithful.
> A French poodle, it's well fed, brushed and people pet it.
> A house bird because of the love people give it.
> The bed my children lay on so I could still be close to them.
> A house, so I could watch people's lives and be close to home.
> A fairy, so I could watch over the kids and other people.

Two-thirds of the working class women gave responses which indicate a desire to continue to be with people, to nurture them, to be nurtured by them, or to have power over them. Only one-third of the middle class women gave such responses. Instead, they were more likely to give responses which represent a desire to escape,* or simply for contentment all by one's self:

*For a discussion of spatial symbolism, see Chapter III, "The Lansons: Equanimity and Its Vicissitudes," in Hess, Robert D. and Handel, Gerald, FAMILY WORLDS. Chicago: University of Chicago Press, 1959.

A bird because it can fly wherever it wants and see the world.
A cloud because it is so light and frothy and free.
A cow so I could just lie around and eat grass.
A flower that blooms for years.

The middle class women are able to use this chance to fantasy about what they might otherwise be, and often think only of themselves in such a fantasy. The working class women still prefer to see themselves closely tied to people and they don't so often want to "get away from it all."

In the life of the working class wife, the ties that matter can be disrupted for little reasons and for big. Disruption can be final because of death or desertion—or repetitive because of recurrent jealousy or friction. The stories cited (and dozens of similar ones in our data) indicate something of the potentiality for disorganization that hovers close to the lives of these women. This is perhaps nowhere better expressed than in this story to the card depicting the woman with downcast head:

Oh my I tell you, it reminds me of when I was goin' to have my baby. I didn't know what to do. I was gettin' myself ready, and my two boys ready. And I didn't know what to do. It reminds me of myself. My husband's father was dyin', and he was gone, and I was tryin' to get my uncle.

Looking at the working class wife's life in terms of her central concerns, we find that *her life has a somewhat elemental character.* Her central concerns are close to the most basic human events: birth, illness, accomplishing the tasks and chores of daily life. Everybody has these concerns to some extent, but they tend to be much more central for the working class woman than they do for middle class women and, more generally, women of higher social status.

The personalities of the working class women tend to be relatively less developed and elaborated, and hence, less involved with more "civilized" concerns such as group life and its ramifications. Their aims and interests tend to be closer to home, less far flung, and to have fewer points of anchorage. Their energy goes into maintaining life and improving it within the framework that is taken for granted, rather than altering the framework.

The life of the working class wife is characterized by much uncertainty. Though her life is fairly circumscribed, and seems to her often routine and dull, she nonetheless has a sense of uncertainty. This partly derives from the fact that most of her energy goes into day-to-day living. She does not have, or make use of, large time perspectives that give her a sense of ongoingness and a sense of moving through life on an assured course. This shows up, among other ways, in the fairly marked tendency not to give endings to thematic apperception stories, except when pushed by the interviewer, and often not even then. This reflects the uncertainty of these women as a group. Thy can look at a picture and propose what might be going on, but they do not know how it might come out. At the same time, they do wish to follow the rules set down by the interviewer on the form of story to be told, and they do wish things to work out smoothly and pleasantly. Often, therefore, they attempt to meet both of these requirements by saying simply that everything will work out all right.

The evidence indicates that working class wives do indeed lead difficult lives. As a group, they tend to find the world an uncomfortable and rather trying place. This is in contrast to other groups of American women we have studied.

However, it would be misleading to suggest that their lives are nothing but hardship and distress. They certainly find occasions for enjoyment and there are situations which give pleasure. This, however, is not the prevailing tone of their lives, but rather a somewhat mitigating circumstance. As we shall point out in more detail in the next section of this chapter, these women have a capacity for accepting a great deal that comes their way. But this acceptance is not the same as genuine contentment or deep satisfaction with their lot.

Her Basic Aims and Resources

To the working class woman, life is a somewhat chancy affair. She is basically a person who waits for what it brings to her door, rather than marking out her own path, and she is never quite sure of what it will bring. Because of this fundamental stance, her life is doubly vulnerable. On the one hand, it tends to be unrewarding: dull, routine, and lacking in deep fulfillment. She does not have much sense of going anywhere, of developing, of progressive inner enrichment. On the other hand, life is unpredictable: open to sudden deprivations and unhappy turns of fate. Such a woman gives much evidence of being familiar with unhappiness, if not resigned to it. While there is an element of resignation in this outlook, there are also elements of vitality. The working class woman does hope for ways to surmount, if not alter, the circumstances of her life.

Two major aims are evident. *One central motive is the search for a stable world.* These women want to reduce their vulnerability. Something of their inner need in this direction is evident in stories given to a rather weird picture of cloud formations overhanging a snow-covered cabin in the country:

Looks like something on a lost island, a ship lost at sea. Radio warnings. Somebody is out to rescue them. I'd be terrified to be way out there.

I can't see any people. Just winter and cold. Maybe it is about to have a snowstorm and lots of people will get hurt.

What could this be? A storm? A house? Oh, now I know. It's a storm coming up near a lake shore. There is a small house, a cabin. The people in it are frightened. So much storm and what will it do to the house? Will they have to leave? Will somebody come and get them? And how will they get the kids out? I bet you they are really worried in there. What weather! I never would like to live next to the lake *that* close.

What is that supposed to be? Looks like a modern art finger-painting. That is real weird, something haunted. There are two people in the window. It is a weird night, like Halloween. Spooky. I would be scared to live in a house like that. That must be far out in the country somewhere with never a soul in sight to see you. Hard to get a doctor, too. This type of house would not be what we want. Ours ought to be friendly, among other houses, with streets and a telephone so you can talk to people.

I don't know. It looks like a house. There's windows. Looks like they're in a tough spot. Not in a house on land but in the water. I don't know how they feel, but I'd be scared. They'll probably be rescued and everything will come out all right.

The personal references in these stories, the spontaneous comments about how "I would feel," testify to the reality of the apprehension concerning the potentially devastating effects of external forces. The weird stimulation of this picture is handled quite differently by a working class woman who feels rather more secure than most:

It looks like a cozy little home. There's a storm brewing on the outside. It looks like the light's on. Looks like it could be warm and comfortable inside like there's no worries on the inside. Safe from the storm and so on.

Not only are working class women seeking greater stability. *They also want to add some brightness to life.* They do not expect that it can become altogether rosy, but there is hope that the dullness can be relieved. They do not expect that this will come about through any alteration of attitude on their part, but rather that external events can occasionally be bright. This hopefulness is illustrated in these stories told to the picture of the woman sitting with chin in hand, staring off into space:

The only thing I seem to see is she's thinking about something.

They just don't mean anything. She's studying about something. Maybe she's looking forward to something.

Oh, you know. You are always the hero of your own dreams. She is married, a mother with preschool kids. Having a quiet cup of tea and thinking: Oh, if Saturday night we could just live it up. Payday is coming and she might make it at that. When is payday, I wonder?

The working class woman has many personal resources that she can put to the service of her aims, resources that help to temper the difficulties of her life. We have emphasized the preponderant importance of the external world, and have pointed out that this basic relationship to the world has several implications. This principle has bearing in the present context, for in keeping with her perception of herself, in relation to outer reality, is her deep conviction that, *with good fortune, one can be saved from or spared unpleasantness but one cannot be personally successful against it.* If one cannot be spared, one can hope that there are ways to live with what does come. Just as she looks outside of and beyond herself for the initial determinants of her life, so she looks for the powers that can revise it. She has a number of techniques for this.

Perhaps the most frequent is her inclination to wish unpleasantness away. *Wishfulness is her most easily summoned resource.* She wishes that just as life has taken an unpleasant turn, it may next take a pleasant one. She hopes that from somewhere, someone or something will appear that will relieve her ache or solve her problem. Her wish may be extravagant in the sense that she looks for a force of superhuman efficacy. It is, however, not always extravagant in the sense that she wants immense realms of gratification that are inaccessible. The content of her wishes may be relatively modest, as in the just quoted story of the woman hoping that payday will make it possible to live it up on Saturday night.

The importance of such wishfulness is illustrated in the comment of a woman who told a long story but did not give it an ending. Pressed by the interviewer, she added:

Oh well, a happy ending. I do not like endings to be unhappy. Not in the movies or anything. There is too much of that in real life to have it in stories or movies. I definitely want happy endings.

In addition to simple wishing, many of these women also make use of the more formal technique of praying. There are frequent references to praying and putting faith in God to see one through or drive away the source of difficulty.

While wishes may or may not come true in the end, life still has to be lived and difficulties have to be lived with. We spoke earlier of the working class women's familiarity with unhappiness, and this very familiarity becomes an important source of strength. Attuned as their expectations are, these women tend to have a fairly considerable *fortitude*. It is as though they know it all so well that nothing new can really throw them. This is not to say that they are insensitive and do not have feelings when some new untoward event comes their way. Rather, their response bespeaks a cerain quality of *realism* and *practicality*. They know life is not a bed of roses and they feel they cannot let it get them down. Throughout our material there is evidence of a *determination to keep going*, a resolve supported by the kind of wishfulness we have described. This they have to do. They will continue to look for alleviation and improvement, but in the meantime, they will carry on. They often feel dismay or anxiety or uncertainty as to how it is possible to carry on—feelings exemplified in these stories (to the picture of the woman with chin in hand):

> To me this looks like a hard working mother who is trying to support her children alone. She is wondering how she can manage without a husband to guide her. She is trying to decide if she should continue on or perhaps re-marry. She hasn't made her own mind up as to what to do, and that is the way my story would end.

This same woman also exemplifies the search for stability and the determination to keep going in her story to another picture (a picture of two shadowy figures):

> What in the world is this? It is one of these modernistic conceptions of a husband and wife looking towards the future together. The feelings are that as long as they are together they can work out anything. They know whatever problems they have they can overcome and reach their goal.

Further illustrations of wishfulness and uncertainty are provided by these stories:

> I'd say that poor lady has some troubles on her mind. She is tired and would like to get away from it. I get that way myself at times where I'd like to just get away. Her mind is just wandering and how can you have an outcome.
>
> Looks like me at times. Wishes her bills were all paid for. Like me, she's just sitting there and waiting. Real dreamy.
>
> I'll bet she can't make ends meet, just like me. Maybe someone is ill in the family and she is quite worried. She is wondering how things will work out and I'm sure all will be well. It usually is when you are the most worried.

To be able to believe the best, even when matters seem at their lowest ebb, represents a degree and kind of strength. In any case, the need to carry on is evident. For example:

> She looks like she is thinking or very worried. Something must be troubling her. I look like that sometimes when I don't know what to fix for a meal. She might figure it all out or just go on working and skip the worry.

On the surface, it may seem paradoxical to describe these women as both realistic and wishful, but the seeming paradox is resolved by recognizing that the two tendencies function in two different contexts. The realistic, pragmatic quality of personality is the way, by and large, that they meet everyday life. They do not and cannot kid themselves about what is going on before their eyes. They do not wear rose-colored glasses in the present. They do not insistently believe the best of others, any more than they do of themselves. They know that people act from dubious motives as well as those that are commendable. They know, too, that stress, strain, and hardship are part of life, at least of their lives. They are generally candid, even outspoken persons, with little inclination toward or skill in the use of euphemism.

In all these ways, then, these women are realistic. They clearly see what life brings and they know what is required of them to keep their heads above water.

Wishfulness, then, is operative primarily in regard to change, rather than being a self-deception about the present. The women are partially sustained by the belief that things will get better, that life will take a new turn toward the sun.

One very important way the working class woman has for alleviating some of the harsher aspects of her life is to make herself and her surroundings as attractive as she can. If we recall the interview excerpts at the opening of this chapter (pp. III-6, 7) it can be seen that these women tend to be highly self-conscious, sometimes in a quite uncomfortable way. Prettying up themselves and their surroundings reassures them that life is not so bad, after all. By giving themselves a lift in this way, they feel better able to cope with things.

> Well, she's a young girl. It looks like she's meditating on what she should wear. She's thinking about something pleasant, and it's probably what dress her new boyfriend would like.
>
> I don't know. She's probably got all her work done, her housework caught up. Wondering what her husband's doing. Pretty, isn't she? Kinda old-timey lookin'.
>
> This is a teen-ager thinking about a prom. She looks like her mind is way off—how her dress will look, will she have a lot of

dances. She hopes to have a good time, but isn't sure. She is in fact quite pensive about it.

Often the need to feel attractive is realized more extensively in fantasy than in outer behavior. That is to say, this self-consciousness may inhibit the woman in her manifest efforts to make herself attractive, though the latter are not at all precluded.

An analysis of a group of figure drawings collected from a small group of working and middle class women has particular bearing on the point under discussion and supports a view of these working class women as coping with a sense of personal unattractiveness by attempts to achieve a more favorable self-regard.* From the analysis we note a trend toward romantic idealizations leading to wishes for beauty. The women's self-concepts tend to veer between the unrealistic and the unattractive. Nonetheless, a certain optimism is implied by these strivings.

In some of the drawings a generally unattractive image of the self is projected. More commonly, some effort is made to develop a feeling of prettiness and beauty. Curly hair is carefully drawn; breasts are developed; expressions are made cheerful and outgoing; long eyelashes are given; cute up-turned noses and cupid's bow mouths are common.

If we bear in mind the working class woman's multiple vulnerability, as well as her self-consciousness, we can understand her inclination to romanticize herself as a tendency toward protective *egocentricity*. She is a good deal less certain about where her favorable experiences will originate than she is about the unfavorable. Therefore, one of the ways in which she responds is to confer favorable ones upon herself. She tries to enhance her attractiveness in her own eyes, with the hope that others, and particularly her husband, will be able to see her as she wants to see herself. This hope that her wished-for view of herself will become and remain visible is another manifestation of the general orientation to the external that we have observed in so many forms and contexts. Concern about loss of attractiveness is indicated in these stories to a picture showing a young woman, and, in the background, an old woman wearing a shawl over her head.

> Looks like the younger gal doesn't want to look at the old woman because she may look like that in a few years.

> Is that an old woman trying to remember how she looked in her early thirties? The expression in the older woman's eyes shows she thought she was once a very attractive woman. No amount of remembering will ever make her look like that again.

---

* The drawings were analysed by Sidney J. Levy, Ph. D., Director of Psychological Services, Social Research, Inc.

The only thing I can think of, the artist has painted a woman as she is today, and how she will be in years to come. She is laughing at herself for changing so much.

This woman is trying to think of what she is going to look like when she gets older. She is worried about it.

Several times we have pointed out the potentially disrupted and unsettling character of the working class woman's life. A great deal of what we have said and diversely illustrated is summed up in a story such as this, told to a picture of a shadowy silhouette figure:

What am I supposed to make out of this? This looks like a man in trouble. I don't know what kind of trouble. He just looks like he is in trouble. Home life, maybe. He is worried. He is in darkness. He looks like he has got these hard lines. He is still worried. Well, he has been working for ten years for the same company. They are laying off people. He has been with them ten years. Now he is getting laid off. He does not know if he can get another job. He does not know if he can any more. That is a crisis that passes. There is light in the picture. He will get a job in the steel mills or something. He will rebound. He will get a better position than he had, if he will go to school. Something better for himself. He takes up a trade, let's say. Generally, most people have a little nest-egg to tide them over. He will be set.

To this vague picture, this woman has little difficulty detailing a troubled life. Our attention is drawn not only to the account of hardship but to the quality of dramatic suddenness. In the telling, she is deterred by the need to repeat that after a long period of presumed stability, there is a sudden and unexplained intervention by which the stability is overturned. From stories such as this, we learn that *the readers not only fear, but are also fascinated with, dramatically impressive events.* It is as if they cannot let alone events which are drastic or impressive or strange. They have a positive interest in concrete and detailed accounts of such happenings.* At times they experience wonder and even awe. Such events give testimony to the overwhelming power of the external world, and this is a power with which these women have repeatedly to come to terms. As we have seen, it is a task which is never finished and must be confronted over and over again in various forms and representations.

This dynamic motive provides certain definite kinds of gratifica-

---

* This kind of interest is not restricted to the readers. It probably underlies and supports such diverse kinds of reading as mystery stories, science fiction, human interest stories of many kinds, news stories of the kind that predominate in what is known as the "sensational" press. It is undoubtedly an important contributing motive in the reading of the FBG magazines.

tion. First, there is the implicit realization that *this could happen to me, but it's not; this time it's happening to someone else.* This should not be construed as a gloating over someone else's misfortune, but more simply a kind of relief that one is not the victim of all the terrible things that can happen.

Thus, a second kind of gratification is provided. This is *the realization of not being alone in a catastrophic world but together with others who are in the same boat.* Deeply unpleasant experience is potentially isolating. The temptation to wonder "Why me?" is frequent. Adaptation to reality is served by knowing that others have troubles, too. Difficulties can more readily be regarded as part of life which all face, rather than something that sets one apart.

A third value that derives from this fascinated interest in drastic experience is that the person *learns what to do "if it should happen to me".* Without being aware of it, the woman frequently utilizes such encounters as a kind of preparation for a time when she may have to face a similar situation in her own life.

The working class woman's life circumstances—her closeness to and expectation of difficulty, her interest in direct human happenings, her relative isolation and apprehension of loneliness—contribute to a particular kind of emotional interest in others. As we have seen, she is more than ordinarily responsive to misfortune, so that *pity and sympathy for the unfortunate are among the most readily experienced emotions.* These women readily feel an interest in the troubles of others, and they readily understand what it means to be in difficulty. Sympathy and pity are not threatening or inwardly disruptive emotions, and they provide a way of mastering anxiety that might be aroused through too great an identification with the troubles of others. Perhaps the most important function served by these feelings, however, is that they provide a line of contact with people. The emotional capacities of the working class woman are not richly elaborated; she does not develop highly diversified or nuanced ties to others. Pity and sympathy are feelings that she does know and understand, that are familiar, and that are available to her. They are for her unambiguous ways of being socially related to others, of feeling close to them.

OBSTACLES TO REALIZING HER AIMS

We have discussed what the working class woman's psychological situation is in the world, what her aims are in relation to it, and what resources she has to cope with her situation. In this section we shall deal with some of the psychological obstacles against which her efforts must contend.

We have pointed out that she is heavily reliant on the external world and is oriented to what it brings her. Another way of stating this is to say that she tends to be a *psychologically passive* person. There are several aspects to this:

1. *She accepts things as given.* She is inclined to take for granted the world as it is. Whatever her wishfulness may be, it is seldom elaborated in fantasies as to how it might be different. Less illness or more money, for example, would, she feels, make her life easier, and these are certainly important. But she does not conceive of a truly different order of things. Partly this is due to and finds expression in the fact that

2. *She has little interest, energy, or skill to explore, to probe into things for herself.* Her energy is largely consumed in day-to-day living. She has little inclination or training to stand back at some distance from herself to re-assess her situation in large terms. She is very much open to suggestion and amenable to guidance that is presented in terms that fit in with her needs and with her view of the world. But by and large she does not venture to experiment on her own initiative. In part, this reflects the fact that

3. *She tends to have a negative view of thinking.* Mental activity is arduous for her. Her ability for inference, particularly in unfamiliar areas, is limited, and she tends to experience discomfort and confusion when faced with ambiguity or too many alternatives. She does not know how to estimate long range consequences of situations. By and large, the working class woman is a person who wants to have things she can believe in with certainty, rather than have things she has to think about. Thinking is associated in her mind with discomfort, and hence preferably avoided. Comments such as these are indicative:

> Looks like a girl deep in thought; doesn't seem to be too happy.
> They are feeling fine; not thinking anything.
> She seems to be concentrating as hard as I am. She looks like she might be troubled.
> Thinking deeply, a little sad.
> She's sitting thinking and remembering.
> She seems sad, but not too unhappy.

The juxtaposition of thinking and sadness suggests that the working class woman assumes that thinking is occasioned and instigated by unpleasantness. She would as soon avoid the one as the other. She does not welcome being alone with her own thoughts. Related to this is the fact that she tends to have relatively few useable generalizations about the world. Events are regarded either as highly personalized or as somewhat vague, magical, and diffuse. Her view tends to be that things happen either because some identifiable person did something

59

or else they happen as the result of inexplicable forces like fate, luck, and God's will. Faced with forces such as these,

4. *She does not have deep faith in her personal efficacy.* She feels that she tries to do the best she can with what she knows; for the rest, she can only hope that the larger and effective forces will move with and for her rather than against her.

Now this reminds me of those women who have to wait on their men that's at sea. Looks to me like she's looking out over the water. I call that picture, 'Waiting'.

That looks like a worried mother. That's about how I look when my daughter takes the car out and is late. (Anything else?) I think she is thinking about her children, how she can make them a little happier. And if she is like me, she is worrying herself sick and usually nothing too serious happens.

She seems to be concentrating as hard as I am. She looks like she might be troubled. Everything always comes out OK. That's the way I like things to come out.

You tell me why you're putting people through this. How can anyone tell what that lady's thinking? Her son overseas, her husband in the hospital. No, not that. She doesn't look too worried. Don't ask me what she's thinking 'cause I don't know.

All of these aspects of psychological passivity that we have been discussing may be summed up by saying that they amount to certain *limitations in self-command.* (Psychological passivity should not be understood to mean lack of physical energy.) These are also limitations of action. While great energy may be expanded in day-to-day living, her action is limited in the sense that she has a very narrow range of alternatives, and she has *little capacity to initiate new directions on her own.*

There is another important way in which the working class woman's command is limited. Effective human action requires organization—either internal personality organization or external organization of people into a group or, more often, some combination of both. We have shown that in a woman of this type, capacities for effective action are relatively modest, particularly such capacities as initiative, assertiveness, self-confidence, thinking and intellectual appraisal. These may be designated "instrumental" capacities. But these ordinarily must be supported by a well-organized emotionality, which is to say that purposeful action requires that a person have his emotions well in hand.

In comparison with the middle class woman, the working class woman's emotionality is not well organized or easily controlled. It will be recalled that in the stories which we analyzed in close detail on pages 46 through 48, the working class woman reacted to the stimulus of the picture in a much more emotional fashion. They were not in such full control of their feelings as were the middle class women. Similarly, the stories quoted at the opening of the section on basic aims and resources may be recalled for their personal references and the sense of emotional immediacy felt by the working class group.

This immediate emotional responsiveness to stimulation bespeaks a lesser degree of inner self-restraint. When a working class woman experiences some emotion, she is more likely to get carried away by it than is the middle class woman. Further, *strong feelings can be elicited by less intense stimulation, as compared to the middle class women.* A middle class person looking closely at the working class woman would be somewhat inclined to judge that she does not have a sense of proportion in emotional matters. This may be illustrated by stories to a picture showing a woman with her hands at the neck or head of another person (sex and age are not clearly indicated), both standing at the foot of a staircase. In the population at large, as in the present study, two main interpretations of the picture occur in the stories told: (1) the woman is attacking the other person; (2) the woman is helping the other person who is ill or has tripped on the stairs. In our study, the working class women markedly interpret the picture in the first way; the middle class women in the second. These working class stories will illustrate the point:

> This looks like two ladies fighting. And one is pulling the other's hair. (Fighting over what?) One probably left something on the stairs and the other fell on it. (Outcome?) Right now one is angry. But she'll soon get OK.
>
> She is choking the life out of her. Looks like the girl has done something she ought not to do and tried to sneak by her mother on up the stairs and her mother caught her. Well, all I can say is that girl is in for a bad week with her mother. Probably she won't let her go to the dance anymore or roller skating. The mother probably don't like for her daughter to stay out so late at night. Maybe she does not approve of the fellow the girl goes with.
>
> It seems like they're having an argument. It looks like she's trying to choke the man. Well, maybe she wanted something for the house and he didn't. I think he'll buy it at last.
>
> Oh, boy. Looks like they are going to kill each other. The man looks like he is going to strangle the girl. Could be her husband, could be husband and wife, could be husband and lover. She could be unfaithful in either case. Looks like a period picture to me. (Meaning?) They are wearing old-fashioned costumes. (How will it come out?) Well, I don't know. He could kill her or else some-

one could rush in and save her. (Which do you think?) It could be either one. I read a lot of murder mysteries. (Interviewer adds: She told me at the door as I was leaving that her husband allows her to buy only two magazines a month, but will let her buy any number of books. Says she buys magazines secretly and reads them when he is not at home, hides them at other times. Says she does not know why he does not allow her magazines, but allows her to spend money on books. She likes magazines because 'they have more news, more things in them.')

The first three of these stories are notable not only for the violence imputed but for the strength of the feeling in relation to the relatively trivial instigation. We are, of course, not inferring that the working class woman actually chokes her husband when he refuses to buy something that she wants for the house. (More usually, she sees herself as the *object* of his aggression.) We interpret the material at a higher level of generality and say that the working class woman has strong feelings which are readily aroused and which she has more trouble keeping in check than the middle class woman does. Here are some middle class women's stories to the same picture:

Oh dear. How can I do that. It looks kind of strange. But I can't tell if it's a child or a young girl. It looks like the other person is looking to see if the child has something in her eye, under good light. I'm sure she will find it. From the appearance of their clothes, this picture must have been taken a long time ago. It's not up to date.

Goodness, it looks like a child or adult has fallen down the stairs. A woman is trying to comfort her, or find out what happened. The one who fell is standing up so she can't be too badly hurt, just standing up. Shows concern on the woman's face. That woman's hand looks horrible, like a bad case of arthritis.

It looks like, from the expression on her face, that the man was ill or injured. There's a staircase. He may have fallen. (How?) Well, he was coming down and tripped on the telephone cord. (Outcome?) He had a serious injury but he got well.

The volatility of the working class woman's emotions contributes to her sense of the world being chaotic. Not only is she unsure of what's going to happen next, but she is not sure of how she's likely to feel. The fact that there is a lack of nuance to her emotionality (her feelings tend not to be characterized by shadings but by an all-or-none quality) contributes to her view of the world as chaotic. Her inner feelings thus tend to corroborate her external perceptions. She puts considerable energy into restraining the expression of her feelings, though it is likely that she is somewhat more openly expressive than is the middle class woman. The observer would very probably find the working class woman to be fairly spontaneous in her outer behavior.

The difficulties the working class woman experiences in maintaining control over her feelings pertain not only to hostile feelings such as those just illustrated. She also feels rather more difficulty than does the middle class woman in maintaining control over her sexual feelings. *She seems to feel somewhat more vulnerable to sexual temptation than does the middle class woman, though we have no evidence that she actually goes astray any more frequently.* If we look at the stories told to a picture of a seated girl looking up at a man who sits behind her, we find that some women from each class tell stories that see these people as engaged or married. But then there is a type of story which is largely absent from the middle class group, though not infrequent among the working class:

> This is a very young girl. The fellow is quite a bit older and he looks like he is trying to seduce her. She really thinks he is God's gift. She is very impressed with him. He thinks she is an easy conquest. (What else about it?) He probably got her into his bachelor's apartment, will seduce her and then forget her. She will be broken-hearted for a while but will meet someone else and unless she learned a lesson, the same thing will happen again.

> It looks like an older man enticing a young girl. (What will happen?) She's just sitting there calm listening to him, but I think she's going to swallow his line.

> She looks like she's fallen in love, but he looks much older. She's thinking how nice it is to have him near her and kiss her. He's thinking the same. I think she'll get wise and find somebody her own age before it's too late.

> This looks like a fly-by-night affair. The pose alone explains itself. She looks so much younger than the fellow. She looks quite innocent to me, but not the fellow. Looks like a hotel room or one room apartment.

The wish to do the right thing comes through in these stories, and attitudes of disapproval toward such dalliance are clearly indicated. Yet the sense of temptation is marked, and the storytellers have no difficulty projecting such feelings into the picture. The middle class women tend to resist this picture much more and to insist that the situation is not a real one. For example:

> Now here's a sweet scene. Looks like a posed photo to advertise a movie or play. She's a child. He's an older man, whispering

sweet nothings into her ear. She's not smiling. He is. Maybe she doesn't like him as well as he likes her.

Looks like in a play or something on the stage, or a movie. He's telling her the usual baloney—'I love you.' And she says 'Me too.' And they talk about 'Let's run away.' And probably they will run, unless there's another woman in the picture. It's just a love affair. This man looks like John Wayne. The girl doesn't look familiar.

The working class women's tendency to a somewhat volatile emotionality is one of the factors that contributes to her moral concern. She wants to be a good person and to do the right thing. She is more often than not dismayed by some of the feelings that she finds in herself from time to time. She does not want to hurt others and she does not want to give in to temptations. Like most people in our society, she wants to be a decent person, respectable and unashamed. She differs somewhat from the middle class woman in the way she maintains her sense of moral goodness in that *she is governed somewhat more immediately by what others will think of her.* The middle class woman is somewhat more likely to be troubled by her conscience if she feels an impulse that she knows is wrong or does something wrong; she will find it difficult to live with herself even if nobody else knows. The personality of the working class woman is less stringently organized. She adheres to some definite moral rules, but in order to help her live up to them, she needs to remind herself that she will be visited by punishment from others if she transgresses.

This *fear of moral isolation* is understandable when we recall that she feels her ties to the larger society are not altogether satisfactory to her. (This point will be further detailed in the next chapters.) It is also understandable in the light of her general orientation to outer events.

This outward orientation has several facets, as we have seen: (1) She believes that most significant action originates from the world external to herself; (2) she relies upon being presented stimulation rather than initiating courses of action herself (and thus her passivity is one of her main controls); (3) she is more interested in what goes on in her immediate surroundings than in her own thoughts. Now we may add a fourth point: that she is more concerned about being punished by others than she is about punishing herself. The internal pressure to be moral is less strong than her need to receive external acceptance and appreciation. In this connection, we may also recall her tendency to be uncomfortably self-conscious in a group. To a picture showing a girl, with many hands pointing at her, working class women tell stories like this:

I see a girl standing. A bunch of hands is shaming her. Looks like she's about to cry. Looks pitiful. I feel sorry for her.

I would say she feels like everybody is looking at her, and she is doing the wrong thing and she doesn't have any friends. Everybody is trying to tell her what to do.

Looks either like they are pointing at her or ridiculing her. It reminds me that she doesn't have any friends. Looks like she had done something they won't approve of.

She seems worried and depressed. People are pointing their finger at her and accusing her of something. Maybe she has a very harsh tongue and has been talking about the neighbors and they're all very angry with her. Possibly they'll want her to move and don't want to have anything to do with her.

Well, I'd say probably all her life she has been pampered and spoiled. She's real pretty and I'd say the hands represent men in her life, and that she has used every one of them in one way or another. And now she looks like she's thinking of what she has done and is sorry she's hurt so many of them and wished that she could do it over and change the way she acted.

The middle class women also give stories indicating concern about what others will think, but they are more likely to see the pointing hands as symbolic of the girl's inner state:

The hands are pointing an accusing finger at the girl. She has stolen something and the hands are her conscience eating at her.

She must be having a bad dream with all those hands. She's got something on her mind or she wouldn't be dreaming. I think she'll just wake up, I hope. With all those hands she'd better hurry up.

The working class woman is not always certain that punishment will follow transgression, and she sometimes feels that it should not. She often feels that there are mitigating circumstances which should be taken into account. (This is a manifestation of her less stringent personality organization that we mentioned a moment ago.) *Sometimes she believes that a first offense should not be punished on the ground that it is a first offense.*

This is a fellow who has probably done something wrong. The police is bringing him to his mother, before they take him down to the station. It was probably his first offense. He got off with just a warning.

Sometimes she believes that one mistake is helpful to a person because it teaches a lesson. She is much more ready than is the middle

65

class woman to believe that a person is entitled to make a mistake or two; and she does not feel that this warrants judgment as to character. These beliefs add a dimension of complexity to her moral outlook, but they can probably be understood in terms of her feeling that life is already hard enough and that what she needs is less trouble rather than more.

These mitigating beliefs are efforts to relieve her burden, ways in which she seeks to feel that she does not really deserve to be shamed and pointed at so much as her apprehension portends. She wants to be good, but she also wants the world—particularly the world of others who may judge her—to be reasonable. To facilitate maintaining her self-esteem, *she engages in moral comparison of herself with others.* It is relevant to mention here a finding presented in greater detail in Chapter VII. Forty per cent of the working class sample agrees with this statement presented in a list of statements about religion: "The worst hypocrites are those inside the church. A lot of people go just to show off their clothes or how respectable they are." This is a comforting belief to the working class woman. It helps her to feel that others are no better than she, and that she is no worse than they. It is not amiss to propose that the working class woman is often envious of the respectability that women above her in the status order seem able to take for granted, as she believes, while she has constantly to struggle to convince herself and others. Of course, many learn to live with this somewhat negative evaluation of themselves, just as they have learned to live with many other negative circumstances. As one said: "My mother didn't go to church the last fifteen years of her life, but I bet she gets to heaven faster than I do."

This woman, and many like her (presumably among the 60% who did not agree with the interview statement quoted above), reveals her sense of moral deficiency, while her tone also conveys a certain amount of reconciliation to it.

The working class woman wants to make her world a more liveable place. She wants to feel more at home in it; she wants to be a respected member of society. She applies her energies to these tasks, contending with limitations in herself, yet also drawing upon genuine personal resources.

CHAPTER IV

THE MAN IN HER LIFE

The primary family of wife, husband and children is the core unit of our society, and the stage on which, over time, the most important actions of its members are played out. Whether we concern ourselves with such broad social phenomena as social mobility, such social problems as crime and delinquency, such psychological issues as the genesis of mental disease, or the economic questions of saving and spending, of consumer behavior, or mass media habits, we must look at the family and its functioning if we are to fully understand the human behavior which interests us.

We know that the human personality is most forcefully influenced in its formative period by what goes on in the family, and that in later years the deep and persuasive motives which characterize the person are played out in family life, and in turn have their influence on the children's personalities. In previous chapters we have examined the daily routine of the working class housewife, the personal characteristics which condition her performance of that routine, and the motives and goals toward which she strives in her daily life. In this chapter, we take a closer look at how the working class wife regards herself in relation to her husband and children, and how she regards them.

Our analysis of the daily routine of these women has shown that they are heavily involved in the triangle of childcaring, housekeeping, and husband-tending. The first two activities certainly absorb the greatest amount of energy, and it is in these activities that the working class housewife finds her most central role, and works out a satisfying sense of self. Her relationship to her husband is less time-consuming, and we will see that it contains a good many more uncertainties and anxieties.

Exploration of these women's personalities has shown that their world view is a highly personal one, and that they perceive the *people* in that world much more clearly, and find them much more meaningful, than the more impersonal forces of social institutions. Their world is thus closer and more personalized than the world of middle class women; the borders of their "social life space" are narrower and they tend to relate more intensively to fewer people than do their middle class sisters. It is in the light of these differences in the world view and life space that the following analysis of the wife-husband and mother-child relationships can best be appreciated.

Americans take marriage very seriously, and for them the husband-wife relationship is an intensely personal and meaningful one. The support which one partner gives the other over a wide range of activities and problems is perhaps the central source of security and feelings of well-being in adult life. The spouse inevitably takes over many of the functions of the parent in assuring the individual a relationship in which he can confide and be confident, in which he can feel accepted as himself, and find his preferred activities, his hopes, his fears, and his foibles accepted, taken seriously, encouraged or constructively criticized. If home is one's castle the spouse makes it so, for if he or she does not provide this atmosphere of acceptance, security and interpersonal closeness, the home is not a place where one can relax and be one's self. This is just as true for the wife who stays in the house all day as for the husband who goes out and comes back. For the wife, the house, much of the time, is simply a place of work; it is through her interaction with her family that it becomes a home.

For the working class housewife, marriage, being a wife and having a husband is perhaps even more meaningful. These women have always known that their reason for existence is to be wives and mothers, and from adolescence on, much thought and fantasy has gone into that someday when . . . There is much less, as we have seen in the previous chapter, of a conception of self apart from these central roles of wife-mother. These women, by and large, move fairly directly from the status of daughter to that of wife and mother; they tend to marry quite soon after leaving school (mainly high school). The increasing frequency of steady dating in high school serves to make the transformation from daughter to wife less disjunctive. Their short work experiences, in a factory or office, have been more "a marking time" than anything else. Traditionally, working class women marry younger than women of higher social classes. We know that since the end of World War II the disparity between working class and middle class women in age at first marriage has lessened, but it is still present. For example, in 1940, more than twice as many women twenty to twenty-four years of age who had not graduated from high school were married, as women who had attended or were attending college; in 1950, slightly over one and one-half as many in the lower group were married.[1]

In light of what we have learned of these women's personalities, we can understand this demographic fact. The working class woman does not feel comfortable without a clear-cut familial role; when she

---

1. Paul C. Glick and Hugh Carter, "Marriage Patterns and Educational Level," *American Sociological Review*, Vol. 23, No. 3 (June, 1958), pp. 294-300.

outgrows the daughter role, she moves as quickly as possible to the wife-mother role.

Thus, the husband is a central person in the lives of these working class women; the relationship is of crucial emotional and realistic significance to them. This is true as much because the woman is deeply uncertain of her "place" in the husband's life, as it is because he offers her the most tangible opportunity for love, security, and defense against the potential chaos and havoc wreaked by "fate." Their husbands are vitally important to their sense of emotional well-being. This is particularly so in the evidence that marriage provides of their personal acceptability to the wider society.

Because these women feel as unsure as they do about themselves and their worth, about how acceptable they are to the world around them, they are heavily dependent on *having* a husband as a sign that they are full members of the society, and mature women. Having a husband, being a good wife to him, and receiving affection and recognition from him all serve as proof that they are worthwhile persons, and real women.

Yet these women frequently feel isolated from their husbands in many but vague ways, and retain lingering doubts as to their "hold" on the husbands' affections. They frequently appear afraid to act openly in a fashion contrary to their husbands' wishes, lest a permanent alienation of affections results.

The middle class women's husbands are also important to them, but with this difference: these women do not feel so isolated from their husbands' lives and they exhibit far less anxiety over whether their husbands are pleased with their every little act. The middle class women thus manifest greater confidence about their place in their husbands' affections, as well as a greater degree of self-confidence in their ability to "go their own way" and get by with it. They appear to be less willing to sacrifice their own interests in order to please any particular husband. They also appear to have greater intellectual resources with which to "understand" their husbands, and they believe their husbands to be more "understandable."

Before examining how the working class wife relates to her husband in several particular areas—his work, managing the household finances, division of household responsibilities, recreation, and religious participation—it is necessary to examine her deeper-lying feelings toward men, her image of what they are like, and her implicit conceptions of the relationship between men and women, husband and wife, if we are to understand why she behaves toward her husband as she does. It will be apparent that her feelings in this area are not only consonant with her total personality as we have described it in the last chapter, but actually are an integral part of that personality.

69

The working class woman sees men as dominant and controlling. Men, including her husband, are in a sense personified representatives of the external world, and she tends to feel that she has no more effective power with them than she does with any other force or power in the world. She is hopeful that her own husband will be benign toward her, but she counts it as a blessing rather than her natural right when he is. She is grateful when she has such a husband, and she often does, for not every working class husband is as assertive as his wife's preconceived image would have him. Her expectation, nonetheless, is that men are likely to be controlling in ways that may hurt her. She is inclined to see them as insensitive and inconsiderate, sometimes teasing, sometimes accusing, sometimes vulgar, and always potentially withholding of affection.

The wish to receive attention and not to be ignored is manifest in this woman's story to the picture of the girl with the hands pointing:

> Well, looks like she's been out with a lot of guys. Priest or preacher's hands. All the guys are pointing to find which to marry. She talks to the priest or preacher, and is told to marry the one she loves. Besides, money isn't important. Lots on her mind. Don't feel right. Goes out and tries to find out. First guy has ideas that are just not for her; he doesn't want a family. The second never asks her opinion about things. The third guy is the one she thinks about most; Tony asks her opinions. She loves him. Fourth is not the type. Decides to marry the third guy. Go to the minister and they marry.

It is also clear that one cannot expect much from most men. The story teller is quite content that she finds a man who asks her opinion. By implication, most men would not; it is much more likely that they would not be responsive to her needs and wishes.

To a picture showing a woman's head against a man's shoulder, we find some stories that indicate expectations along this line:

> Looks to me like he is tender and loving, which is something unusual for a man. Looks like a nice way to comfort one another.
> It looks like an old couple. He's embracing her for some reason. I don't know why. Maybe just because he has loved her so many years. He just wants to hold her close.

Tenderness, care, affection are exceptions; and in the eyes of working class women, the woman who is sure of receiving these from a man is fortunate; often this kind of woman considers herself lucky to be able to settle for permanence in a relationship whether or not it also has elements of the closeness and tenderness she longs for in fantasy (although their personalities often are such as to make it difficult for them to respond in kind were they to receive these).

It is hard, these women feel, to get a husband to do what they want or to change his ways. Men go their own ways and as often as not the wife feels she has little influence. She seems unable to free herself altogether from the view that men are quite independent and can easily leave. This is frustrating, yet seems to be accepted with resignation rather than with a sense of defeat. A picture of a woman clutching the shoulders of a man whose face and body are averted as if he were trying to pull away from her, elicits stories such as these:

Wife discovered her husband cheating. She looks like she wants to forgive him, but he don't know what he wants. I guess that's it.

Looks like she is trying to explain something to him. He doesn't want to listen to it. That's all.

She's pleading with him there. [Over what?] Doesn't want him to go, maybe. [Go where?] Oh, anyplace. [How end?] He'll go anyway. He looks like he'd do what he wanted to.

Oh, golly. I don't know. Looks like a nice argument and she's trying to reason with him. From the picture behind, the argument is over a woman. She's pleading with him, or he's mad at her and she's asking forgiveness. [Mad at what?] She's said something cross and is sorry. [Outcome?] Well, his head is turned away. He'll not easily forget.

Oh joy. Looks like an argument. Probably over another woman. [The situation now?] She's trying to coax him back. [Outcome?] She might win, but I doubt it.

The sense of inferiority to the male is marked, even in the stories with a hopeful ending. No real independence of action is attributed to the female. The man has the strength and the control over the situation.

The middle class woman is readier to assume that a woman can set a train of events in motion by her own acts and initiative. To the same pictures, they tell such stories as this:

Oh dear. I don't get much out of this. I'd say a terrific argument. They're married. The picture looks like a couple of movie stars. He's going out and slug somebody. Maybe he caught her running around with someone, caught them in the act no doubt and she's trying to restrain him from being foolish. They will make up. It only looks bad and really isn't probably.

The middle class woman typically deals with such problems in two ways. She seeks to direct and control the man's behavior, and feels reasonably confident she can do so. And, one of her ways of

controlling is to minimize the significance of emotional outbursts—
"it only looks bad and really isn't probably."

The working class woman feels that she has to put up with
brusqueness and inconsiderateness. Sometimes she also feels that she
has to accept rough behavior from her man in order to hold on to
him. Such expectations are reflected in stories like these:

> I got a pretty good description for this one. She just had a
> fight with her husband. He just walked around the block. It looks
> like he might sock her around a bit. She looks a little mussed up.
> She is thinking—the heel I married. A guy like that. Gee, I should
> have left him long ago. He probably will come home drunk about
> one or two A.M. and they will make up and everything will be fine.

> Looks like he is up to no good and she is trying to reason with
> him. Maybe he is fighting a drinking or gambling habit he has
> and wants to go out. She realizes if he does that he will go back
> to his old habits. She is pleading with him to stay home with her
> or else take her with him so she can help him. He will tear away
> from her and go out to indulge in his bad habits. When he comes
> back, she will forgive him as she always has.

> He's disturbed about something and angry. What's on the wall?
> A picture of another woman or what? If I could make out that
> picture, that would help some to tell me what's wrong. She is
> pleading with him. Telling him not to be ridiculous. She is trying
> to talk him out of something. Telling him to control himself.
> Maybe she is afraid he will get out of control and she won't be
> able to handle him.

The actual frequency of such behavior cannot be judged. What is
important in this context is that these women anticipate its possibility.
It is not unknown in their environment, and it is a latent possibility
within the realm of their experience. They are likely to have a sense
of relief and good fortune when husbands are good to them.

Further insight into the ways of dealing with and responding to
husbands comes from a question posed to the women in our study
sample. Working and middle class women were asked to put themselves in a hypothetical situation in which a woman asks advice from
a friend about a problem with her husband. The question asked was
this: "Let's imagine for a minute that two women are talking who
have been good friends a long time—and they can talk quite easily
together, and often discuss their problems and difficulties. One woman
tells the other that she has a problem with her husband. Imagine
what this problem might be, how it came about, and what the other
woman would offer in the way of advice."

By and large the problems presented are the same for working class and middle class women. For example, some women in each group propose that the problem is drinking or running around with another woman. Even in responses comparable on this point, however, significant differences are evident. The working class women tend to see the problems in more extreme terms and they respond much more passively to the challenge the problems present:

> Let's say her husband is a bad drinker. When he gets in a beer garden he gets interested in women, not because he wants to but he overindulges and is taken away—a sort of supernatural mind. He hasn't done anything to be ashamed of yet, but she's under the impression if he doesn't stop drinking, things will get worse. He goes straight to the beer garden after work and they have no children, and if he doesn't cut this out, she's going to leave him. He is nasty and beats her up. [What will the friend advise?] Well, the other woman would say, "I wouldn't blame you for leaving him, but first explain to your minister or priest. But if that doesn't help, pull out before you have children." If he hasn't changed after all these years, it will be hard to change him unless a miracle turns up.

These women tend to pose one of two solutions to their problem with the husband: either put up with it, accept it, and suffer if necessary, or, if things get too bad, leave him. They do not seem able to think through ways of dealing with the problem more actively. Leaving the husband is not, after all, a sign of active mastery of the problem or of independence, for this solution is posed only when the husband is described as unbearable, where there is no other choice. There is thus an either/or character to their predispositions in case of conflict. It is assumed that the wife's role is to put up with things if she possibly can; if not, she may leave.

In contrast, the middle class woman sees herself as taking a more active role with such a problem. She wants to probe into the cause and to see if she can be helpful in altering the husband's behavior. For example, these women gave such responses as these:

> The problem might be that her husband has taken to drinking a little more than he should and she might be worried he might continue. Is that enough for the problem? [Yes. How did it come about?] How did he start drinking? Well, he was used to having a drink occasionally and the men at work would ask him to stop on his way home from work and he started doing this. And he asked if he may go out once or twice a week with the boys. The wife feels it's just a little too much. [Advice?] Well, she should try to get her husband interested in a hobby and try to make

things at home as pleasant and interesting as she can; get tickets for a play or something like that and take him out in the evening and see if that doesn't help.

Well, I think everyone has a problem today. Especially wives. It could be drinking or gambling or another woman. And children. [How come about?] There's usually a cause for any problem. It's best to get to the cause and eliminate from there. [Advice to woman?] Of course, you can always seek a family counsel agency or your clergyman. I wouldn't seek help from relatives; rather an outsider. And I wouldn't tell too many friends.

And another middle class woman indicates how a situation might be worked out without forcing it to an all-or-none, either-this-or-that conclusion:

Well, let's say that her husband wants to go fishing. He has two weeks vacation and he wants to go fishing for the two weeks with "the boys." His wife wants him to take her and the family on a trip and they have quarreled about it. The other woman would probably suggest that the husband go with "the boys" for one week and maybe the family the following week. That way, both would be happy.

The working class woman feels her relationship to her husband is subject, or at least potentially vulnerable, to great ups and downs. Her own feelings are unpredictable; men are unpredictable. She believes that husbands usually do not want to feel that they are at all controlled by women, particularly by their wives. (A few women complain that their husbands are still too strongly attached to their mothers). Men are seen as self-seeking and pretty much able to have their own way. They are not very amenable to wifely influence.

Despite such problems with the husband, he means a great deal to her. Most often, she would like to have more contact with him rather than less. He is her best antidote to loneliness, and an important focus for her fantasies and daily energies. She may be somewhat resigned to, but she is not pleased with, the extent to which he can move out of range of her. Still, her own capacity for intimacy (in the sense of emotional exchange and ready self-disclosure) is not great. What she wants is to have him around more and show interest in her, rather than any more intensely emotional relationship.

Our evidence indicates that the way in which the working class wife relates to males is not simply a phenomenon of her adult years, but goes back into childhood. She has early been passive toward men, expecting most, if not all, of the assertiveness to come from them, yet having to be wary lest she surrender too much too soon. Wishing to avoid temptation and the trouble a young girl can get herself into, and being passive, she has not been able to allow herself to develop a sense of full companionship with males. (The extent to which the latter would want it is probably a factor here also.) A rural-looking picture of a boy and a girl, the latter with face averted, elicits data that cast light on the relationship with males. A story by one woman exhibits a wish for gratifying contact together with the reluctance or inability to participate:

Looks to me like he's probably asking for a first date and she is pretending like she isn't too interested, but is hoping he persists.

The following middle class woman defines the basic situation in almost identical terms, but she is able to provide the depicted girl with active motivation and a means for companionably joining in:

This little boy, he is just trying to be friendly. Maybe he is having his first crush, and she is a shy child. He maybe asks her if she will go to the movies with him. I suppose she says that she wants to ask her mother, but finally she agrees to go with him, if her mother agrees, too. She finally goes with him.

Working class women tell stories to this picture that suggest girlish awkwardness, as well as an inability to be in command of themselves when a male is assertive toward them:

This looks like two farm children ages ago. And he has either stolen his first kiss or showed her something that turned her stomach. He looks disappointed in whatever happened. She is feeling and looking very coy. So it must have been a kiss.

They look like farm children. It looks to me as if he has said something that she is kinda embarrased about and she looks rather shy. They usually always come out all right in the end.

It looks as if maybe he asked her to go someplace with him or something. She acts like she is shy and bashful. [Anything else?] He may be asking her to be his girl. [How come out?] She is going to do whatever he asks her to do.

I would say these are two rather rural young people—brother and sister in some sort of trouble. The girl has already done something from the apologetic guilty look on her face. It has irritated the brother no end. She respects her brother and she is afraid she has lost his respect forever.

The most usual modes of reacting to males, then, have been shyness and retreat, or acquiescence and admiration. These women show a great deal of anxiety about their acceptability to men, and a tendency to feel they must give in, or at least not respond assertively

75

if they are to have a chance with the man they want. At a very deep level, assertiveness signifies to them alienation from men, and thereby loneliness. No matter how much "husband managing" may be required in the adult housewife role, the working class wife is uneasy about her assertiveness, and unsure how far she can go and still retain her own husband who is, after all, one of his sex. She feels that men as a group cannot be stood up to, and the necessity to do so in the give-and-take of marriage is a tense business for her because of this.

When we turn from a consideration of the subjective aspects of the woman's relationship to men in general, and to her husband, and look at the ways in which husbands and wives interact in the working class, we find a pattern of relative isolation, and a tendency for their roles to be rather sharply demarcated. In a variety of areas, the husband's work, the family finances, household chores, we find the husband and wife going their separate ways. The couple's day seems to be spent in isolated activity, with a minimum amount of time spent around shared interests. There seems to be a greater division of labor and interest between husband and wife in the working class than in the middle class. Often we find the wife a little unhappy about her isolation, but feeling that this is the way her husband prefers it.

These women often wish for more intimate interaction with their husbands, and a chance to share his experience away from home with him. More often than not, their experience is along the following line:

> I wish he'd let me take an interest in his work. But he doesn't want to talk to me about it at all. He just grunts when I ask him about it. He never has wanted to discuss it with me.

In such circumstances, they feel that the most they can do for their husbands is to keep their clothes neat and clean, so the man will not look "like there's nobody to take care of him," or do a good housekeeping job so that the husband can go off to work in a "good frame of mind and won't have to be worrying about what's going on at home."

Often it becomes apparent that the working class wife must stay at home while her husband "has fun." Sharing of recreational and sporting interests is not common. The wife and mother tends to be almost totally absorbed in her homemaking chores and interests; her husband has outside recreational interests and often does not want her to share them. Even vacations are not always family matters:

> My husband goes in field training for the national guard during his vacation and I stay home—so you see I don't get much of a vacation at all.

76

> My husband takes his vacations during the deer hunting season, so all I do is stay home.
>
> He takes his vacation during the fishing season and I just fool around the house while he's gone.

Middle class wives seldom report separate vacations—the husband may get some time away for himself, but some sort of family vacation is mandatory. Many working class wives, in contrast, say that the only change in their lives wrought by the passing seasons is the coming and going of the husband for one or another sport. The wife considers herself lucky if there is one season when her husband has nothing sporting to do.

> My husband fishes in summer and hunts up in the mountains in winter, but I stay home in either case.
>
> There's not too much difference between winter and summer. My husband still spends all his spare time making model cars, boats, and airplanes.
>
> In winter he doesn't fish, so he stays home and I enjoy his company.
>
> In the summer my husband plays baseball a lot. Oh generally five times a week in the evening. He coaches a little league, too, on his own. He eats and sleeps and lives baseball. I go with him. When the baseball season is over, him and his buddies, they go out and start with football. This fall I will have to stay home with the baby. [What is winter like?] We watch TV instead of playing ball.

In times of prosperity at least, many working class husbands have a long work week, either on one job, or with an additional part-time job. This tends to keep them away from home more than is true in the middle classes, both in the evenings and on weekends. It would seem that when the working class man is free his desire for relaxation and pleasureable stimulation tends also to keep him away from home. The wife's isolation is compounded since, as will be shown in later chapters, she has so few outside interests herself. She knows few people aside from her relatives, and does not participate much in organized club activity. She is, then, excessively dependent on her husband for contact and attention, and has a fairly steady sense of frustration and disappointment because his interests are such that he does not provide these.

It is interesting to note in this connection that when these women are encouraged to talk about the kinds of sexual problems a wife might have with a husband, the most common difficulties revolve around the husband's physical demands without giving his wife a feeling of being personally loved and cherished. She often feels her husband treats her as an object for his own personal gratification without the kind of tenderness she so much wants. But, she feels she cannot complain, because there is always the possibility that he will seek sexual gratification outside the home, and she will be further isolated. Thus, working class housewives specify common sexual problems with husbands as follows:

> A very good girl friend of mine came to me about a problem she had. She was upset because the only time her husband made love to her was in bed. He never showed any affection otherwise.
> You get problems like this. In the morning she has a lot to do, is tired, but he is always bothering her. He wants sex in the morning. Of course, he has had a good night's sleep and is ready to go. The poor wife has been up with the kids half the night and as I said is tired. She should have the husband get up during the night. Maybe he would be too tired to want sex.

Another isolating influence in the lives of many of these women arises from the fact that their husbands are of different faiths—usually marriages in which one spouse is Protestant and the other Catholic. Often the religious difference remains a source of concern (probably more for the wife than the husband) and serves to heighten the wife's feeling of distance from her husband. Such marriages seem more common among working class than middle class marriages. (More will be said about the subject in the chapter on religion).

Differences in religious identification not only isolate these women from their husbands to some extent, but also creates a sense of isolation from the church itself when the women allow this difference to keep them from attending religious services.

The wives generally tend to be hopeful that their husbands will eventually give in and join their churches—but occasionally they find it necessary to abandon their own faiths.

> I figure that he will go Catholic. I'm Catholic—but my husband isn't. I figure he will get religious later, though.
> Right now my husband does not go to church. I think that if he changes his religion he will turn Methodist and then he'll start going. I'm Methodist and he's Catholic. I think he will probably change.
> I'm a Catholic. He's a Protestant. He wants children brought up in his way and me mine. Then one of us will have to give in when the children get ready for school.
> I was a Lutheran, but my husband ain't about to change and

78

he's a Catholic, so I'm taking instruction. I don't know whether I'm going to be a very good Catholic or not. I disagree on some of their instruction.

I'm sorry to say that I haven't been to church since my marriage. My husband doesn't go to church. I went quite a bit in my childhood and when I was in my teens—but I haven't been recently. I feel bad about it.

Of course, this number of working class wives who are separated from their husbands in religious enthusiasm or conviction does not represent a majority, but it includes a considerable number, and constitutes one more way in which the wife can feel isolated or separated from her husband.

Often these women feel that their husband's behavior is inexplicable or that the husbands act in an irrationally willful manner. Some of them, who might like to join clubs, can't get their husband's approval.

My husband dislikes clubs. I really think clubs are a good thing and if most husbands felt like mine who would ever get things done?

Others, who would like to go to church, don't go because their husbands refuse to accompany them.

We used to go—but for some reason my husband won't go. I'm ashamed to say it.

We go to church whenever I can get him in the notion of going—but that's only once in a while.

Every Sunday the kids go—and sometimes I make it too. But my husband never goes. He used to go, but he quit—don't ask me why. He just did.

Other working class women would like to be normally sociable, but their husbands will not cooperate.

My husband doesn't ever want to go anywhere—he sure makes me mad. We go to my mother's once in a while and even that bores him.

It is not only that the husbands do not do what the wife wishes; this, after all, is characteristic of husbands. Rather, it is the note of arbitrariness and the inexplicableness the behavior has to the working class wife. Middle class wives are much more likely to search for, and find, a "reason," and to actively strive to modify the husband's behavior in terms of that motivation. Working class women, in contrast, tend to accept such behavior on its face, to feel that that is the way husbands are, and they cannot really be understood. This inevitably increases their feeling of isolation from him, since some con-

79

viction that one understands another and why he behaves as he does is fundamental to rapport and mutual confidence.

Given these feelings of isolation, of apartness in their separate roles, one may wonder what working class wives do to get along comfortably with their husbands. As will be shown, one of the main things they do is to set up a way of relating which structures the isolation in terms of clearly defined roles and responsibilities for each marriage partner. They organize their routine so that life can go on smoothly, though separately. The middle class wife would be much less tolerant of such arrangements and, as will be shown below, seeks a greater degree of interpenetration of the roles of wife and husband.

Submissiveness is another way working class wives deal with their husbands. Where the wife does try to get closer to her husband and his activities, she usually does it in a submissive way. That is, she simply goes along with him, doing what he wants to do, or often simply watching him do what interests him. Thus, one woman describes a typical weekend's activity as follows:

> During the weekend I cater to my husband's wishes. I watch him work on the truck and enjoy the companionship. I have to buy parts and special equipment in town during the week and then he spends the weekend cleaning and adjusting the trucks and keeping things in working order. Then, if he does anything around the house, I just follow him around. He says he doesn't want me working or cooking or washing while he's home. I guess I just don't do anything but what I know he wants me to do when he's home on the weekends.

In general, a pattern of separateness rather than sharing characterizes household responsibilities. The husband has his, usually only a few chores; the wife has hers. In many working class homes there is a sharp demarcation in terms of inside or outside the house. The husband may take over some of the inside chores if the wife has a good excuse for not working, as when she is ill, or has a new baby. But this is recognized as an exception to the normal, proper way of doing things.

> My husband and I have this understanding. He does the yard and I do the dishes. Occasionally he will help me with the housecleaning when things have gotten ahead of me, or when I can't do the job alone—such as moving the furniture.
>
> My husband takes care of the garden and the lawn, and I worry about the inside. Occasionally we help each other, though. It's not beneath us to help one another.
>
> My husband takes care of the outside of the house. I take care

80

of the inside—well, I really go to the edge of the back porch. He puts the older child to bed and I put the younger one.

That one woman needs to comment, "It's not beneath us to help one another" points to the strength of the rule which normally separates their activities. That this pattern is not universal is, of course, also clear. Some working class wives talk of sharing the chores with the husband, although one sometimes gets the impression that it is more a case of her sharing his chores than his sharing of her duties. Both middle and lower class wives, of course, have husbands who will take no responsibility around the home, but these are rare.

In most middle class homes there is some division of labor between husband and wife but the rules tend to be more flexibly handled: middle class wives tend to see a greater interchangeability between the marriage partners in handling the work that must be done. There is much more interest in doing things together, whether it be the dishes or painting the walls; "togetherness" is largely a middle class value. The middle class wife seems to take it for granted that she can call on her husband for many more chores, especially ones which are normally considered feminine, than does her working class sister. Similarly, they seem somewhat less uneasy about undertaking masculine chores such as repairing, painting and yard work.

I usually do the dishes, but he cooks the Thanksgiving and Christmas dinners, as well as some of the weekend meals whenever he's not too busy. He loves to cook—and I really don't happen to like it at all. He loves to fix a roast and all the trimmings. Now take the lawn. It's really a family project. He cuts the grass himself —but that's pure recreation for him because when he is out working in the yard I am right out there too with a thermos of hot coffee, and I talk with him as he is going past with the mower.

We do some things together and some things separately. I consider the yard his responsibility, but I help out and wind up doing it more often than he does because he's out of town so much. He takes care of the car and the repairs and he built the garage, but we both did the porch. I help on his projects outside a lot, and he'll leave his tinkering for a minute if I need anything done. I do most of the running with the children, but whoever is best suited does the job really. I take them to dancing school, but he takes them to football games.

There is then, in the working class, a sharper division in who does what around the house. At the same time, working class women are often happier with the quality and efficiency of much that their husbands do around the house than are middle class women. Since most

81

working class men work with their hands, they often do a better job at the physical and mechanical chores than do their middle class, white collar counterparts. Working class women frequently point with pride to their husbands' mechanical skills. Many middle class women, on the other hand, complain about their husbands' ineptness at physical labor, and with mechanical tasks.

Another area in which differential preferences for division versus sharing manifests itself is family financial management. Working class families seem most commonly to invest major financial control unilaterally, while middle class families seek sharing of financial responsibility and decision more conscientiously. In the majority of working class families, the control of the purse strings lies in the hands of either husband or wife, with the other partner having a distinctly secondary voice in how the money is spent. (This does not mean, of course, that the controlling spouse does not try to take the other's views and desires into account). In general, the wives seem to be dominant in financial matters. They tend to feel that "earning the money is the man's responsibility; spending it wisely is the woman's duty." In our study sample, about half of the working class women exercised dominant financial control, and over a third described a pattern in which both husband and wife had considerable say in how the money was spent. In only a small percentage of either middle or working class families was the husband's voice dominant.

Working class wives describe their control of the husband's paycheck (and their own, if they work) as varying from autocracy to a system of general authority subject to an occasional veto:

I have the final say-so on our money. My husband just signs his checks and gives them to me.

I have all the say-so. My husband is very easy to get along with. He never questions me about what I buy.

I do the finances. I pay who we think should be paid when, and that's it. My husband is like a lot of Irishmen and he says, "If a man goes out and earns it, a woman should know how to spend it."

My husband takes about three dollars and gives me the rest. He usually checks though to see if what I'm getting is reasonable. If I buy something he thinks is senseless I have to take it back.

My husband always tells me that I know how to handle the money and what I can afford, and if I want it and know I can pay for it that I should just go ahead and buy it. But I don't really buy anything unless he says it's all right. I ordered a rug recently, but he hasn't said yes or no yet, so I am not going to buy it until he finally says yes.

It's my job to handle all the finances. Pay all the bills and so forth. He brings home his paycheck and I take care of all the rest. Lots of men are like that. Now I'd never go and buy more than ten dollars worth without asking him. That way he could never say that I got us into trouble.

These women believe that the control of the family purse-strings are generally theirs through husbandly default (as when the husband tells her that "a woman should know how to spend the money") or else the control is theirs because the husbands are incapable of maintaining a sound disbursal policy:

I handle all the money. I wouldn't have a thing if I left it up to him. He's easy come easy go—and has no idea of how to handle the money he makes.

I tried letting him have charge of the money—but we got into debt over our ears. Now I'm in charge and we're about to see daylight again.

A twist on this old complaint that "I woudn't have a thing if I left it up to him" appears in the thoughts of some women who report they "wouldn't have a thing" because their husbands are too lazy to bother with making any purchases in the family's behalf.

I pick everything out that we are going to buy and then take him down to sign for it. You've got to give that husband of mine a push or he wouldn't ever go no place or get us anything.

Even when the wife asserts that her husband is the financial arbiter in the family, she still admits an important role for herself in making the intial choice of items to be purchased:

My husband generally goes along with me if I want to buy anything. If he can afford it he'll get it for me—or else he'll tell me I have to wait for a while. I let him handle the finances.

He makes the money so he handles it. We do go shopping together though. And if we buy a refrigerator or something bigger he decides what we get. If it's something smaller he lets me make up my mind generally. But whatever it is we get, we both go shopping for it.

The working class pattern for family financial management is very different from that reported for middle class families. The latter most commonly seek to share all decisions over major purchases and husband and wife come to some measure of agreement over the portion of the budget which should be allotted to the wife for her daily and monthly use in purchases of goods and clothing. It might be said of the middle class husband that he serves as "architect of the family's fiscal policy," determining the proportion which should be saved, designing the insurance program, and planning how to invest any extra money. The wife, on the other hand, serves as the purchasing agent with the limitation that her degree of authority over purchases is in an inverse ratio to the expensiveness of the item.

> My husband gives me an amount each month and I try to stick to it. If I have some left over I am free to do with it what I choose —but I usually save it in an account I have. He handles the mortgage and the banking and all that kind of thing. He has to mesh those things in with his business operation, and try to invest our money wisely, and consider the tax problem.
>
> I take care of all the household expenditures and the children's things and some of the clothing. My husband then handles all the big money like the mortgage, taxes, insurance, and all that.

Sometimes, even more of the spirit of cooperation pervades the family's financial management, in which event the housewife is able to describe the family's pattern of fiscal arrangement along these lines:

> All the routine household buying is my job. We take an evening off and have a family conference and it includes the school-age children also. Then we decide on special things. We size up the situation and see if our budget can take it. I feel special projects are a family thing. I wouldn't want to be handed money without knowing the total score of where it comes from and what our setup is. I like to know all sides of the financial picture, and the children should know what we can and cannot spend also.
>
> Neither my husband or I have a final say-so on the expenditures. We have a sharing agreement on all money matters. We just discuss it, like everything else. I know all the details. He knows all the details, and we usually can agree quite easily for what and how we are going to spend it.

It is probably true that the planning of purchases, savings and disbursements is more complicated in a middle class family, even where income is not markedly greater. As will be shown in later chapters, working class families tend to concentrate expenditures into fewer categories of goods and services, and more in terms of immediate consumption goals. Middle class families are more likely to be involved with a complicated insurance program, educational expenses, and a wider variety of special consumer goods. The premium on close cooperation between husband and wife is consequently greater. Also, the husband will want a greater voice than his working class counterpart since the family's expenditures have greater relevance to job success and career advancement as will become apparent in the discussion below.

A husband's main task is to work and earn the family's income. Working class wives do not feel it is their "place" to take any considerable interest in their husbands' work or career. They do not feel that his career will particularly benefit from any concern that they might demonstrate or any advice they might give. Rather, they believe they can be of greatest assistance to their husbands by "tending to my own knitting," which is to say by "keeping the house clean . . . the children neat . . . my husband's clothes in good shape . . ." and by remaining "good, respected women."

In our study sample, middle and working class housewives were asked to choose among several alternatives describing how a wife can be most helpful to her husband in his work. These choices involved various versions of two basic approaches to the husband and his job. On the one hand, the wife can take an interest in his work, discuss it with him, listen to his problems on the job, and be a good hostess in entertaining fellow workers. Or, she can regard the job as the man's concern and instead concentrate on caring for his needs, doing a good job of housekeeping, caring well for the children, and being a good, respected woman herself. Over two-thirds of the working class women in our study sample believe that the latter pattern is the best, while over two-thirds of the middle class women emphasize taking an interest in the husband's work and being a good hostess.

Working class women see little to be gained from "interfering" in the husband's job concerns; indeed, they are fairly sure such interest would be rejected by the husband himself. Instead, they feel they are doing their best for him when they manage the home so it gives him no problems. They say things like this:

> I think a wife should tend to her own business as far as the husband's job is concerned. Making money is his responsibility, so a wife shouldn't interfere.
>
> I just think a wife should stick to caring for her home and children and always being respectable.
>
> A wife should not start meddling in her husband's work affairs. That's no good.
>
> The man should do the job he likes. The woman shouldn't push into his work. Some women ask me why I let him do such dirty work (he's an auto mechanic) —and come home looking like a grease monkey. Well, that's what he knows how to do and likes it—so, it's all right with me.

It's the man who has to earn the living. I'd hate to make my man do something he didn't want.

Thus, they feel they do best when they simply ignore what goes on in their husband's life when he is at work. Indeed, some working class wives have difficulty saying exactly what their husbands do at work or where his company is located. Few have ever seen his place of work. One thing the wife can do to help her husband, then, is a negative contribution; simply let him alone. The more positive constructive contributions they feel they make are indicated by such comments as these:

The most I can do is keep him happy and clean and his outlook good. If the man is in a good mood when he goes to work he can perform a better piece of work.

I believe in keeping affairs at home running so smoothly that he doesn't have to worry about them. It's essential to the husband's frame of mind to know he is not coming home to a pig sty.

He always wants clean clothes and everything—it makes a difference. If you don't keep a man's clothes neat the man looks like he hasn't got anybody to take care of him. I never saw a man yet who didn't think a woman should keep his house and kids clean.

My husband is on the road, and when he gets home he likes to find the home has been well taken care of. He wants to know that his child has been tended to properly and that his wife is a good respectable person.

Apparently, these women believe that a happy, unworried husband will do the best job of bringing home the bacon. Furthermore, they believe that their efforts at keeping his clothes clean, at rearing the children properly, at remaining respectable women, are the very best proof of their interest in their husbands. They are thus showing a real interest in the man, if not in his work as such. "I think if a man knows his wife is taking care of his children, he knows she's interested in him too."

Even those women who advocate taking an interest in the husband's work do not typically show the middle class pattern described below. Rather they think of taking an interest in terms of reciprocity —"if you don't he won't be interested in you." These working class women's interest in the husband's work is not aroused so much by a belief that by being interested they can help him in a career, but rather by the belief that being interested and willing to listen is a sign of their affection for him.

For the working class wife, the husband's job is a necessity. It takes him away from home to earn the money that the family needs to keep going. She hopes that his job will not too demanding, and that he will come home in good spirits. Preferably, they should live close to his work (or he should get a job close to home) so that he does not tire from traveling back and forth. Overall, however, what goes on at work is of minimal interest.

For the middle class wife, however, the job has much richer meaning. It is a more integral part of the family's life, and the interpenetration of family concerns and career concerns is much greater. The wife considers herself more responsible for the husband's work performance and success. She must be understanding and helpful when he has problems there and she must do a good job of representing him socially to work associates, clients, the boss, when that is necessary. For herself, the middle class wife often finds some knowledge of her husband's job intellectually stimulating, it helps her avoid being "just a housewife."

CHAPTER V

NATURE'S LAW: MOTHERHOOD

A great deal of what the working class wife holds dear is located in her children. This is a central attitude, even though children are also a source of frustration. In talking of their children these women reflected many conflicting attitudes. At one and the same time, they felt "tied-down" by their children, they considered them a "terrific nuisance and bother," yet they were exaggeratedly concerned over their physical well-being and happiness, and called them the "most prized possession in our house." If they were less devoted to, and less deeply involved in the task of caring for, their children, if they were able to reduce their anxious worry over the children's well-being, the women would not be so tied down by their children. It is precisely because they are so involved in their children that they are so heavily caught up in child-caring chores.

When asked, "What would you say is the best thing that ever happened to you?," a large proportion of these women say having children.

> I guess the best thing that ever happened to me was getting married and having my family.
> My baby.
> When the baby was born, my little boy.
> We got married and I had a baby.

To be sure, they also find children troublesome and wearing on the nerves, but most of them, at least part of the time, find children intensely appealing. They have always wanted children, and most of those who do not yet have children are regretful. They feel that having children is a fulfillment of themselves, and signals the realization of what they were always meant to be—mothers.

Just as marrying signifies to her that she is truly grown up, and a socially acceptable person, so having children establishes her in her own eyes, and, she hopes, in others' as a normal, respectable woman. The working class woman tends to feel that she has only her body, her energy and her good conscience to offer as evidence of her worth —having children is the most dramatic and absorbing accomplishment she can offer to the world that she has done well. Thus pregnancy and childbirth have a strong fascination for these women, and they are perhaps more deeply involved emotionally in these physical experiences than are middle class women (which is not to say that the latter are not highly involved, too).

The activities of motherhood provide continuing evidence of the personal worth which childbirth symbolizes for her. In all of her activities centering around the children she communicates to herself and others that she is continuing to be a good woman, doing what God and nature meant her to do.

The working class woman looks for gratification from her children in the present rather than the future. She tends to regard her child as something that should give her pleasure, even as she cares for it. She has some tendency to regard children as though they were a combination of animated toy, stuffed animal, and sparkling bauble. A child is for her, in one of its major aspects, a passive object to be hugged close, or to deck out in appealing clothes, or to be enjoyed for its antics. Though she knows that children have minds of their own, she does not always have this fact clearly fixed in her own mind, so much does she want the child to be a source of pleasure and only pleasure. She knows, too, that this cannot be the case, and she learns to live easily enough with the reality. But, this does not mean that she abandons the notion that the child should somehow be primarily a source of pleasure to the mother.

Working class mothers feel protective toward their children. They are very concerned about looking after their children and seeing that no harm comes to them. Most mothers of whatever group, of course, feel this way, but what is to be emphasized with regard to these women is that protectiveness looms larger in their outlook because it is not accompanied by more active fostering of development. These women tend not to see children as already being persons—individuals with an integrity of their own and worthy of respect. They are not greatly interested in a child's individuality except perhaps for his entertainment value. They are interested in his behavior mainly in terms of such broad categories as being good, not being ill, getting along with others.

As an expression of her protectiveness, the working class mother devotes many hours a day to the physical care of her children. She considers the time she spends in feeding them, dressing them, bathing them, and bedding them a central feature of her day. She also reports that she finds life with her children one running battle to "get them to eat," "get them to bed," "keep their clothes clean," or "keep them from fighting with one another." In addition to serving as mediator or arbiter in disputes between children and with the children, she also serves as first-aid nurse in bandaging the wounds and "kissing all their little hurts and bruises."

Both their concern for the children's wellbeing and the extent to

89

which this concern ties the woman to her home, is shown in their comments about the way they worry over the children:

> My husband calls me a worry-wart. I won't leave the children at home by themselves. They might find a match and the whole place would be on fire before I got back. I am going to see that the children are raised right. They're not going to have broken arms and things like that, because I have neglected them, if I can help it. I always keep an eye on them.

> I always want to be home at noon—no matter what else I might have to do. I like to keep the children home for a full hour at lunchtime so they will rest.

> Saturday night I give the kids a good bath for Sunday School. Then on Sunday we all have breakfast, then I dress them and they're ready for Sunday School. Maybe you think it's funny I feed the kids before I dress them—but I'm always afraid they'll get messed up before we leave. After I get them dressed I put the TV on while I get dressed and the kids watch it.

Many a working class mother finds the television set the housewife's greatest blessing because the TV set keeps her children out of physical harm's way, as well as out of "her hair."

> The thing we have in our house that I like best is our TV set. It keeps my big boy from running around out in the streets and the little boy will sit there for hours watching the cowboys.

> I like my TV set better than anything else: it goes day and night and keeps the children quiet. They all watch it until 6:30 and I can keep them still and get my work done.

Motherliness, in the working class mother, is most strongly evoked when children are very young or are ill. This does not mean that they wish their children to become ill. It means that when the child is ill, just as when he is young, he is most available to the mother, and most in need of her. Her pity and sympathy for a child in need of comfort provide a contact that is deeply meaningful to her and not easily attained under other circumstances. These women respond most fully to someone they feel needs them. It is of considerable interest to note how some of these working class mothers respond to the question: "When your children are grown, what changes do you think there will be in your way of life? What kinds of things would you like to do that you have never had the opportunity to do until now? Why those especially?"

> I can get up and go when I want to without a little kid hangin' on me and I can go without stoppin' to think about if they're goin'

to get cold before I get there. I'd like to get out and join some homemaker clubs and go to the Children's Hospital and help out a little bit. [Why?] 'Cause I love kids. I just love little babies so much that I could squeeze 'em to death. I could spend my life around kids, but let five or six grownups be around me and I get scared to death.

I think that I will join some kind of something to keep busy. I don't know. I always have been interested in kids. I would like somehow to do something for the kids. Work in a hospital or orphanage. Stuff like that. I have always been interested in kids all my life.

Travel a bit more I guess. I would do more volunteer work in the hospital. I take a training course every Tuesday at St. Francis Hospital and I would love to do more of that, but I can't see paying someone to take care of the children while I'm working for nothing.

I'll have more time to fool with my flowers and be a *wonderful* housekeeper. I'm in no hurry for this time to come. I like it fine just like it is with all the confusion. I'd like to have time to help anybody who needed help. A day or a week. Someone who was lonely or blue. I'd like to have the money to do for others.

The urge to work in hospitals is not widespread among these women, but the protective, mothering attitude which underlies it is.

The psychologist will see two elements in this highly ramified protective behavior and the anxiety which stimulates it. First of all, there is the realistic concern inspired by the problems of caring for children compounded by the relatively less stable world in which the working class child is brought up, and the predisposition of the working class woman to feel that the world is a rather dangerous, unpredictable place. Secondly, however, he will wonder at the intensity of this protectiveness when he notes that middle class mothers tend to take a more matter-of-fact attitude toward sheltering their children from danger. It seems quite likely that because these women invest so much of themselves in their children, and find it so difficult to have an identity apart from that as mothers that they must also sharply repress the inevitable hostile feelings mothers have toward unruly children. Much of their almost phobic concern for the children may stem from their own aggressive wishes toward them since their personalities allow them few resources for handling such feelings other than by repression. The middle class mother, on the other hand, is more likely to express such feelings verbally, and also to provide herself with other outlets for her energies so that the mother-child relationship does not have to serve as the stage on which so much feeling is acted out.

91

The working class mother feels it is difficult to influence the behavior of her children. She knows not why or how, but somehow that passive object that can be plunked down in front of a TV set becomes activated in his own manner, to the despair of his mother. Children are sources of inexplicable motion, and these mothers often feel at a loss. They expect children to get into minor mischief, and *hope* they will do nothing worse. To a picture of a woman facing a policeman and young boy, we find stories like these:

> Looks like the boy has played hookey from school or something and the law's bringing him home. The mother doesn't look too surprised. In fact, her expression shows, "Oh, this again?"
>
> I may be a fatalist, but it looks like my son, and the policeman is bringing him home to tell me what he did. In other words, he's been running away and getting into mischief. But it will all turn out okay.

The mother is often uncertain in disciplining her children. There is a variety of feeling, from discussing misbehavior as something that will be outgrown, to clamping down hard the first time and thus making sure "it won't happen again." Working class mothers have few tools for evaluating behavior and may try to operate by some rules of thumb. Often, their mood of the moment dictates how they respond. This variation is evident in these stories to the picture described above:

> Policeman with a little boy bringing him home to his mother. I imagine he has done something but I don't know what. Probably talk to the mother. If it is the first time, he'll just talk to them.
>
> Boy was caught doing wrong and the officer has come to the mother. The boy will get a scolding or something to correct the situation. I would do the same thing if an officer brought my son home. [Little boy sitting by his mother said, "She'd skin me alive."]
>
> I imagine he's in trouble. I imagine he's stole or lost. It could end two ways. He could be sent to reform school, or he is just given a talking to or scolding.
>
> This is a story about a policeman who brought the mother's little boy in for some wrong doing. For something he did wrong. Don't ask me what. It all depends on what type of a mother she is whether she will take the boy's part or the policeman's. I'd probably take the policeman's part, though.

On the one hand, the mother's inclination to excuse, to make allowances, is marked. On the other, she feels it necessary to take the side of authority. She does even when she excuses misbehavior, struggling to reconcile her need for external reinforcement of the moral order with her sympathy for a child in difficulty. Presented with the policeman's picture, these women are decidedly inclined to take for granted that the boy has done something wrong. Middle class women, on the other hand, question whether or not the boy has done wrong, and they are not content simply to excuse or simply to punish. They want to understand the situation in order to decide how it can best be dealt with:

> This little boy has been picked up by the police. I am just deciding what he could have done. His mother is standing in the door, wondering what her little boy is doing in the custody of a policeman. If he would have done anything wrong, he wouldn't bring him like that to the door. I think he just got lost. Even so, he looks old enough to know. I suppose if the mother finds out what was wrong, she will say, "Come on in." But she still would want to know just how he got where he was. And she will try to get all the facts from the policeman, too, so that she can see to it that it doesn't happen again.

Thus, the middle class woman is more likely to perceive her child's behavior as complex, requiring understanding. The working class mother is more likely to see her child's behavior as mysterious, beyond understanding. The latter, consequently looks for rules or authoritative guidance which she hopes will work and take hold on the child.

The working class women want their children to grow up to be "moral, upright, religious-minded" and happy adults. The different orientation toward their children which is reflected in the accounts of their daily activities—the concern of the middle class women over providing their children with "worthwhile experiences" and the desire on the part of the working class mothers to protect and nurture their children, and to "raise them right"—emerged clearly in other phases of our investigation. For example, all of the working and middle class women were asked, "What do you think is the most important thing parents can do for their children in bringing them up?" In response to this question, the working class women overwhelmingly chose the parental path of "teaching children right from wrong so that they will grow up to be moral, upright and religious-minded adults." The contrast women were less often inclined toward this notion, and exhibited much greater preference for a course of action which involved "giving their children a wide range of experiences which will help the children grow up to be well-rounded adults."

The table below shows the pattern of preference for four different modes of child-rearing which were expressed by the two study groups:

Percent in Each Group *Choosing Response*		Alternatives to: "Which of these statements do you think comes closest to describing the way you would try to bring up your children?
Working Class	Middle Class	
15%	44%	Parents should give their children a wide range of experiences which will help them grow up to be well-rounded adults who will feel comfortable in a variety of situations.
74%	54%	Parents should teach their children right from wrong so that they will grow up to be moral, upright, and religious-minded adults.
1%	—	Parents should help their children find out what they are most talented at, and then concentrate on developing these talents so that the children can do well in the world.
10%	2%	Parents shouldn't worry about their children becoming famous. Just teach the boy a trade and the girl how to be a good housewife, and then they can make the best of whatever comes their way and live happy, contented lives.

In both groups there is a majority favoring the plan of parental action which aims at "right-thinking, moral and religious-minded adults." (When we look at only those contrast cases who are definitely "above middle class average," we find that 64% express the intention to aim at "well-roundedness" and only 37% are concerned with "uprightness." In general, the higher a woman ranks in social status the more likely she is to choose the first alternative and the less apt she is to exalt the teaching of "right from wrong.")

The working class women reject the notion of "concentrating on the child's talent" because they feel that their children ought to be allowed to choose their own occupations—just as they believe their husbands should be given free rein to be cooks or truckdrivers or mechanics, if that's what they can do best and enjoy most.

You should let them choose what they want to do in order that they can have a happy life.

The parents should study their children to find out what they are adapted to, but they shouldn't tell them what vocation to choose. That should be left up to the child.

Parents shouldn't try to force an occupation or trade on the child's mind. I want to let my daughter make up her own mind about all important matters—like being a schoolteacher if she wants, instead of a ballet dancer like I might want.

Take each child for what he is and don't try to change him.

These mothers consider a "happy, contented life" more pleasant and desirable than a striving for mobility and accomplishment. They do not care if their children are not famous, as long as they are happy and good, and value their mothers.

94

It doesn't make any difference to me what my children will become, as long as they're honest and happy. I don't care if they're famous or not.

I don't worry about their becoming famous. Naturally, I want the boy to go to college, and the girl to be good.

All I want for my children is a happy, contented life. I don't want riches or fame for them.

I wouldn't be broken-hearted if they didn't become famous. You get famous sometimes and you don't appreciate what you've gotten. If they're just healthy and happy I'll be satisfied.

It may be that the child will accomplish, but then it will be natural; striving does not help:

If they're smart, the kids'll become famous—you don't have to worry.

If they are going to become famous they will do so regardless of what you do.

Working class mothers are not attracted by the more complex training and direction because they are confident that a training in how to recognize right from wrong is the best guarantee of successful, happy adult lives. Perhaps a wide range of experiences carries some dangers of being led into things the children know are against what their teachings have been.

If my children grow up to be moral, upright and religious-minded, they are pretty sure to be happy.

If they know right from wrong they can handle almost anything that might ever come up.

I think if you teach them right from wrong they'll naturally grow up to be good housewives or husbands.

I feel that if they are taught wrong from right they will be successful adults and good persons. Maybe you could encourage them to develop a talent—if it's in the right direction.

Middle class mothers say many of the same things. They are not eager to "push a child into something he doesn't show a talent for," they also believe in fostering knowledge of "right and wrong." The differences between the two groups appear to be a matter of degree. The middle class women are likely to believe that a "wide range of experiences" will naturally include experiences which will give practical instruction in ascertaining "right from wrong," and they believe that such experiences are a more realistic basis for a successful adult than any other program of parental action. They believe that "if an individual feels comfortable in different situations, then he is probably

95

going to be successful at whatever he does" and that "children cannot always feel comfortable in new situations unless they have a sense of values to rely upon."

The evidence from this analysis suggests that working class mothers are guided by the desire to bring up *happy* children, *good* children and *religious* children. The goals of middle class women in child rearing (insofar as they are different) are *adjusted* children and *successful* children. The middle class women seldom mention "happiness" as a prime goal for their children.

Many working class mothers demonstrate the extent of their desire that their children grow up to be "religious-minded and upright adults" by sending the children to church every Sunday, even though they themselves do not go. They feel that religious training will help the child all through life, providing the child with a beacon light, so to speak, to guide it through life's certain storms.

I want my daughter to go to church and Sunday School all the time. It's a good thing to have. Someday she might really need religion to help her through some trouble.

I make sure that the children go to Sunday School every single Sunday. They haven't missed in four years. I'm ashamed to say my own record isn't so good—I can't get my husband to go with me usually, and I don't want to go alone. It makes me feel a little better that I have sent the children.

I'm not too interested in church myself, and I wouldn't go except for the children's sake. I think children should attend— it's something they ought to have. It'll help them all through life.

Middle class mothers are apparently more concerned with the purely social character of the experiences their children have. This conclusion is implied from the concern which these women show over the character of the neighborhood and the kinds of children who are in the same schoolrooms (or Sunday Schools) as their children. Middle class women believe that "being near a school with a fine-type of youngster" should be a very important consideration when choosing a neighborhood in which to live. They want to send their children to schools with a "fine-type of youngster" because they believe children are most easily influenced when they are young—they are outside a lot and associate with other children, so you've got to make sure that they are associating with the right kind of children."

Working class mothers are less inclined to worry about a school's social reputation or whether it contains a "nice-type of youngster" because they believe that "kids are kids regardless of where they live." They contend that "kids are about the same in all schools . . ."

"every school has fine youngsters . . ." "and there's always kids you don't care for in any school." Furthermore, it's "hard to know what kind of children you're going to find before you move in any place." (The main limitation these mothers placed on the kind of youngster they wanted in their children's schools is a color limit: "I couldn't raise children near a Negro neighborhood.")

This concern of the middle class parents over the nature of their children's social experiences is merely one aspect of these parents' primary desire to produce a child who will fit into the middle class mold as an adult—a child who has been "properly educated," who can be "comfortable in a wide variety of social situations," who has "nice manners," and who will later in life reflect credit upon his parents. The working class mothers' relative lack of concern for these matters and their greatest emphasis upon the child's happiness and contentment seem to represent less concern over the child's eventual financial and social status. Where middle class women tend to judge their adequacy as parents by the child's subsequent maintenance of middle class status, working class mothers judge their parental adequacy according to the child's subsequent "happiness" and basic "goodness."

Finally, it is apparent that working class mothers want to be needed and loved by their children in a way which middle class women do not. The latter are more desirous of aiding their children to achieve goals which they themselves never achieved. If their children accomplish "fame" or manage to maintain a high-level "middle class social status," the satisfaction which the mother will feel over the credit this does their abilities as mothers will be a sufficient reward—they will not care too deeply if the children do not reciprocate with undying love. One suspects that such reflected glory would not suffice for the working class mother; she would almost feel her sacrifices were gainless if her children did not recognize them and reward her with their affection. This feeling is not always directly manifest in her words—but perhaps statements such as these can indicate its operation:

> The main thing is showing them you are interested in every-thing they do and especially letting them know you will always be there when they need you.
> The things that will count most in raising your children is giving the kids what they want, even to the point of denying yourself for them. That will be the most important in the long run. They'll always remember what you did for them in their childhood. Take my husband. Last month he needed shoes very badly, but instead he bought a $25 swimming pool for the kids instead.

97

The difference between middle and lower class mothers in their approach toward their children is nicely reflected in the fact that the latter relate to their children with "gifts" hoping for a reciprocal gift of their affection, while the middle class women guide their children with goals, seeking the satisfactions attendant upon their realization. When the women in both groups were asked what ways of spending their money gave them the most pleasure, and what ways of spending their money would be of greatest long-run importance, there was a striking difference in the response pattern. The working class mothers gain their greatest pleasure whenever they spend "to make the kids happier;" the middle class women feel they have spent most wisely whenever they have provided their children with an experience which will benefit them as adults.

Working class mothers commonly mention that money spent in one way or another on their children gives them the greatest amount of immediate pleasure. Sometimes the money they have enjoyed spending most is very simply that spent on doctor bills and hospital bills in the process of giving birth to the baby, of bringing them into the world, thus providing themselves with a tiny companion.

> Babies are the most fun to spend money on. Having the babies. They are so nice after they are here. You are happy you have got them, after they are born. I guess that I have gotten the very most pleasure from saving up and paying for the babies.

Other working class women believe that it is the gifts and toys and clothes they buy for their children which give them the most pleasure:

> Anything that I have spent for the baby. I spend a lot on the baby—new dresses, and a nice new toy every week.

> I just love that baby buggy. I decided on it myself and no one else has ever used it. I won't even let anyone touch it. I certainly wouldn't ever lend it to anyone. I like the buggy so much I guess because I like the baby so much. I love anything I get for her— her play pen, well just anything. When she was small I put her in that play pen and she sure looked something special.

> Buying things for my kids gives me the most pleasure. The kids enjoy everything we get for them so much.

One man spoke up for his wife and said:

> The thing that gives that woman the most pleasure in this world is buying clothes for the kids. I never saw a woman get such a kick out of doing for the kids. [The wife replied] I suppose he's right. I do enjoy buying for the kids, and for him too, though. It's really buying for the whole family.

98

Unlike these women, the middle class women do not often mention money spent on their children as presenting them with the greatest amount of pleasure. Usually, it is money spent on their own clothes or a special item of luxury for their homes which gives the most "pleasure." On the other hand, when it comes to the money which means most to them in the long run, more than half the middle class women in our study sample turned to their children and claimed that money saved up, or spent presently, in behalf of the child's development is of the greatest long run importance.

Frequently, this money of "long run importance" is that being put aside for college years, but equally often it was money expended on a day-to-day basis. In either event, the expenditures are designed to provide the children with the kinds of "experience" (either purely educational or indirectly so) which reputedly give children "poise" or "know-how" or other personal qualities of life-long benefit.

Any investment in the children is well worth the money. When you give them music and dancing lessons, or when you take care of their eyes and straighten their teeth, you are really helping your children acquire poise and self-confidence.

The money that will have been spent to greatest benefit in the long run is the money we are spending right now for the children. We are giving them piano lessons, teaching them tennis, square dancing, and spending quite a bit on their scouting activities. It's all being spent in a way that will benefit them in later life. It gives them those little extras for character development that will follow them to the end.

Middle class mothers want to give their children "those little extras for character development;" working class mothers would rather shower their children with extra-special pleasures. The former *invest* in the children; the latter *indulge* them.

These differences in immediate versus long-range orientation are apparent in working and middle class mothers' orientation to the school and their children's education. In general, working class mothers think of schools as a somewhat necessary evil. It would be nice if children did not have to go away from home to get the knowledge they need, and to have the social stamp that one is a good American, which high school graduation provides. However, this is something the mother cannot herself provide, so the child must go to school. The school is generally not an institution on which they look with confidence, but rather with a kind of wary hopefulness. As will be shown later, not as many working as middle class mothers belong to PTA's. When they do belong, their interest tends to be in their own child rather than in the school as a community interest. Thus, while middle class mothers are likely to talk of the PTA as encouraging better schools, better teaching, better parent-teacher relations in the community, working class mothers are more concerned to have a chance "to know what my son is doing in school and meet his teachers," or "to get reports on how my kids are making out in school." When middle class mothers talk of learning through the PTA of their own children's experience they are more likely to be interested in the quality of experience and training their children receive, and not simply in knowing "how he is making out."

Much of the way the working class mother regards the school in relation to her child stems from her own feelings about schools, and her remembrance of how it was for her. Going to school was not generally a satisfactory experience for the working class mother, while her middle class counterpart tends to value her education as having been a training ground for middle class life, and a symbol to others that she is middle class.

The working class woman feels that the requirements presented by the school have to be met, and yet she feels that neither she in the past, nor her children now, can expect to feel at home in school. School provides one more indication to her that it is difficult to feel fully a part of society. These stories to a picture of a young girl at a school desk vividly portray her feelings:

> She is in school, depressed. She does not seem to know what she is doing. Looks like Joycie, my older girl. Looks like she has not done her homework, like Joycie always does. My, she is sad. But I think it'll come out all right. She'll learn some more that evening and then she'll get better grades. [Joycie, also present, in the kitchen at that moment says: "How come I always flunk my tests? Mine never get any better!"]

> Looks like she is worried about a test. She does not know what to do. Looks like she is being homesick. She looks so sad. A typical cute little girl. I guess what happened is that she does not know her homework. Like some do, they rush with their homework and then they really don't know any of it next day in school. It's hard on some kids. She looks as if she'd be very close to her mother. Maybe she is missing her right now.

> The little girl looks like she has an arithmetic problem and she really doesn't know how to work it out. She's trying to solve it. Right now she's feeling she can't possibly solve it. I think the outcome will be that she'll solve it.

Such stories testify to a feeling of limitation—a struggle to deal with the problems that society sets before her. She feels that at least in intellectual matters—comprehending what is required in school assignments and how it relates to life—she is no more than modestly successful. Why this is so is partially illuminated for us in the other theme that emerges strongly in the working class woman's stories to this picture. In sum, it is this: these women are so concerned about and preoccupied with the stability of their basic human relations that they have not the freedom to commit energy to impersonal tasks such as school learning.

It's a little girl in school, worrying. She looks so sad, holding back the tears. She's not paying attention to the teacher, not looking at the blackboard. Something terrible happened at home and she's thinking about it. She will hate to go home when school is over.

She is a child with problems at home. Not thinking about schoolwork. She is in a daze, in a different world. Possibly her parents are divorced and she misses the companionship of her father. Or her mother. Poor little kid, she sure looks lost.

I can see quite a pathetic situation in this. She can't seem to concentrate. Just torn up over the whole affair. This young girl is very unhappy. Heartbroken. From my own experience, I would say it took a long way around, but everything turned out all right for her.

These dominant themes attest to the working class mother's feeling that school is important because one should do what the teacher expects, but is not something with which one ordinarily can identify. For the most part, she appears to feel that it has minimal relevance to life after leaving school. She is more concerned with hoping that her child will not be unhappy while he is in school.

It's a very sad young child, worried. Looks like a school test and she is scared to death. Reminds me of myself when I was in school—never knew the answers. It's a terrible thing to feel that way. How they torture the kids in school.

There are, of course, many working class women who desire their children to be socially mobile, to move up in the world, and who look to education to help accomplish this. These women are not so likely to shower their children with gifts, and tend rather to concern themselves with providing the child with the same kind of worthwhile experiences that middle class mothers seek for their children. Even when their own experiences with school have not been gratifying, they will encourage the children as best they can to profit more from the experience, and to grow up to a "better" life than their parents have.

101

Most working class mothers, however, do not feel there is anything basically wrong or undesirable with a working class life for their children. Even though they may fantasy wistfully about the child obtaining a college education and bettering himself, they seldom take organized action toward such goals. Most of them raise their children to the life they themselves know and in the ways that seem natural to them. It does seem natural to her to raise her children on "gifts" (both material and emotional) and a hope for their happiness in adulthood while her middle class sister strives to provide her children with the kinds of experiences she believes will build "poise," "self-confidence," "good adjustment," and "success." The reward the working class mother seeks for her efforts is *reciprocated love; reflected glory* is the secret hope and vanity of the middle class mother.

The working class wife and mother lives her life closely tied to the day-to-day experiences within the family, and her children and husband occupy her energies and emotions, her inner life and her routine behaviors much more extensively than is true for the middle class woman, as we shall see in the next two chapters which concern patterns of formal and informal social relations. It is within the family, then, that she must achieve whatever gratification her world offers her, and it is on the basis of her feelings about her family, and her conjectures over how her actions will affect them that she makes her decisions, whether these be to go or not to go to the doctor, to buy this brand or that, vote for the school bond issue or not, to go to the movies or read a magazine. Similarly, her response to the persuasive appeals of advertising, public relations or political platforms has its origin in the feelings, attitudes and strivings which stem from her life within the family, and from her feelings about what is appropriate or gratifying or permissible for her as her husband's wife, her children's mother.

CHAPTER VI

FRIENDLY RELATIONS

We have already dealt with the meaning of children and husbands in the lives of working class wives. Now we turn to the world of "other" people, of people outside the primary family. Other people, in this sense, include relatives, neighbors, working companions, old school pals, social acquaintances, and the whole realm of anonymous others. The working class women reveal quite a different pattern of behavior toward the world of such other people than do middle class women: the former spend more time with relatives and are more emotionally involved with them than are middle class women, and they have much less to do with non-relatives. For working class women, relatives are the most important other people beyond the immediate family of husband and children. For middle class women, relatives are very often less important than non-relatives.

Working class wives are family-type people and relatives are the people they like best. In Chapter II, we noted how often a working class wife reported that if she went visiting during the week, it was usually with a mother or sister or in-law. Also, in a large number of working class households, "getting the whole family together every weekend" is labeled "automatic." (The whole family refers to the extended family: parents, married sisters and brothers, aunts and uncles and the grandparents.) In fact, whenever working class women mention doing anything with other people (going on a picnic, shopping, getting together for dinner, or celebrating a holiday) the other people are relatives more often than not. In the middle class woman's recital of her day, weekend and year, she talks about being out in the world of other people and places more often than do working class women, and relatives enter her recital far less often.

In talking about their preference for "family-type" people, working class women give us many clues to the motivations behind their preference. In the first place, they feel more comfortable in the presence of these relatives, and they tend to have more in common with them than they might with other people.

> We're always visiting our relatives. My brothers and sisters and his brothers and sisters have kids about the same age as ours, and we're more comfortable there. We're all in the same budget bracket and we like doing about the same kinds of things.

103

We are a close family and enjoy ourselves. Our relatives are in neighboring towns and we spend a lot of time with them. We spend more time with our children than anyone else.

We enjoy being with our relatives most. Oh sure, we are friendly with the neighbors, but the people we see are mostly relatives. My husband has a lot of relatives here, and we go up to my home every weekend.

We have big family reunions once a month and then we all get together and drink coffee and talk about the children and the house and who got sick and who's having a new baby—things like that.

The tone of these remarks in explanation of why they are "family-type" people is considerably different than that taken by the middle class women who use the same phrase. Many of the latter interpret "family-type" as signifying the kind of people who act in the spirit of "togetherness," who generally participate socially as a family unit. In this image of the family, they do not include any individuals beyond the immediate circle of husband, wife, and children. They do not mean "clan," as do working class women.

Mostly we do things as a family-group ourselves, but not necessarily with relatives. I think we're what you'd call family type people, but you can strike out that part about the relatives.

We're a baseball-minded family. That's our social life. Whenever our boys are playing ball there we are watching them. The family's all together. Actually, though, we have a more varied life than that description implies.

The affinity of working class women for their relatives as social companions is shown even more vividly by their answers to questions about the people they see most frequently. In our study sample, almost half of the people mentioned by the working class wives were relatives, while only a fifth of those mentioned by middle class women were relatives; further, over three-fourths of the working class women included one relative or more in their answer to the question, but only a third of the contrast women named any. When they were asked to "name the person you like being around most," slightly more than half of the working class women chose as their favorite person a mother, sister, or aunt; while only a fourth of the middle class women did so. (Many of the working class women concentrated their votes on their husbands and children, despite the instruction to "keep your choice outside your family.") When working class women describe the way they feel about these relatives, they claim that they can "relax with them," "have fun with them," or "feel at ease around them."

I have a favorite aunt and a girl friend. Both are very similar in a lot of ways. You can relax with them and have fun.

I like my sister-in-law most. She's kind of gabby and puts me at ease. I'm kind of quiet—but around her it seems that I talk more and enjoy myself.

I like my mother most. She is always ready to pick up and go shopping with me. We have a lot of fun shopping around. I never spend the morning here at home when school is on. We go out together nearly every morning, then she comes home for lunch with me. I really like to go out with her.

There is another sense in which the working class wife is a family-type person, and that is in the continued meaningfulness of the ties to her own parents. On the part of at least some of these wives, there is a *tendency to remain strongly attached to their own fathers.* Their fathers seem to have been quite significant figures in their lives, and somewhat idealized attachments to them seem, in many cases, to remain. To some extent, this idealization is transferred to older men generally, contributing to the feelings of temptation the women sometimes have toward them. A picture of an indistinct figure standing outside an open bedroom door elicits:

You want me to tell a story about this? I could take two on this one. Could be two different things. I will say the man standing there could be looking in on his wife or daughter or son. I will make it his daughter. To see if she is tucked in. Make sure the light is out. To see if she is covered. He checks her everyday like that. See if everything is OK.

This reminds me of a true experience I had for myself. How old was I when I had mastoid, Ma? (Her crippled mother sits watching the children and never says a word.) I was about six. Well, I was very ill and to the point that they thought that I might . . . they might lose me. I was very close to my father then, and I could feel his affection in everything he did for me. He is not the type to be too demonstrative. I lay in bed and he came home from work and I remember when I was half asleep and awake and I knew he was standing there. I overheard my mother tell him she thought I was worse. It was winter already and it was dark and he was standing in the doorway. He stood like in that picture. He was not realizing that I knew he was there and I, as little as I was, I knew what he felt. He was worrying about me and his love for me and he wanted me to be better. He stood a few minutes there. I called 'Hi Dad.' He came and kissed me. I made up my mind I would get well right then. (Great feeling and tears in her eyes.) I made up my mind to get well because I knew he

105

loved me and wanted me to get well, and I wanted to get well right quick for him and I did.

The image of the protective father is a potent one. From everything we have learned about these women, we would conclude that they continue to wish to feel close to a fatherly figure. Whether or not they are able to do so in actuality, it remains a meaningful note in their fantasy and probably is one cause for their frequent wistful disappointment that their husbands are not as attentive or affectionate as they would like.

Working class women also feel a sense of closeness to their mothers, but negative aspects of this appear more often, taking the form of difficulty in breaking away from mother (both before, and after, her death). These women tend not to value individualism. They continue to feel an obligation to conduct their lives as their mothers would wish (though they do not always do so). Comments such as these convey this feeling:

Mother would have a fit if she knew I wasn't going to church all the time.

Since my mother passed on, well, they had the body at the church. I can't bring myself to go. It reminds me so much of her.

Maintaining the image of mother contributes some sense of stability to the life of the working class woman. She feels in this way that she has hold of something solid. At the same time, she often feels that she would like to escape from the potency of this force which seems too influential. When her mother lives close by, there is a problem in the relationship with her. When her mother is no longer present, it becomes a problem in her internal psychic organization.

Despite feelings of closeness, working class wives often do not want to live near their relatives because "it might breed trouble." In view of the frequent demonstrations of affection for their relatives, we might suppose that these women would argue that the most important consideration in choosing a neighborhood in which to live would be the possibility of proximity to these relatives. However, quite the contrary is the case. Few rank being near relatives as important considerations. Almost half of the women in our study sample rejected the idea of living in the same neighborhood with their relatives. Those most vehemently opposed were, in many instances, the same women who announced in another section of the interview that they were "family-type" people.

The notion of living near one's relatives is rejected largely on the score that "living too close to your relatives breeds trouble." These women feel that when their relatives are too close, they try to exert too much influence; they interfere too much with the wife's right to live in her own chosen way.

You can have too much of relatives. It doesn't work to be too close. We used to live right across the street from my parents, and my father was always telling my husband how to do his work, and it made my husband mad, of course. Then they always used to notice whether a light was on in our house—and if we stayed out later in the evening than they thought we should, they would begin to worry about us. We moved away from them, and now we get along just fine.

I want to be a safe distance away from them . . . If they're next door you can run into trouble.

I'd never want to live near the relatives. As it is we get along fine, but if we were closer we might not.

I wouldn't want to live in the same block. A few miles away is all right. I wouldn't want to be living right by them, even though I do love them dearly.

Working class women do love their parents and relatives dearly and want to keep it that way, so they choose a modicum of physical separation in order to retain a maximum of emotional integration.

You appreciate them more and they appreciate you more if they're not too close.

I want my relatives just close enough to visit every now and then, but not too close to spoil the chances of enjoying them.

One source of the working class wife's concern with maintaining close ties of affection with her parents and inlaws, siblings, aunts and uncles, seems to be the feeling that outside this family circle she is friendless and lonely. Many working class women are family-type people through default. Their best friends are within their family less through choice than by virtue of their social isolation from any other kinds of people.

About the only ones I know except my relatives are some of the neighbors here—well, a girl across the street. I hardly know anybody. People move in and out so much. I'm just nobody— why did you ever pick me to talk to about these things?

I don't really see anybody anymore. My girl friends don't come and visit me anymore since they got married themselves. Our neighbors aren't much for us. They're mostly older people. I guess I enjoy my husband's aunt and uncle most.

107

We don't visit too many relatives because there aren't many here in town. But that's who we do visit whenever we go visiting.

Indeed, some working class women are family-types because they are deeply fond of their parents and siblings, but others are family-types because there is no other "type" available to them. At least within the circle of the extended family they find the security, affection, and acceptance which is so much more difficult to obtain from the wider world of "unknown" other people.

By and large, then, it is necessary to conclude that the working class women feel isolated from the world of non-relatives. They may not in fact be isolated, but they tend to feel that it is harder for them to "get acquainted" than it is for average people; and they are fearful that they lack the personal skills for making friends easily. If they are anti-social, it is less because they feel hostile toward other people than it is because they fear other people's hostility or lack of interest in them. If they succeed in being "social," it is frequently accomplished by an act of gift giving, or by the demonstration of an extremely solicitous concern, behind which is implied a hungry "do unto others as you would have them do unto you."

In many ways, the world of people outside the family is a perplexing place. At the very least, the working class wife does not feel readily secure with others. She has a greater inclination than does the middle class woman to assume that others would not be interested in her. Her sense of being actively rejected was illustrated in Chapter III, when we examined how she interpreted a picture of a solitary girl sitting in a doorway. If we look at stories to a picture showing, in silhouette, a group near a wall and a person standing near them, yet somewhat apart, we find this same sense of separateness. Working class women, much more often than middle class women, are apt to tell stories like this:

It just looks like there's a group of people talking and one is left out. Just left out of the conversation.

Is that s'posed to be me, by myself? I think they're all going to church, bein' glad to go, wonderin' if they'll feel better.

A group of people are shunning some poor soul. This one man seems to be alone.

A group of children turned against one of the others. Why they did it I wouldn't know. But you know how kids are—they fight today and then tomorrow they'll all be playn' together again.

These are teen-agers. All boys except the stand-offish one who is a girl. One of the boys is her brother, and of course he taunts her even more. They left her out because at this young age boys think girls put a curse on them.

108

Middle class women show greater variety in how they interpret the relationship of the single figure to the group:

> It seems like a group of young boys gathering at some sort of church. Appears like there's a guard standing in the doorway; maybe a soldier.
>
> The big decision: to enter the group or stand alone on own worth. Possibly this type that would stand on own convictions regardless of what others would think.
>
> This indicates story of an individualist. One apart from the group, very obvious. (Outcome?) Not too well. Probably not come out well at all. Individualists don't fare too well in this world.

Thus, middle class women are more likely to see this solitary figure as being such, either because he is fulfilling some particular formal role which requires him to be apart; or because he chooses to keep himself apart. They can conceive of people wanting to keep themselves apart from the group and of forming independent views and convictions, even when they do not think it wise. When they do interpret the picture as a scene of rejection, they are likely to see it not as something personal and immediate, but as an example of a larger organized framework of events:

> It makes me think of segregation. The one little boy over here, and looks like a group that won't have anything to do with him. He's probably colored and would like to join them, but he knows he's not wanted. He'll go home and talk to his mother about it.

With underlying feelings such as we have described and illustrated, it is not surprising that the working class woman has greater association with kin than with outsiders.

Among the working class wives who think of themselves as family-type people, there are many whose self-placement in that category reflects more nearly a poverty of other-type friends than a powerful attraction to relatives, as we have already noted. This point can be further clarified, however, by illustrating with some additional quotations the "longing" desires which many of the family-type women expressed for friends outside and beyond the circle of relatives.

> Actually, though, we don't go anywhere too much—not even to our relatives since I've had these little ones. I don't even know my neighbors as well as I'd like to. Oh, we speak, but I just don't seem to have time to do anything more.
>
> All of my relatives are here in town and I guess we visit them a lot. But I sure wish we had more company over here.

109

We really don't visit our relatives much. And they don't come here. We just don't go out hardly at all. We don't have much to do with my husband's work people either. It's just the lady in this house—our landlady—that we have struck up much acquaintance with.

We seldom go out and really have only a few friends. My husband and I are both very hard to get acquainted with.

Even those who speak of their friends as coming from a great variety of sources seem to describe their relationships with other people as a vague "catch-all." When asked to clarify, they remark:

Most of our friends are not from our families so we're not 'family-type people.' In fact, until recently we didn't have much time to go anywhere or didn't know much of anybody.

Really none of those descriptions fit us. We just have some friends around town we visit every now and then. We'll talk to our neighbors on occasion too. Sometimes we go to Longview to visit our relatives. We've just met the friends we do know in several different ways but there aren't an awful lot of them.

The working class women who have met "friends in several different ways" reflect quite a different attitude toward these friends and the process of friendship selection than do the middle class women. The latter find mental stimulation in acquaintance with a wide circle of individuals. They also appreciate the variety and quantity of companionship.

It's good to know people from many sources—you learn from people who have different interest from yours. We have a great assortment of friends.

We have some dinner friends, a group we enjoy as a discussion group, and we have another we play bridge with and others we read plays with—these are larger groups—but we also have friends and couples we visit with.

For one there is business associates and their wives—my husband is in the builders' association and we have lots of social functions with the builders. Then we have friends since school days, we both knew them—couples we double-dated with when we were going together. Then another group is our beach group. They are all permanent residents in the cottages there. We have a dance club, my husband's athletic club, and we play bridge with certain couples. But we also like doing things alone, just the two of us for dinner. Then we can talk over our problems.

When working class women describe their friends as the kind of people who "act the same" as they do, the similarity in behavior is, in some instances, almost mystically similar; but for the most part, the similarity they are seeking is in age, budget bracket, or recreational interests.

> We don't like people who drink or have wild parties.

> Most of our friends are from our same social and economic standing. We grew up with them and we all understand one another and know just about what kinds of things we can all afford to do.

> Most people we go around with are my own age. That makes it so nice—I think that you can be really good friends with only people your own age. The younger ones have different worries— take the unmarried girls—and the older ones don't enjoy things so much anymore.

> I have two girl friends who adopted children and we have a little mothers' club together. We're all about the same age and so are the children. We play canasta and poker, we belong to the same church too, and the children were adopted through the same doctor and they were baptized the same day. When we get together as couples the boys talk fishing and we talk sewing.

Middle class women who describe their choice of friends on the basis of "acting the same and doing things together" display some of the same attitudes as working class women. We can probably assume that the working class women who chose this particular alternative are the more socialized segment of the group. After all, there certainly are a number who are not as lonely and friendless as we find the group as a whole is. However, these women do seem to demand of their friends a somewhat greater degree of "similarity" in tastes and habits, in budget and even in children's christening dates, than do middle class women. *When they are able to cross past whatever barriers of shyness they may possess, they do so most readily with people whose social characteristics are most nearly identical with their own.* For example, they discuss their experiences in clubs with such comments as the following:

> The clubs I'm in have mostly friendly women. A lot of them are Italian women like I am. They discuss what goes on and we have interesting activities. I don't get out too often so the club is really ideal for me.

> I like to have contact with other women so I can have a chance to compare notes on home ideas, children, and other kinds of problems. The women in my clubs are plain, ordinary housewives like myself.

111

I enjoy being with other women when we can see how each other does things. We can talk about our houses and our children. The women in these clubs are a nice bunch of women, they're neat and clean like I try to be.

Working class women are not essentially antisocial people. That they are more lonely than hostile, is shown by their response to the notion of seeking a neighborhood on the edge of the city where people would not be breathing down their necks. Whereas, in our study sample the number of middle class women, expressing a desire to live on the edge of the city, exceeded the number who rejected such an aspiration, the reverse was true of working class women: a larger number wanted to avoid the city's edge and its implication of physical isolation from other people than were attracted by whatever advantages such a location might possess. These working class women felt that such a course was "escapist," "snooty," or downright unfriendly.

That sounds out in the sticks—as if you want to be a hermit.

People have to learn to live with one another—there's no point in trying to get away from people.

That sounds too snooty—it sounds like you don't like other people.

Furthermore, some of them, who already complain of being lonely, think that moving to the edge of the city would be the worst possible way for them to overcome this lack of friends.

I want people around me—I'd like a few more than I have at present, if they'd be friendly.

If I couldn't walk down a street and say hello to a few people it would drive me insane.

I'm alone a lot as it is, what with my husband driving trucks out of town, and I like to have neighbors.

I wouldn't mind if people were breathing down my neck a little more than they are right now.

Working class women very much want to "do unto others as you would have them do unto you." In their search for friends working class women recognize the value of doing for others and "respecting them as you would like to be respected yourself." They sometimes reflect an almost paralyzing fear of hurting someone else's feelings, lest in turn their own would be wounded. They are unusually conscious of this equation in human relations, of the transgressor transgressed.

You might call me a pacifist. I believe in getting along with people. There's nothing that hurts me more than having to argue

112

with someone. If you treat someone with respect, you can get along a lot better in life. You should treat them the way you expect to be treated yourself.

My husband and I try to be neighborly with everyone and do whatever we can for the people we know. We don't ever like to do anything that might make people dislike us. We just try to be friendly and hope that other people will treat us the same.

Finally, they are fond of bestowing physical tokens of their esteem upon other people, as well as displaying the more purely behavioral signs and symbols of friendship. We may recall how many of the readers found their greatest pleasure in "buying something for the kids—well, really something for the whole family." They do not draw a boundary line for their gift giving; they enjoy gift giving on any and all possible occasions and sometimes say that the money they have spent most pleasurably was "whenever I've given people a gift and made them happy." Perhaps the classic statement made by a working class woman, in reference to her fondness for gift giving, came in reply to the question: "What would you do if you had $1,000 a year less income to get along with?" She says:

I'd have to spend less money on the gifts I give to all the people I know. I'd just have to try to make my heart a little smaller.

If the working class woman is a "big-hearted person," it is no derogation of her to say that she would be delighted were "other people's" hearts as big as her own. Her great fear is that their hearts are more than a little smaller.

113

CHAPTER VII

NOT ALL AMERICANS ARE JOINERS

So far, we have looked at the working class wife in relation to the close and intimate social world around her: the family, relatives and friends. In this chapter, we examine her relationship to formally organized associations and to the church. Certain clear cut differences emerge between working class and middle class women. It will be apparent that these differences are closely related to, and arise from, some of the personality characteristics of working class women and the realistic concerns arising from their roles as wives and mothers.

First, let us look at their participation in the voluntary associations which are so important a part of American community life, and which have been so fully discussed by social commentators as representing the main avenue available to wives in our society for directly experiencing the larger world of the community and the nation, and for influencing that larger world. Next, we will examine these women in relation to their churches, and their attitudes toward religion, in general. Here, we will be particularly concerned with the extent to which the social organization, the church, is successful in representing and satisfying their religious feeling.

CLUBS AND ASSOCIATIONS

The working class woman is not a club woman. Only one out of every four in our study sample is actively engaged in the enterprises of any woman's club. Three out of every four currently are not taking any active part in a club, although many have done so in the past and many intend to do so in the future. Many of these not currently busy in club work maintain at least a dues paying relationship to some organization or other, in anticipation of picking up on their activity at some later point in their lives.

The working class wife does not take active part in clubs because she believes she is "too tied down with young children" to give time to "things like clubs." She believes that her family, her husband, and her home should come first in her attentions—and that clubs should only occupy her time after these other obligations have been fulfilled.

When she reaches the stage of being a "liberated mother," that is, when her children are all in school on a full time basis, she does tend to become more actively involved in clubwork, in line with her ex-

114

pectation that this will be the case. In our study sample, almost half of the liberated mothers are active club members, in contrast to less than a fourth of "tied down mothers." Most of this increase in club activity of the liberated mother is concentrated on one type of club: the Parent-Teacher Association. In fact, the frequency of the liberated mother's involvement in the PTA makes her a more active woman than any of the other working class categories we have studied: "free wives," "young brides," or "deserted mothers."

Unlike the working class woman, the middle class wife is almost invariably a club woman. In the matter of her enthusiasm for club life, the working class woman registers a quite different attitude than does the middle class wife. More than three out of four of the middle class wives in our study sample are actively engaged in club work; and in their case, the extent of activity seems to be relatively un-affected by "motherhood stage." Almost all, in each category, are active in one kind of organization or another, but we note that the working class women who are active at all participate in fewer clubs than middle class women. The great difference between these two kinds of women is in the extent of activity.

The clubs which attract the loyalties of the working class women and middle class women are somewhat the same. Overall, Parent-Teachers Associations and church guilds are the most popular kinds of organizations for both groups. Actually, there is only one kind of club in which some middle class women take part, but in which no working class woman claims membership, and that is the golf and country club.

However, when we look at the distribution of types of clubs belonged to by the two groups, we do see some differences, in spite of the overall similarity. For our study sample, half of the clubs which working class women belong to have to do with the children—either the PTA or a scouting organization. Conversely, over half of those to which middle class women belong emphasize self-improvement (such as lecture clubs) or adult socializing, even though they may have subsidiary concern with children.

We can sum up by saying that the working class wife is less likely to belong to voluntary organizations. When she does, she generally belongs to fewer than do middle class women; and the ones she does belong to are more likely to be child-centered than adult-centered.

With respect to many of these club types, there is also a distinct difference in the particular species of organization within the broader category, which attracts the two groups. For example, the working class wife, if she is in an occupational auxiliary, is typically in the Non-Commissioned Officers' wives club, or the "fire ladies," or the "policemen's pals." The middle class woman on the other hand, is more apt to be a member of the dentists' auxiliary, the Rotary-Anns, or Ki-wanitas. If the working class wife is in a "card" club, it is probably devoted to bunco-playing; if the middle class woman is in such a club, she probably plays bridge or mah-jongg at her meetings. If the working class woman goes to an alumni meeting, it is probably to a high school class reunion, or a group which went through nursing school together; but when the middle class woman joins an "alumni" group, it is most likely a college sorority group, or the American Association of University Women. If the working class woman takes an interest in politics, she will look to her neighborhood precinct club to satisfy her appetite; while the middle class woman joins the League of Women Voters or the Twentieth Century Republican Women. If the working class woman's husband takes her along to one of his club parties, it will be held at the Moose, Eagle, Elk, or American Legion lodge. When the middle class woman's husband escorts her to a club party, they will probably go to the country club, the Shrine hall, or to one of the local hotel banquet rooms.

The working class woman often believes that her home and family come first, and that clubs are for women "whose kids are grown, so they have time to kill." She says that she is not in clubs because she either does not have time, or the money, or the means of transportation. She believes that her responsibilities to her children or to her husband come before any purely private pleasures she might obtain from "getting out of the house for a minute just to socialize with some other women."

It's hard to go any place when you have children. I can't afford to pay baby-sitters, and I'm not the type to go away and leave my husband alone with the children. My husband comes home tired and he's worked long hours so he doesn't like to be left with the children.

I don't have time for clubs—what with the baby and all. It takes too much of your time—and that's not good if you neglect your husband and family.

With six people at home to take care of, I don't see as how I'd have the time for clubs.

I don't have the time or the money or whatever it takes.

They're outside of my reach financially.

I don't drive for one thing—and it is awfully inconvenient.

We live too far away from anything, and I don't have the car here at home during the day, so I have no way of getting back and forth.

I'm more or less confined to the house because I've had my children one after another and I don't have any transportation.

116

I'll take care of my kids before I'll let clubs come into the picture. I have a young baby and just don't have time. I think a home and husband should come first, anyway. I won't join as long as I have to hire a baby-sitter. The baby is the mother's first responsibility, I figure.

I'm not in any clubs yet—but maybe when the boy goes to school. My family comes first, and if you don't take care of the family, what's the use of having them.

Frequently, she remains out of clubs in deference to her husband's opposition to them, though not always with complete pleasure in accepting his notions.

My husband wants me home—I don't think my husband appreciates clubs. But if that's the way he wants it, it's OK by me. I think husband and home should come first.

My husband dislikes them. He doesn't want me to be gone when he's home—and most things are at night. Actually, I think clubs are a good thing, and if most husbands felt like mine, I wonder who would ever get things done.

Inasmuch as she excuses her own lack of participation in the club world as an example of how she puts "family first," she believes that most club women are those who "neglect their families," or else they have no "young children, they have a lot of free time, the car at home, and don't know what else to do with themselves." Here are some of the things they say about "club women" as a breed.

Club women are usually ones who are not so interested in their housekeeping. They would rather be anywhere other than at home.

Mostly women that have a lot of spare time, they've got their families raised, and they don't have enough else to do to keep busy. Sometimes, women get in too many and can't even do their work at home properly.

Club women are mostly women whose children have started to school, and in that way these mothers are beginning to get a little freedom.

In these remarks, such as "mothers beginning to get a little freedom," and "mothers whose families are raised," we catch hints that the working class wife hopes that maybe her day (for getting into clubs) will come when she too achieves the freedom of having the family raised.

The more prosperous working class woman who lives in a new suburb, and thus comes into more contact with the middle class, is less likely to reject club participation on the grounds that she doesn't have the time or the money, and is more likely to excuse her lack of interest in clubs by pointing to various undesirable aspects of the clubs themselves—the "politics," the "back-stabbing," and the "snootiness" which characterize some clubs and club women.

> There's too much politics in clubs. Everybody is trying to get ahead of everybody else—and I'm not that ambitious.
>
> Clubs tend to be made up of catty women who don't accomplish anything but a lot of talk. The women just talk about one another. Some of the women go just to hear the dirt so they can peddle it around.
>
> I steer clear of clubs. Your club women are snooty a lot of the time. They always seem to believe that the women who aren't in their clubs just aren't good enough to be in them. They won't even bid you the time of day. I've seen a lot of nice sweet people join clubs and their personalities changed after they'd been in the clubs a while. Those snooty club women really make me mad.

Some middle class housewives feel they "can take clubs or leave them," and if they "prefer staying home," it is because "that's what interests me most. If I belonged to clubs, I wouldn't have time to read and do other things I like to do."

In rather distinct contrast are the attitudes towards clubs expressed by many at the lower edge of the working class. At this very low status level, women quite often admit that they "would like to be in a club or two" (if they had the time), but they "haven't ever been invited" and are "too bashful and backward" to push into one.

> I'm just not the type to go out and meet people easily. I haven't gotten to know anyone here as yet, and I haven't ever been asked to join a club.
>
> I don't think I'd be very good at a club. I'm too self-conscious. I've been thinking of joining, maybe that will help me.
>
> I'm ashamed to say I'm not in any clubs—it's usually the very social type of person who joins clubs and I'm not that type. You have to have the knack for getting in those organizations and becoming officers in them. I'm not smart enough to hold an office.
>
> I read a lot about clubs in the newspapers. There's really no reason why I'm not in any club, except that I'm not the going type.
>
> You have to have an interest and be a pusher to be in clubs. I like to be told what to do. You have to be good at public speaking and I'm too nervous for that. You also have to be a good hostess—as there are times when you may have to give a tea or bridge party.

118

The lower status working class women believe that the club world is far above their own social level, inhabited by "Mrs. Roosevelts," or "the wives of small town mayors," and "society people who have lots of money and throw fancy parties." Rather wistfully, these women talk about having "never met anyone who belonged to a club," and express pride whenever "my daughter is just the opposite from me. She's not afraid of people at all."

The working class women who are actively engaged in club enterprises are of two minds about their participation. One group sees their activity (particularly if they are members of a PTA or church guild) as representing an expression of their great concern for their families and children. Unlike those who believe that they are "putting their home and family first" by staying home, these active women contend that they are "putting family first" by going to a club meeting.

> I go to the PTA in order to know what my son is doing in school. I meet his teachers and know the school system. I go to the church because I like the idea of getting together with other Christian people and teaching Christian living to children. Any group I'd join would be one where I felt I could get clean enjoyment out of life.

> Women who are really interested in their children's welfare join the PTA. I always learn something from attending and enjoy the entertainment afterwards.

> My husband and I are in scouting because we felt that if the kids had to participate we should too. The people who are in these things are those who feel it's their duty to their families.

Then there is also a less nobly motivated group of active women who admit that their activity is designed to "get them out of the house" and away from their families. They believe that women are essentially social creatures—and express the opinion that their desire to be out socializing is a normal human tendency.

> I like clubs because it's kind of a diversion to get away—it's the only place aside from a baby shower that I go without my husband, and it's just sort of a change. I think anyone is glad to get out once in a while.

> We're all just normal wives in my club—we like to gossip and forget about house and husband for a while. We're home most of the day otherwise . . .

> Truthfully, I just like to get out of the house and get some adult companionship. My husband isn't home much, so he isn't very good company.

119

The women in my club like getting out for an evening, relaxing, and having a good time—and talking. We like to get out of the house and be with other people for a change—isn't that a good enough reason for having a club.

The attitudes middle class women hold toward organizational activity are sharply different from those of the typical working class woman. Middle class women certainly believe that their club activity constitutes an expression of their concern for the well being of the families, their children, and the wider community. In fact, the urge to "devote my time to some good cause" is most often claimed by middle class women as the motivation for their club memberships.

I enjoy working in a club that has a purpose. I am interested in what's going on in my community—in the schools, and the other organizations which are doing good. I think most women in clubs are the civic-minded type, who are well educated and good-intentioned.

The actual rate of working class women's membership in organizations and the type of membership they have, and the nature of the comments of those who do belong to somewhat formalized groups, testify to one of the most significant characteristics of the group: *they have difficulty feeling themselves to be full-fledged members of the wider society.* Their sense of participation is a rather marginal one. They do not readily identify with purposes larger than those that develop within face-to-face groups such as their own families or, in some cases, with church groups. As the comments indicate, the groups they do join are likely to be for personal gratification of a fairly direct sort. Similarly, participation in such groups as the PTA is construed in terms of knowing what their own children are doing. They are far less likely than middle class women to think of themselves as civic-minded or participating for a purpose conceived of in abstract terms. The community beyond the group of people they know personally is a quite vaguely defined entity that they do not easily relate to their own lives.

Middle class women want also to widen their intellectual and social horizons. They join clubs to "meet interesting people," "to hear about current events," or to "find out about other things and to make new social contacts." Unlike the working class woman who is new in town and does not know about any clubs, the newly arrived middle class woman makes it her business to immediately join a club and strike up acquaintances: "I'm new here in town and I needed the contacts." And unlike the working class woman who is "too shy to go out among people," the middle class woman who feels that she is more backward than she would like to be, tries not to let that prevent her from joining an organization. In fact, it may precipitate her choice of one.

> I'm shy and bashful, and so I'm in the Toastmistress Club because I want to learn how to talk.

It is this kind of diversion—mental stimulation, personal improvement, or widened social acquaintanceship—that motivates middle class women to seek involvement in the associational apparatus.

Few middle class women give the need to get out of the house to avoid "the monotonous life of the housewife with small children" as a determining factor in joining a club. Perhaps less often they feel this life to be monotonous—because they feel less tied down by these responsibilities. The effect of young children upon the middle class woman's social life is typically only a curtailment of social life, rather than a total confinement. For example:

> I've slowed down since the baby and don't take in every single meeting now, and I'm not holding any office for the time being.

On one thing, both middle class and working class women are in complete agreement: "club women can be catty." Middle class women are ready to admit that "sometimes women are just in clubs to try to outdo one another in dressing up," and that, "some club women are only looking for social prestige and want a leadership part." Unlike working class women, however, middle class women go ahead and join these clubs, because they feel they can handle the situation and obtain benefits in mental stimulation or make social contributions, regardless of the personalities of some of the other members.

THE CHURCH AND RELIGION

Working class women are deeply religious women. Almost all working class women believe "Religion gives me peace of mind and helps me face troubles." Most of them also feel that "religion is about the most important thing in my life." Religion means many things to them; it gives them a feeling of "being at peace with the world;" it makes them "feel closer to God;" it blesses them with a "sense of happiness;" it bestows upon them the "strength to cope with life." The greatest benefit they derive from religion is without doubt, however, "peace of mind," and "help in time of trouble." Perhaps this one example will clarify the need for God's help sometimes felt by a working class wife.

> I have to be religious—it's the only thing left, believe me, after everything that's happened to us. My husband is a registered opto-

metrist. He had an office, but had to give up. He couldn't get a clientele going in the neighborhood he selected. It was a bad section of town. I had surgery three years ago and have been sick ever since. We've had to move from house to house. There's been death in the family, and we've tried to give the kids—who really aren't our own—the best. It's been almost too much. More and more I've been asking for God's help. He's got to start helping soon.

In somewhat less dramatic voice, many others chorus this application to religious experience for the answer to trouble.

A sense of peace and happiness comes over me while I'm in church—a feeling of being closer to God. I forget all my troubles, and it gives me hope. I don't worry so much. I believe that God is going to get things right.

To me, life without the church and without God would not be worth living. Our present world is nothing but chaos, and I would that a lot of us go to church to help find the answer to this chaos.

When I go to church I let my husband stay home with the children because I can get more praying done if the kids aren't with me.

Religion not only helps in time of trouble, it also helps the working class wife "stay out of trouble." It gives her a "standard to live by" and "live up to."

Going to church gives you strength to cope with life. It prepares you to be a proper person for the next week.

Religious people are different. They are able to endure things when the going gets rough. We all need religion or we'd wither on the vine. We'd be half alive so to speak. If I didn't have any standards to try to live by I'd be dead.

If you don't have any beliefs you'd be down in the gutter like some people are. Religious people are less liable to temptation.

Everyone should have a fear of God and fear the evils of the devil—if you have this fear you'll live better.

Religion also provides her with a vision of what life might be like without these standards.

To some, the feelings which are gained from attendance at church or other religious rites are somewhat more exhilirating and mystical than these more temporal concerns with trouble and temptation.

When I go to church and see the processionals, I feel like breaking down and crying, it's all so inspiring.

When I'm in church I have a sense of awe, as if I have been with God, in His presence—and I come away feeling kind of holy.

I feel like I'm in sixth heaven when I'm in church—as if I am in a different world. When I come out of church I feel much better, my whole being feels better. I try to have a lot of faith. I just feel safer in church.

These, then, are the most common meanings found in religion: "peace of mind," "help in time of trouble," "strength to cope with life," "standards to live by," "power to avoid temptation," and a "sense of awe in God's presence." In these regards, working class women are not very different from middle class women. The latter also gain a sense of well being from "having gone to church," and they, too, feel that religion gives them "standards to live by," and that "religion can help solve problems." However, they do not report such mystical or awe inspiring experiences with religion.

Yet, working class women are not church goers. Less than half of the working class women in our study sample go to church as often as two times a month. The typical working class wife only goes to church "occasionally," "maybe once a month," or "just for the big holidays, like Easter and Christmas." Still, she thinks "the church is a good and worthwhile institution, and most people would be better off if they attended more regularly." Almost all feel that "the church ought to be the center of a family's life outside the home."

The relationship of the working class woman to organized religion, as represented by the church, more closely parallels her relationship to other associations, as reported in the previous section, than it does to her attitude toward religion and the ideal church.

The church-going behavior of middle class women presents a decided contrast even though their attitudes toward the importance of the church are very similar.

The typical middle class woman describes herself as a "regular churchgoer who does not miss more than one Sunday a month." More than half of the middle class women in our study sample place themselves in this category, and three-fourths attend church at least "twice a month" or "better."

This wide difference in their church attendance patterns is not mirrored by any striking difference in the attitudes of working class and middle class women toward the church as a "good and worthwhile institution" or as the "center of a family's life outside the home." Both groups are strong defenders of these propositions. Both groups are fairly willing to counter with the belief that "you don't have to go to church to be religious—as long as you live right." Working class women are slightly readier to accept this limitation on the church's importance, than are middle class women, while the latter somewhat more often proclaim the church's unqualified merits.

123

All of these differences in the group's attitudes are slight, though, as compared with the working class woman's willingness to denounce the character of some churchgoers with the epithet of "hypocrites." Almost half of the working class women in our sample felt that some of "the worst hypocrites are those inside the church," while three-fourths of the middle class women would not agree that this was so.

Now, in view of the basic similarities between middle class and working class women in their evaluation of the church (with the exception of their attitudes toward the character of some churchgoers) and in view of the strong relationship between social status and church attendance, we would suspect that the working class woman is not a churchgoer for approximately the same reasons she is not a club member. She is afraid that she might somehow feel out of place in a church, and furthermore, she is too tied down with young children and other responsibilities at home to take the time or make the effort to go to church. That the working class wife does go to church more often than she goes to club meetings is evidence that she feels religion more important in her life than the pleasures of club activities.

Actually, their failure to make it to church regularly causes many of these women to "feel guilty about it," and to apologize to their consciences. One echoed the feeling of many when she reported:

> I really am ashamed to have to tell you that I never do except when I'm down home with mother. I go all the time when I'm there for the weekend. She'd have a fit if she knew I wasn't going every Sunday up here too.

A large number express the hope that when the "children get older I'll be able to start up regularly again." Apologetically, they cite their good records in getting the older children in their families to go every Sunday as evidence of their enthusiasm for church-going. As one mother said:

> Somehow, after I have gotten the girls all ready and on their way to Sunday school, I can't seem to get myself dressed in time to make it to church.

Still another considerable group of the Sunday stay-at-homes told of difficulties with their husbands on the church-going issue. Often "mixed" marriages appear to be the cause of defection from the ranks of church-going regulars.

> My husband is Pentecostal and I'm Episcopalian—we can't agree on which to be, and so we don't go at all.
>
> I think we'd go more often if we were the same religion. I'm

Catholic and he's Methodist. He's agreed to raise the kids in my church—but he won't join himself. I think I'm going to win eventually though.

But, in many instances, an inexplicable hostility on the husband's part toward church is claimed.

I don't drive so I can't go unless my husband goes. We used to go every Sunday, but then he quit. Don't ask me why—he just did.

I'd go if my husband would go—but he likes his Sundays off and doesn't want to spend time going to church. That's the only reason why I'm not there every Sunday.

Some of these women feel they "might be out of place" in church because they don't "have any clothes good enough to wear" and fear that some people there would say things, like "she doesn't have another dress to her name." But this is not the reason many working class women would feel out of place. They feel they should not perpetrate the hypocrisy with which they accuse some churchgoers; they seem to feel that it is wrong for "ritually impure" persons, as themselves, to go to church unless they could be altered by the experience. Yet, note the mildness of their "sins."

Even when I do go to church, it doesn't seem to change me. I'm not an angel. I've got a pretty bad temper.

Unless you intend to lead a Christian life it's futile to just go to church and then come home to do the same things you did before . . . I smoke a little and get a little wicked in my talk, and I don't think I can change.

Working class women who are not presently going to church generally hold out this consolation for themselves: the present condition is only temporary; sometime in the future they're going to start up again. The future circumstances which are expected to permit this are either "when the children are older," or when the husband "decides to give in and join my church," or when she learns to drive the car.

You should have asked me how often I go to church fifteen years ago. I used to go every day and twice at night. I even sang in the choir. But now I'm too far away—I'm learning to drive though. And when I've learned, I'll start going to church more often.

125

CHAPTER VIII

MORALITY AND HOPE:
THE CASE OF *TRUE STORY*

Just as behavior in the consuming area differs from one social class
to another, behavior in relation to the mass media varies. We present
here a case study of one magazine, *True Story*, which, we know from
audience studies, appeals particularly to working class women. These
studies suggest that over 75% of the housewives who regularly read
True Story are of the working class (and over 80% of the readers of
the magazine are housewives). They also indicate that the overlap
between readership of this magazine and the more middle class women's magazines is rather low. Thus, although not all working class
housewives read this particular magazine, or one like it, we can say
that we are dealing here with a particularly working class phenomenon. (It has been estimated that over two-thirds of the working
class housewives, who read any magazines at all, read one of the
"romance" or family behavior type.)

It will be worthwhile, then, to examine the readers of this magazine, and the way they respond to it, in terms of the kinds of social
and psychological characteristics outlined in previous chapters. The
data for this analysis come from a research carried out in 1955. The
study involved over three hundred detailed interviews; half of these
with readers of *True Story* and half with non-readers (most of whom
were middle class). The interviews were gathered in Chicago, Battle
Creek, Michigan and Erie, Pennsylvania.

In the following sections we will concern ourselves with the conceptions which readers and non-readers have of the magazine, with
the socio-psychological functions which reading the magazine serves
for its readers, and with the attitudes they have toward, and the use
they make of, the advertising carried by *True Story*. Although we do
not have research evidence to support the belief, we are certain that
the findings reported here for *True Story* would hold in broad outline
for other magazines of this type since we know that their audience
tends to be very similar in social status and age composition.

CONCEPTIONS OF TRUE STORY

Both readers and non-readers of *True Story* derive their conceptions of, and main ideas about, the magazine from what they believe
true of its stories. The stories are the main focus of interest and give

the magazine its character. The magazine is read by those women who find the stories have an especial appeal. The non-readers, in turn, generally reject the magazine (with varying degrees of intensity) because of what they believe the stories are about and their attitudes toward such content.

Readers' attitudes are typified in these comments:

They are true stories about romances, good times, destruction and other things. They are very interesting stories.

Well, the main thing is that the stories in *True Story* are stories that actually happened to people. They are true life experiences. It's very enjoyable reading as you can see someone else has a lot harder times than yourself.

And non-readers' comments are typified by these:

I just doesn't appeal to me. I don't think they should be around the house. I like fairly good literature, especially for the children. I suppose it's all right, but I never bothered with it.

I don't know, when I was a kid in school I thought they were just the thing. But now I can't stomach them. There's too much sex in it. Then I haven't looked at those magazines in years and years.

It is quite clear that overall rejection of *True Story* by non-readers is based on their conception of the magazine as primarily containing stories which have to do with sexual relationships. These same stories, on the other hand, represent the main value the magazine has for its readers (although they show general interest in other features of the magazine). For them, the stories do not deal primarily with sex, but are concerned with a range of topics of importance and human interest.

Other features tend to reinforce and fill out the meanings supplied by the stories. Particular items like "The Village Pump" (a correspondence column), the various inspirational, religious and advice articles fill out the readers' conceptions of the magazine.

I like the articles by Don McNeil, they are very interesting.

I always read the "Village Pump," you get a lot of ideas from it, it's nice to know about what other women are doing and thinking.

It has some good religious articles. I read those too.

Some of the articles on medicine and things like that are interesting. It tells you about what to expect and what to do about it.

Non-readers seldom seem to take into account that *True Story* contains anything but the "true stories."

The home features seem rather well attended to, although they are definitely not the main source of interest in the magazine. The women who also read the women's service magazines are less likely to take serious interest in the homemaking features, although their general interest in anything that has to do with the home leads them to read *True Story's* home sections in addition. For the majority of readers who do not read any of the service magazines, the homemaking features are very much a part of the magazine and they tend to follow them quite regularly.

Well, I mentioned about the recipes. I like them very much. The women's columns are very good. They have little household hints. (Like what?) Oh, like how to keep a cake from falling, and what to do if you're having trouble getting a soft creamy icing. Just little suggestions that are helpful.

I like the home column. I use the things on cleaning and the recipes are all right. Home spare time work ads though are the bunk. The doctor's column, they make sense.

I read the recipes sometimes and tried them things. Well, the ones on child behavior help me to understand my three-year-old better. Paterns I use sometimes, or a new pill or cure that they discover, I learn about them.

They have good articles on diseases. I like the patterns too. I love to crochet and they have some good ones. I like the recipes. I try them sometimes. Quite often they have articles on how to remove stains, too.

This, then, roughly covers the prominence of the various features in *True Story*. Our research was not designed to investigate exhaustively the attitudes toward particular parts of the magazine. However, this much of attitudes toward the specific contents had to be covered in order to have a basis for thinking about the meanings of the magazine, the image which it has for its readers and non-readers. In summary, the major definitions of *True Story*, for both readers and non-readers, are influenced primarily by the conceptions these people have of the stories and their meanings. The non-readers have very little conception of any other parts of the magazine, but the readers do read other features with interest.

True Story is realistic. The readers, for the most part, see the magazine as a realistic one, dealing with people's actual problems in a sensible and realistic manner. There is much discussion of *True Story* being concerned with real life situations—not with just the bizarre and infrequent, but with common and everyday situations.

128

Thus, when we asked women whether they could make up a story out of their own lives which could fit in *True Story*, we found that although they were reluctant to say (or admit) that they themselves had been in *True Story*-type situations, they often said that some of the things that had happened to people they knew would fit very well.

> Oh, I've known about things like the True Stories. (Pause.) Well, you know you hear about things all the time—you can tell those stories are true, there are things like that just happen. Well, like wives getting abandoned or raising children. Not things that happened to me, but things you know about.
>
> I don't think they compare with me. I haven't had as much trouble as they have in those stories. But some of the problems I guess I've had. My other marriage broke up. I guess I could write about love and romance. Just about my romance and marriage.
>
> The stories seem real. They're interesting. One seemed like my life once, but just sometimes. (Tell me more.) Well, just parts of the stories sometimes seem like that.
>
> Well, I never thought about writing a story. I like to read but not to write. I don't even get my letters written. Some of their stories are like my life, I guess. Some of the problems. We always manage to work them out though; maybe not the same way they do in the book. Well, in a certain way they compare with my life, everybody has problems.

Of course, not all women are even willing to come this close to saying that *True Story* bears a resemblance to their lives. Nevertheless, women do say that the stories are realistic—if they aren't like their own lives, at least they are things which happen and which one can expect to happen. There is much discussion of "liking to read about other people's problems." The general feeling of the readers that the stories are realistic and sensible is well summed up in comments like these:

> *True Story* is, well, it's down to earth more. They devote their time to facts you know, it's there and you deal with it, and sometimes it's love and sometimes it's sad—just like life generally.
>
> I like to read *True Story* because I know they are true. *Intimate Romances* I just read to have something to read. It's better than the other romance books that are out. (How do you know *True Story* has true ones?) I take it for granted. They are more realistic then the other stories, they could be true.

In sharp contrast, the non-readers think of *True Story* generally as being somewhat bizarre, different, as not dealing with down-to-earth actual situations. They do not have to quarrel with the "truth" of the stories to feel that they are unrealistic. It is simply that the non-readers do not believe that *True* Story deals situations which are important and significant ones in their own lives.

> Oh, I used to read them. (What do you think about them?) Well, a lot of times I think it's just some fanatics who have written stories about themselves. If you read one story, you've read them all.

> I don't care for it. It's mostly love stories. The people are always breaking up and married people are always cheating or getting into trouble. One story is the same as all the others.

> It's just a bunch of love stories.

The idea was often expressed that *True Story* contains stories which are "just a lot of" something or other. The word "just" gives us the cue that non-readers dismiss *True Story* situations as really not pertinent to their lives, as having no real meaning for the world they live in.

True Story is human, concerned with people. Very much a part of the idea that *True Story* is realistic is the notion that it is a magazine which is, first and foremost, concerned with people, their lives, and their problems. Over and over, readers make some reference to the people involved in *True Story.* They are aware of the relevance to human problems rather than to the more impersonal ones. They see it as a magazine which sharply focuses attention on *human events,* on things that happen *to people,* on how *people act,* how *people feel,* etc. Non-readers also think of it as people-centered, but because they do not think of it as realistic this has little positive meaning for them. Their stereotype of the kind of people who appear in the magazine tends to be along negative, or at least indifferent, lines.

We see this conception operating most clearly when we ask readers to describe the kind of person who is interested in *True Story,* the "personality" of *True Story.* They tend to see it as a magazine for a woman who:

> . . . is interested in people, and nice to everyone.
> . . . wants to be nice to all the people she knows.
> . . . is someone mostly interested in people.
> . . . is interested in other people and helpful to people.

True Story is youthful. Both readers and non-readers agree that *True Story* is for younger people; that it does not seem appropriate for older people. There are differences, however, in *how* young readers and non-readers see the magazine.

By and large, non-readers tend to think of the magazine as a publication for very young people—for teenagers or for women who have not really grown up. Thus, they imagine a reader of *True Story* would be:

> A Miss, probably around 28.
> She's somebody who doesn't know what she wants, or can't find it. Somebody lost.
> She'd be a Miss, about 16. A gullible, possibly lonely girl who craves romance or excitement. I wouldn't judge her too badly because she is still immature.
> She would be a Miss, about 16. She'd be a very lively person trying to get a few pointers on life.

The readers, of course, see this youthfulness in a much more positive way. They believe the magazine is for the younger person, or the somewhat older person who still has much of the young-at-heart in her personality, and is still interested in youthful things. The youthfulness attributed to *True Story* probably derives from several factors. First of all, in our society it is assumed that mature adults really do not have problems. To have and to be interested in problems is presumed a phenomenon of youth, because one has not yet worked out a stable solution to life situations. Also, the emphasis on problems concerning sex and one's relationships to people of the other sex, deepens this youthfulness idea. Adults are traditionally assumed to have solved their problems with sexuality and to have found, through marriage, a stable way of dealing with them. Thus, we find from readers, remarks such as these about the probable readers of *True Story*:

> Well, she's at the marrying age. She'd be going through different falls of love and things like that until she gets settled down. Maybe she'd be a young housewife with perhaps a baby, one that needed advice.
> She would be young, and in love with her husband, and likes to find out how to solve her problems.
> It's for the younger Mrs. between 25 and 35. She's younger but she's not a teenager. She's somebody who likes a home, yet has been places and seen things.

True Story is moral. The readers, in fairly sharp contrast to the non-readers, think of *True Story* as a magazine which points up moral conflicts and points toward a moral solution of them, within a realistic context. This moral realism they tend to think of as somewhat distinctive for *True Story*. They may see other magazines as also being quite moral, but on a more elevated plane, on a plane not particularly

131

pertinent to their concrete experiences and daily lives. Thus, they say things like this:

> This story just shows that helping people and being good is the things that make a person the happiest and then real happiness can come to you.
>
> I thought it taught a very good lesson (a story about a mother who causes juvenile delinquency) because it shows that you shouldn't be too strict, just as you should not be too lenient.
>
> Those stories tell you about right and wrong. They show how what happens when people don't follow the straight and narrow. I think it's good for some of the younger ones to read, they learn more about life and what's good and what's not.

Although they see it as moral, they do not see the morality as obscuring or overshadowing concretely realistic presentation. In this sense, the morality of the magazine is less important to them than the realism (although they would probably quickly reject a magazine in which moral resolutions were ignored).

As we have seen, and with no need to belabor the point, most of the non-readers regard *True Story* as unrealistic; often as silly, often as too sexy. In terms of their values, the magazine could not possibly be moral. Some women reject it outright as immoral, others see it as silly and childish.

True Story is positive. Readers see the magazine as one which generally presents positive solutions, as representing a generally constructive point of view. Non-readers, as we have seen, tend to perceive *True Story* as a much more negative object and tend to project onto its readers generally negative characteristics of immaturity, of "being fanatics," etc.

In describing the magazine and attributing a personality to it, the readers tend to emphasize characteristics of "niceness," congeniality, friendliness, and to describe the stories as working toward positive resolutions. They certainly value this in the stories and articles—the "happy ending" is very important to them.

> All their stories are good. *True Story* makes you learn a lot, all about kinds of people, about their problems, and about how they help one another, what what to do if it's your problem too.
>
> I read about a little blind boy. It stands out in my mind because they were helping him themselves and treating him like an ordinary child. Most of them I forget, but that one really stands out.
>
> I recall a story about a girl who lost her lover and then she was in trouble . . . and when she met this fellow that fell head

132

over heels in love with her and they were married and she was happier than ever before.

In this area, again, the realism of the magazine must be taken into account. It would seem that these people do not think of the magazine as too nice or hopeful or positive. Rather, it is positive within the context of a difficult and often unpleasant reality. They see it as generally presenting a *reasonably* positive outcome.

THE FUNCTIONS OF TRUE STORY FOR ITS READERS

True Story mirrors their conflicts. *True Story* mirrors in good detail the types of conflicts these women have in their lives, and presents these in a social context which is familiar and meaningful. In so doing, it gives them a kind of objectivity in facing their conflicts which it is not easy for them to achieve. By being able to read stories about other women, generally of similar background and often with similar experiences and problems, they are somewhat better able to step out of their own lives, and view the situation through the eyes of someone else. Psychologically, this has a very important function. The more middle class women's magazines do the same thing, but they tend to mirror different conflicts, in a different context, and with different implicit attitudes and values.

This is the central fact about *True Story* for its readers, and the central source for its rejection by non-readers (whose conscious and near-conscious conflicts are usually not the ones *True Story* pictures). It is from this fact that the conception readers have of the magazine runs along the line of realism, "problems" of everyday life, concern with people and their experiences, even though the degree of conscious acceptance of the fact that *True Story* mirrors their conflicts certainly varies from reader to reader, as does the conception of the magazine as mirroring their past or their possible future problems.

True Story does not present standards that are too high. We have seen that *True Story* is considered a moral magazine. It does present standards to the reader, and is valued for this. The morality is one she understands; it is a strict and sometimes rigid morality in terms of what it defines as right or wrong, but it makes allowance for failure to always measure up, and emphasizes the possibility of forgiveness, the legitimacy of extenuating circumstances such as innocence or good intentions. Again, we see the realistic and positive conception of the magazine: it sets reasonable goals for behavior and accomplishment; it does not present ways of acting and feeling which seem too removed from how the reader believes she can behave. One important reason why readers value *True Story* (and often prefer it to other magazines which also deal with women's problems) is that they feel the other

133

magazines set standards that are too high. The readers, conscious of their own characters and social position, are aware that they cannot live up to every aspect of the core culture value system which they see mirrored in many different and subtle ways in these other magazines (and which represent the strength of these magazines with the middle class audience). They feel that *True Story* does not so uniformly impose these standards, but allows for the play of human emotions and some compromise to a woman whose strivings are basically moral.

True Story reassures and accepts. Readers seem to feel that *True Story* does not condemn the things which it delineates; rather, it accepts them as some of the unfortunate events of human life, and reassures the women that there is a way out; catastrophe does not necessarily follow adultery, and a woman can regain her moral status. To the woman who is "hating herself in the morning," or hating herself in advance for a possible "next morning," both the content and the tone of *True Story* are reassuring.

As we have pointed out, the reader is typically of the working class, and lives among people who do not wholly subscribe to, or at least fully realize in conduct, the middle class value system. Her controls, in terms of these values, are not stable and secure, and her psychic economy must make room for possible transgressions of moral standards without an overwhelming sense of guilt or shame.

Repetitively in the interviews, the women recall and retell with evident satisfactions, stories of women who have transgressed, and still manage to live a good life. The happy ending, which reconciles a woman's needs and wants with moral standards, after immoral behavior, is obviously reassuring. Similarly, with the stories which deal with "hard knocks" (the blind child, the alcoholic husband, etc.), the reassurance which comes from the woman's ability to rise above such adversity, gives the reader hope that she, too, can carry on in a world which she often finds difficult.

True Story helps and encourages the woman. She likes to read about "other people's" problems because she has had, or may have, some of the same ones. She very definitely feels that *True Story* increases her store of knowledge about *what to do* in difficult human situations. Since she often feels uneasy about what to do, what to say, how to feel, what moral viewpoint to take, *True Story* serves an important function in her life by giving her an example, a model, by which to guide her behavior (even if sometimes it is only along the line of "Don't do like I did, do like I say"). In doing so, it encourages her to resolve her problems more effectively.

Many a reader seems to implicity assume that she will be in some of the situations the stories portray. She does not find it fantastic to believe that she really may step out on her husband, or have conflicts with him over sexual relations. Given this, her problem is, "Then, what do I do?" She feels that *True Story* tells her what to do through the medium of case histories about women in similar situations.

Some of the readers do not feel so close to these problems. For them, the refrain is more likely to be "I like to read about other people, people whose lives have been harder than mine, and learn about them." For them, there is reassurance and encouragement in the contrast itself—the stories tell them that things could be worse, that they should learn to appreciate the advantages they now have, much as when a parent says to a child, "There are lots of boys and girls who don't have your advantages."

The magazine reduces the sense of isolation and aloneness. Like all of the mass media, *True Story* provides its readers with a kind of symbolic interaction with other people, and a way of seeing oneself in other places. We know from our personality study that these women are inclined to feel isolated, friendless, intimidated in social contacts. It is particularly important to them, therefore, to have ways, if only vicariously, of participating in social life. By reading the stories, they feel more participant and engaged with others. Because of their particular concerns and preoccupations, this vicarious participation takes the form of living through problems to a reasonably happy ending, with a great deal of emphasis on the problem. As noted above, the problem focus serves several functions, but in addition to those specific to the problem and its resolution, the stories do provide this way of feeling one is in contact with people, this way of cutting down for a while on feelings of isolation. In this fashion, *True Story* serves to link its readers to a larger social reality than that of their everyday world. By promulgating a particular moral outlook and regularly providing certain kinds of problem solutions, *True Story* can be said to generate, or at least supplement, the readers' moral tradition. Fostering, in this way, a larger identity for its readers, the magazine can be regarded as contributing to social cohesion.

True Story provides fantasy gratification and thus reduces tension. As pointed out above, readers prefer to talk about the more realistic and moral aspects of *True Story,* or to talk in generalities about it being interesting and exciting. They do not always talk willingly of interest in love stories, or in stories that deal with sexual or aggressive behavior. Yet from their comments, it seems quite obvious that they value *True Story* because it provides them with material for fantasies about adventure, particularly erotic adventure.

They do, however, talk easily about the magazine as being interesting, entertaining, relaxing, and a good way to get away from the daily grind. The magazine is stimulating to them. It talks about situations

135

and actions which interest them and which are meaningful to them because the content parallels their own feelings and wishes.

Dreaming, daydreaming, and fantasy play a very important part in preserving one's stability, and in aiding individuals in controlling their actions along socially acceptable and effective lines. To the extent that *True Story* provides material for fantasy gratification of these women's impulses (and provides it in a positively toned and reassuring context), it gives them concrete aid in managing themselves through reducing the tensions which come from life's experiences.

Such a fantasy function could not, however, be well served unless the magazine was also regarded as moral and respectable, since this keeps the fantasies stimulated from being painful and guilt-ridden.

True Story helps readers organize their past, and the transition from adolescence through single adulthood to stable marriage. By presenting and dealing with many conflicts which revolve around the status of the young woman (from the teenager to the young wife), *True Story* helps the woman to organize her own feelings about herself in this difficult period in such ways as these:

It helps her integrate and justify her past behavior.

The occurrence of many of the late adolescent problems presented in *True Story* is not uncommon among this group. By reading *True Story* the woman learns that she was not alone, that such things are part of normal growing up, and that she can accept her past behavior, and not feel that it has disastrous implications for her future.

It does not push her prematurely into the mold of a self-controlled, non-sexual, middle class mother. That is, it deals with the presence of unfamily-like feeling in young married women, and it tells her that these "adolescent" residues are not to be regarded as abnormal, but should be dealt with as normal, realistic problems of control and affection for others.

If she has become rather highly controlled, it helps her to release, through fantasy, the impulses which she has but cannot express overtly.

An older, more stably adjusted woman may still experience many of the impulses with which the stories deal, but not be close to acting them out. Still, by reading, she can live through some of these impulses in fantasy, and thereby reduce the tension and anxiety they cause.

True Story provides guidance and information for more mundane, day-to-day problems. Up to this point, we have talked about some of the functions of the magazine which are peculiar to its content and character. The magazine (as we have seen in examining responses to

136

the articles and the advertising) also serves more down-to-earth functions. *True Story* is a magazine to which the readers can turn for help in the wide range of problems the housewife in our society must meet: from children to food, etiquette to illness. As we have noted, the women's interests are heavily weighted in the direction of home and family; the help they receive from *True Story* in this area is important, even though it does not stand out as strikingly as do the more emotional functions.

The teenage aura about the magazine also makes some of the older women value it concretely for the guidance it gives them in teenage problems. Frequently, they encourage their daughters (though not their sons) to read it, on the logic that forewarned is forearmed. Thus, the woman with an older daughter often regards the magazine as not only appropriate to her own realistic problems, but also to her daughter's.

ATTITUDES TOWARD THE ADVERTISING IN TRUE STORY

The advertising in True Story, for the most part, is well-attended to by its readers. The advertising in *True Story* is well suited to the overall character of the magazine and to the kinds of women who read it. Readers are often notably familiar with the advertising and able to recall not only the range of things which are advertised, but also a large number of specific brands. Thus, of the readers interviewed, 61% recalled advertised *brands;* 14%, *products* but not brands; and 25% could not recall anything.

The general familiarity with the advertising in *True Story* is revealed by comments such as the following:

> I look at most all of the ads—like the ones about foods. They have menus and how to fix different things sometimes. Yes, I look at the things about chidren's clothes, nice things for the house, etc.
>
> Yes, I'd certainly say the ads were good—especially the ones on soap and things. In fact, I wish they weren't so good. I usually buy what I see advertised.
>
> I like advertising in magazines. I just love it—best thing they can do—especially *True Story*. I can hardly wait for the next one after reading the first one . . .

Personal products, for example cosmetics, are felt to be appropriate for True Story. The *True Story* reader, feeling some special attachment to this magazine (though it may be one of several she reads) expects to find articles of a personal nature. Because *True Story* talks about more intimate things, its readers expect it to advertise personal items such as cosmetics—ranging from soaps and shampoos (which are the most widely recalled of the cosmetic products advertised), to lipsticks, eye make-up, facials, perfumes, deodorants, etc. Nearly half of the respondents were able to name specific brands of cosmetics which are found in *True Story*. These products fit in well with the intimate, feminine, sexual qualities which dominate the *True Story* image.

It's good. I'd say lots of things you'd be interested in buying for your face, hair, and hands. Good too for ads for baby things, foods, and food ads. Prell, Lustre Creme, Lux Toilet Soap, different shampoos.

. . . most of them are about perfumes and lipsticks. They tell you how to make your husband love you. If I didn't know, I sure wouldn't be married today. (What are some of the brands you remember seeing in *True Story?*) Maybelline—they were telling about eye shadow. Revlon was advertising lipstick. Playtex showed their girdles.

Oh, I look at all those different ads in there on makeup. You know different ways to fix your hair and how to put on make-up. I always look for those ads the first thing . . .

The *True Story* reader is concerned with physical attractiveness, and interpersonal relationships between men and women. *True Story's* stories place considerable emphasis on these matters and this is one of its appeals. Readers are interested in their own bodies, how they can retain youthful attractiveness, having babies, keeping their husbands satisfied, etc. They prefer ads showing people, particularly young attractive people, whom they are able to view as figures for identification.

I like ads with people in it. I like to see what they are doing. Maybe where they are—things like that. I like Listerine ads, because usually there's a man and a woman in them. I guess I really don't *not like* anything. I notice people but I look at other things too, but can't think of anything special right now.

I like ads on women's dresses. I like to see what they look like then you know what you are getting for your money . . . all of the pictures of movie actresses and the cosmetics they show. I always look at all that stuff. I look at most all of the pictures, but I don't read most of the stuff they say about it. (Dislike?) Oh, all these ads of pictures of alcoholics and that. Those ads on non-smoking. I don't think that should be in magazines. Oh, I like lots of real splashy color in ads—that helps to sell stuff.

I like a pretty face, and not much writing. I always notice color. Anything plain I just skip. I like the Modess or Kotex ad and that

138

just says 'Because'. It has such stylish clothes and the most beautiful girls. (How would you like to see the ads?) If I were writing an ad, I'd make sure it had plenty of color, pretty girls, and very little writing.

Other personal products are also felt to be appropriate for True Story. These women are able to become quite involved in the stories, and to put themselves in the position of women they read about, to experience many of the feelings which they might have were they in similar positions. This ability to become personally involved is carried over also into the advertising. Personal products, feminine in nature, other than cosmetics, fit well into this setting. These items include underclothing, bras, girdles, hose, sanitary napkins, cleansing tissues, etc.

Oh, they have those "Modess ads—you know, 'Modess Because' and they have Maidenform Bras. What's that thing—'I went dancing in my Maidenform Bra'. (Laughs) And Playtex girdles and baby things. Oh, that's about all I can think of . . .

Personal gratifications and wifely responsibilities lead to strong interest in the food area. The pleasure of eating and preparing tasty meals for the family is important. Their lives are largely confined to their homes and what they sometimes regard as an endless routine of domestic chores. They feel entitled to the few personal satisfactions they get, in a day full of hard work for their families. They are able to derive personal pleasure from preparing as well as eating good food, and thus the readers recall many food ads and recipes.

I look at the foods and the recipes for them—and clothes. Clothes and recipes. With four children you don't get many clothes for yourself.

I get lots of things from *True Story*. Their recipes are very splendid. I made some of their cakes. They have different things to put in turkey to make them look good for Thanksgiving.

I like the food ads mostly—pretty dishes and nice food. I love to look at pretty dishes all fixed up. I can never get them to look like they do in the pictures.

I think it should show what the ad is talking about. Like a picture of food so you would want to try it. I should look good to eat like the one I saw advertising Spry and there was fried chicken in it . . .

Products for children are of real interest to the True Story reader. The woman who reads *True Story* spends a good deal, if not most, of her time at home. She is likely to have young children or infants and to spend a great deal of her time taking care of them. Her time and energy are largely consumed by her domestic duties and there is little place in her world for goings-on outside this sphere. Many of these women devote much of their daily routine to their babies, and ads for food or clothing for infants are of a good deal of interest to them. When asked what advertising they remember from *True Story*, respondents are likely, as we have seen above, to mention things for babies, especially baby food.

There's baby things—Johnson's and other kinds.

Sometimes they have Pet and Carnation recipes for nursing mothers. Sometimes I try those recipes for Billy and me. I like those Playtex bras and wear those rubber gloves. A week is about all I can wear them. I look the Gerber baby food ad over every time I go to the laundry.

I know there's an ad on Maidenform bras. I noticed them in there and bought one. Guess there is one in there on Spencer Baby Clothes too. Oh yes, I know there's ads on baby foods— Clapp's or Gerber's. They both show babies on their can . . . Johnson and Johnson oils and baby powders.

Products for the home are also of interest to the True Story reader. They do nearly all of the purchasing for the household and they often feel that their shopping time is limited—especially those who are "tied down" most of the time by small children. They are able to save time by looking over the home furnishing ads in *True Story* and assess possibilities for their homes.

I like the furniture ads, of course—and homes too. Almost anything pertaining to the home. I benefit by it—either in planning, decorating, arranging furniture.

I like pictures—colored ones especially—kids' pictures are my favorite. And home, how I love pictures of homes and furniture and bedding and clothes.

Well, of course the ads that appeal to me most are those that show rooms. If I see a picture of a kitchen or bath, or any other room that appeals to me, I clip it out and keep it.

It seems to me that any ad that is big, full of color, and catches your eye is good. Some of these ads of furniture, new homes— really almost take the money out of your pocketbook. They're too good. They make people buy that don't have the money. (Appeals?) All the ads on food are very pretty now—like the ads on Betty Crocker and Swans Down cakes. (Doesn't appeal?) I can't say there is much I don't like. I wouldn't say there is anything except perhaps articles that have a lot of writing.

Overall, it appears that the advertising in True Story is appropriate for its readers in terms of social class. They are able to feel "at home" with the kinds of things advertised in *True Story*—in a sense they feel these products are for women like themselves. One important aspect is the feeling that most of the items advertised in *True Story* are not beyond their means; another is that they are quickly and readily understood. In all, the advertising in *True Story* is felt to be appropriate for people like themselves, for housewives whose lives are in many ways similar to their own.

Within this context, however, they want advertising to be colorful, lively, attractive, etc. Even more than most women, the readers like advertising which is visually stimulating; large, bright, cheerful, eye-catching, and in general, colorful. They like pictures which have *people* doing things, ones which communicate action, ones which are dynamic. Advertising which is technical or matter-of-fact is thought to be dull or uninteresting.

Part II

CONSUMER BEHAVIOR

CHAPTER IX

DOLLAR DECISIONS

Everyday decisions to buy this, postpone buying that, and consider more seriously what to do about a clanking refrigerator take place within the context of purchases already made, ones long planned for, certain overall conceptions of oneself and one's family economically, and certain habitual ways of managing the family's income. These hard facts and psychological fancies form the backdrop against which those day-to-day purchases which constitute the flow of goods from store to working class home are acted out. If we are to understand why it is that the working class housewife buys the things she does, when she does and in the way that she does we need to know something about the particular economically relevant context in which her consuming decisions are made.

Working class women, like most American women, are somewhat discontented with their financial status. However, they express more "absolute" discontent than do middle class women, whose discontent is more nearly "relative." The former do not admit that their dissatisfaction is rooted in human nature as do the latter; they do not blame their dissatisfaction on any human weakness to "want more no matter how much you already have." Working class housewives genuinely feel that their incomes are inadequate for participation in many of the normal activities of American life, like being in afternoon clubs, taking "nice" vacations every year, going "out on the town" in the evening every now and then, or stocking their homes as well as they would like. Middle class women believe their incomes are sufficient to any of these purposes, and they proudly point out that their participation or rejection in any of these so-called "normal activities" is more a matter of personal preference than financial considerations.

Most working class women realistically assess their families' incomes as average or a little bit below. Few think of themselves as being much above average (even when their husbands have some of the higher-paying working class jobs). It is not that they believe they are particularly disadvantaged compared to their neighbors and other average people; rather, it is that they feel their incomes just are not large enough to cover the things they think they should buy, and are entitled to have. They tend to think of themselves as people for whom ends meet, but not as comfortably as they should, and sometimes the ends are made to meet by a sacrifice in the mid-section.

Thus, working class women have a strong psychic sense of money deprivation in spite of their relatively good incomes. In comments about their economic position, we find a persistent theme of not having enough to go around, yet we know that they have close to average incomes for their community, and that they amass a respectable quantity of goods. Overall, this sense of economic deprivation seems, to the outside observer, primarily relative. One of its main sources lies in the avidity with which they consume, and the strong desires they have for material well-being.

In the section on the working class wife's relationship to the associational apparatus of American society we noted that they typically claim that they neither have the time nor the money to take part in clubs. These women feel their homes and families come first. They honestly *feel* they cannot afford to be "club-type women," and this creates some dissatisfactions with their "economic lot in life."

> I don't go to clubs because I can't afford the time or money. It's hard to go anyplace when you have small children. I just can't afford to pay babysitters.
>
> I don't have the time or money or whatever it takes. Most of your people in clubs are the kind who have lots of money and can throw fancy parties.
>
> Clubs are outside of my reach financially. I won't join as long as I have to hire a baby-sitter.
>
> There's too much money involved in one way or another, and we just plain don't have it.

For the same reasons that these wives feel they cannot afford club meetings during the afternoon, they cannot afford to go out to parties with their husbands in the evenings.

> We don't do much at all. We haven't the money to spend going out, much less the price of a baby-sitter.
>
> Right now we don't have much money to do anything social with—so we don't go visiting much, and people don't to come here either. Most of the people we know are about like us that way.

One solution to this problem is suggested by a woman who described her family's favorite recreation in these terms:

> Our family likes nothing better than a drive out in the country. It's good, cheap recreation—and no baby-sitters to worry about. We just pack a lunch and go.

Working class women also experience the same feeling of financial inability with respect to "taking vacations" or "going out in the evening." Their husbands are not paid enough during the work year to permit their saving a substantial enough amount for a vacation. ("We just stick around the house and relax. That's the only way we can get by on his vacations—we don't have enough money left.")

These women sometimes complain of lean holidays, and of a lack of opportunity to privately "celebrate" much on other days of the year.

> We've had so much sickness and doctor bills to pay this last year that we wouldn't have had much Christmas or Thanksgiving if my mother hadn't sent us a little extra money. That way we did get to do a few things that otherwise we couldn't afford.

One reason that working class people are "family-type people" is that it is cheaper that way. If some complain that, "if it weren't for all the relatives I keep giving money to, I might be well off," others must surely be "better off" precisely because they have got relatives.

The pervasive concern over their economic status is also shown in a widely-scattered group of remarks which are presented here to illustrate this general point. A woman observes, for example, that "it's cheaper to live in summer" as the principal difference between the seasons.

> It's cheaper . . . in summer. We can eat outdoors quite often. It doesn't cost us so much to stay outside in the evening. We don't use up all that electric power. But now in the winter we're confined inside and use up all those electric appliances—like TV, that's on most of the evening.

Another cites as her reason for maintaining a church membership the belief that a minister makes a good "credit reference."

> One reason church is so important is that most places you go to ask for a loan they wonder what church you go to. Your pastor can come to your assistance if you've been going to his church a while.

Another woman feels that her grocery bills are problem enough to her without a husband adding to the miseries by bringing extra guests in for dinner.

> A husband oughtn't to bring men from work in for meals. A wife has a hard enough time figuring out how she'll get through the week with the groceries.

We do not wish to imply with these quotations and references that all working class housewives are overwhelmed by the inadequacy of their financial resources. Some of them live in very pleasant homes and are able to take vacation trips to Miami every other winter. However, more of them experience the sensation of not having enough money than the opposite one of having plenty to go around. Many are not bowed down by the weight of their financial problems; instead they use this as a challenge to their creative enterprise. If some of them were forced by economic necessity to spend a few of their early married years in stale and stuffy rented apartments, this experience seems only to have whetted their appetites for "do-it-yourself" projects once they have reached the state of home ownership.

In summer there is yard work to keep us busy, then in winter time we try to do things inside the house so we can have time in summer to enjoy the out-of-doors. We lived in an apartment so long that we really enjoy working in our own back yard. We do a lot of puttering here and there fixing up the inside too. My husband figures he can get quite a bit done on his vacation if he keeps busy.

No More Money Tomorrow Than Today

As might be expected, working class women as a group are not confident that their economic futures hold promise of improvement. They are more pessimistic than otherwise over the prospects for their families' financial futures. They neither have confidence in their husbands' increasing earning skills, nor are they optimistic about the general state of the economy. They fear that the future "won't be any better than the present—and it might get worse." They can only "hope" that their economic status will improve in the future—but their predictions betray their essential lack of faith in "hope." ("I certainly hope my husband makes more money—but you can never tell" or "I hope the future's better than the present.")

They generally believe that their fortunes are at the mercy of economic conditions which they cannot control or even mitigate. In these beliefs they are quite different from the (more hopeful but not necessarily more realistic) middle class women. The latter generally express satisfaction with their husband's earning capacities in the present and have confidence in the ever-more successful utilization of these talents in the future. They do not mention the possibility of adverse economic conditions reducing their standard of living as often, nor do they rely upon "hope" alone to grant them improvement in economic status. In short, middle class women are "quite sure" that their husbands—mostly now of junior executive status or at the young-professional-in-the-process-of-proving himself level—would certainly provide them with a more prosperous future.

The doubt which these working class women express over their husband's capacities to earn more money in the future appears to rest upon a candid appraisal of these husbands' career lines—an unblinking understanding of the likelihood that the future will find him doing much the same thing he has done in the past.

He'll be working as a truckdriver the rest of his life and it's hard to tell what he'll be making. It'll probably be about the same though. An office job just isn't for him. He tried it once and couldn't stand being cooped in.

He's been doing the same kind of work since he was 15. He started as a busboy and now he's a cook. I sure hope he makes some more money in the future, but I'm not counting on it—I sure don't know.

The pervasive fear that the future will not necessarily be any more financially fortunate than the present—that the best a woman can do is "hope"—is illustrated by some of the following remarks:

Maybe we won't be so poor in the future. I don't want much out of life. Just enough to get by on. But my husband's a brick-layer and we keep being afraid that there won't be any work. God be willing, we'll still be living here in this house. Maybe if we get some of these bills paid off I'll be more contented.

I don't think my husband will make any more money. In fact I'm pretty sure he won't. I hope to be able to stay here. I would only move if my husband lost his job.

I certainly hope my husband makes more money. But you can never tell. I hope he makes more, because I'd like to buy a house.

I expect to be living here unless I'm forced out by my husband being out of work. I don't think he'll ever really make much more. They give small raises, but it's not enough to make any difference.

He better be making more. I'm definitely not satisfied on his wages now. My kids need so many things. I do hope there'll be a change, although I don't think so. I don't know whether or not he'll ever make any more—and neither does he. It all depends on how the economic situation keeps going.

He'd better make a little more money. He's just about got to make more money, what with three little kids to take care of.

A good many of these women, however, are not so helplessly willing to accept their fate, nor so accepting of their standard of living. Many of the young working class mothers champ at the bit to get out into the working world (again) and add whatever they can to the family treasury.

I hope it isn't going to be the same all the time. I hope my husband has a better job—but I think the best thing is for me to go out and get a job too.

My husband better be making more. I wish I was working. This is boring. I don't like staying at home. When you're out working you make friends and it's more fun. I hate housework.

I guess it will remain about as is unless I'm working. I'd like to make a few changes and try to buy a home of our own.

Gosh, I hope it isn't going to be the same. I would like to get to work, and quit this housekeeping. This is monotonous. I was washing today from 5:30 to 11:30. I'm all fagged out. I'd like to get some work and make some extra money—Boy-ee, that would be great.

In contrast is the middle class women's tone when asked to speculate about their futures. A great majority of them expect their husbands to make more money. They expect their future to bring them larger houses. They expect to find themselves less deeply mired in the "installment-planned" debt, they count on more recreation time, more time to spend with their adult friends, and more time for travel on purely luxurious vacations, such as a whole summer spent at the lake.

I'm sure my husband will make more money. He tells me that we'll definitely move in 3 or 4 more years in connection with a promotion.

I'm quite sure my husband will be earning more money. He's extremely intelligent. He's advancing in his work, and there's no reason why he shouldn't keep earning more.

My husband is going to school now, getting a master's degree because he wants a better job. He is a person who will never be satisfied to stand still.

We're getting ready to move right now. You don't think we'd be moving if it weren't to better ourselves, do you? Obviously we expect to make improvements and changes in our standard of living during the next 10 years.

Once my husband completes his medical training—he's interning now—and gets established in his profession, I expect our standard of living to zoom right up. I certainly imagine that we'll have a nice home and beautiful furniture and all that sort of thing.

Middle class women believe in planning for the future. They also make a fetish of being dissatisfied as the most satisfactory stimulus to moving upward economically.

I always say that as long as I want things and am not completely satisfied with what I've got I'll continue to be happy. I'm always wanting something more or different or new.

Are we ever really satisfied? I think you might as well make a long-range plan even if it does get upset. I want to spend more money in the future on things like the theater or a few more luxuries than we have now. I want to do more reading and maybe I'll take some courses at the university here in cultural subjects.

For the working class wife, dissatisfaction is apparently too real for her to make a fetish of discontent. She typically wants to achieve some state of financial contentment with a nice home of her own, and relief from the ever-present fear that "the wolf may be at the door tomorrow." A typical response to a question about "what use of your money will be most important in the long run" is "money which we save up against the possibility of hard times"—in line with our other findings about their view of the world as potentially chaotic, working class women manifest a severe case of "depression phobia." And yet, as we shall see, these feelings seem to have only an indirect effect on their purchasing habits, an effect which has more to do with *why* and *how* they think about buying than with what they actually buy.

The broadest context for the purchasing decisions these housewives make involves their homes. Not only does most of what is bought find its way into the home to be consumed, but the home—and what it represents—stands as a kind of umbrella under which the variegated acts of consuming take on meaning and significance. It seems appropriate, then, to examine the context of consumer decisions in terms of the way working class women think about their housing, about what basics go into housing, and most importantly, where the housing is located. We are not used to thinking of the neighborhood in which we live as an item of consumer behavior. Yet, a little reflection will indicate that this is true. One pays more or less for the same housing depending on the neighborhood, and the differences are sometimes dramatic. A desirable neighborhood has a price tag built into the rent of an apartment or the asking price of a house, and people in the market for a home usually have some subjective estimate of what they are willing to pay for the chance to live here or there.

Working class women have fairly clear ideas of what they want in the way of a neighborhood, and what they are willing to pay for it. These ideas also tend to differ rather markedly from those of their middle class counterparts. Most importantly, they are strongly motivated to stay away from what one wife called "the slums and the crumbs." Since most working class areas border, and sometimes interpenetrate, slum areas, particularly in older residential areas, this is no idle issue for them.

In their relationship to the surrounding world of people, these women are as concerned with their public reputations for being respectable people as they are eager to be sociable people. A reputation

151

for non-respectability in either their own eyes or those of the public would be perhaps more devastating to their morale than would be a reputation for friendlessness, but both are apparently ever-present fears.

This fear of being identified with the non-respectable elements in society is reflected in the way many of these women respond to questions about what kind of neighborhood they wish to live in. They express the desire to "live near substantial people" as a goal second only in importance to that of "living near the husband's work." Phrased so, this is a more central consideration in their choice of neighborhood than it is for middle class women. For the working class women, a substantial neighborhood seems mainly a guarantee of isolation from unsubstantial people. They explain their concern over the character of their residential settings with worries about neighborhoods where there are "brawls" or "dens of thieves" or "colored people nearby."

I wouldn't want to live in neighborhoods where there are brawls all the time, or that would be near the colored people.

I wouldn't ever want to be near anything but white people.

I don't necessarily want to be near the moneyed class, but I sure wouldn't want to be living next to any den of thieves, either.

I don't think anybody would want to live in a rough neighborhood.

When I say I want to live in a substantial neighborhood, I mean a neighborhood where people aren't crumby—where people keep their houses up in good condition.

I don't want to live in a neighborhood where there is a lot of cursing and drinking—and where the children will learn bad language.

They want to avoid such neighborhoods because they not only fear the reputation which residents of such neighborhoods tend to acquire—unjust as this may be; they also fear that proximity to such neighborhoods might weaken their own hold on respectability.

I want to live in a nice neighborhood where the kids won't grow up having to be ashamed of their parents.

You can't raise kids properly in slums, no matter how hard you try. There are too many bad things happening around that the kids know about—and you can't always keep control of them.

"If you live near crumbs, it rubs off on you." Working class women are not attracted, on the other hand, to neighborhoods of marked social repute. Many reject the idea of living near "substantial people" on the basis that they would not feel comfortable around people who might be "high-toned" and "uppity." "Substantial neighborhood" for them means "down-to-earth" fellow residents, not "wealthy people."

> I wouldn't want to be out of place in a neighborhood. I couldn't be happy in a neighborhood where other people had more money than I did.

> I don't want to live in a ritzy neighborhood where the people think they are better than anyone else.

> That's OK, living near substantial people—if that means upstanding and moral people rather than just the moneyed class.

Middle class women display quite a different attitude toward the advantages of living near "substantial people." Among the advantages of "substantial" neighborhoods for them are the presence of people with "good standards," "high cultural values"—and the likelihood that the "property values will remain high." The advantage, however, which they consider most important is the "presence of good schools" and "nice youngsters for my children to grow up with." Often, middle class women displace their own desires for a reputable neighborhood onto a concern over their children's social development.

> If you find an area where there are a fine type of youngsters, it usually is associated with a nice type of parents.

> If you're in a substantial neighborhood, you'll find a fine type of youngster in the schools.

> There's really no difference in my mind between the two choices. Substantial citizens have a good crop of youngsters, so you would automatically be in a neighborhood with good schools.

In many ways, then, working class women seem more concerned with what a neighborhood is not, while middle class women have specific ideas about what they do want in a neighborhood. The working class woman wants to feel safe, both socially and physically, in her neighborhood, but aside from that she is not too concerned. The middle class woman values the neighborhood for the social contacts it can provide, as well as for its particular symbolic value socially. Given a minimum standard of decency for the neighborhood, the working class woman is more concerned with the house itself, while the middle class woman has a more complex set of expectations for both neighborhood and house.

In Chapter I we have discussed the kind of housing characteristic for working class families. We noted that the majority of them own their own homes, and many more aspire to. By and large their desires for housing are modest; they want an adequate house in terms of rooms for the family, they want something in reasonably good con-

153

dition (and are willing to put a great deal of "do-it-yourself" labor into improving its condition). Preferably the house should also look "nice." Those working class families who do not own their own homes look forward very much to being able to do so, and much of their consumer behavior is conditioned by the planning for that nicer, more permanent dwelling. Major expenditures on appliances, furniture and the like are held up until there is the proper place to put them. Once the "house of arrival" is purchased, the working class housewife's major purchasing interests tend to center around getting it properly stocked. This usually means a television set, one or two radios, a good, but not necessarily the best, refrigerator, range, an automatic washer, a vacuum cleaner and such smaller appliances as a toaster and a mixer. In the first decade of marriage much of the working class wife's planning goes into providing herself with these "essentials" of a well-stocked house.

It seems likely that appliances and food represent the main areas of necessities for working class families. A large proportion of their budgets go into these two areas, and their total expenditures in these areas probably differ less from those of middle class families than in most other areas. Expenditures for housing are much more a function of class—in many ways the working class housewife expects to put much the same appliances in her home that the middle class woman does, and she is willing to sacrifice a more expensive house if she can appliance it as she wishes. Similarly, she is not nearly so willing to cut down on food (and, of course, this is much less possible) as she is to skimp on the house itself. In many ways, then, for working class women, housing and neighborhood form the bare bones on which the flesh of the good life as represented by appliances, food and furnishings are put, while for middle class women the housing and neighborhood are of more intrinsic interest.

The way income is managed has, of course, a great deal to do with what actually gets bought by a family. As pointed out in Chapter IV, the working class housewife is typically the chief purchasing agent of her family, and she is more likely than her middle class counterpart to have major financial control. In some cases, the woman handles parctically all of the purchases, simply relieving her husband of his weekly pay check and disbursing it as she finds necessary. More often she is the family accountant and purchasing agent, but discusses matters with her husband. Less often, is there the clear sharing of money management and shared responsibility most characteristic of the middle class family. As has been pointed out, this is probably partly due to the more complex financial management necessary for the middle class style of life. To a large extent, it is probably also due to the working class husband's preference for avoiding household worries, his desire to earn the money but let the wife worry about how it is spent.

Given the housewife's large role in managing a working class income, it will be worthwhile to consider the techniques she has for doing so. Many of these women struggle to balance their income and outgo by practicing a kind of "tin can accounting."

They tend to rely upon gimmicks such as envelopes, various drawers, or tin cans to help them in budgeting their disbursements. They are not given to abstract thinking and generally find paper budgets or written records more confusing than helpful. Instead, they seek some definite place in which to store their money-with-a-purpose; they find it relatively meaningless to abstractly earmark money in a bank account. For them it is more congenial to guide expenditures according to the amount of money they can observe left lying in an envelope or deposited at the bottom of a tin can set aside for some budgeting category.

The procedures followed by a working class housewife who practices what we have called a "tin can economy" are illustrated in the following remarks:

> I have a silly little system. Whenever my husband gets paid I take away so much for my grocery money and put it in my kitchen drawer. Then I take all the rest and I put it into a tin can. If we can pay a bill in person we take the cash out of the can— otherwise we may write a check on our bank account. I try to pay as many bills in person as I can though, because I don't like spending the money it takes to write a check. Now, whatever is left over in the tin can by the time the next payday comes we transfer into the bank account to pay our future bills. If my husband doesn't have enough money for gas out of his allowance, or if we go out for some entertainment we just take the money out of the tin can. Sometimes there is only a little left in the tin can at the end of the period, and sometimes there is a lot—it just all depends on the weeks. I've tried to budget with envelopes, labeling them for this and that, but then we always took money out of the wrong envelope whenever we ran low, so it didn't really work. Now I've found the checking account together with the tin can the best system.

For those who practice a "tin can" or "envelope" economy, the greatest advantage in the procedure seems to be the vivid statement of their current spending power provided by an "empty" or "full" can. An empty can more dramatically commands, "thou shalt not spend," than does a nearly red bank balance.

155

I have this system where there is an envelope for each thing that I have to put money away for. There's one for the mortgage, another for the utilities, and so forth. Whenever I receive a bill I put it in an envelope and the next time my husband receives his pay the money goes right into that envelope clipped to the bill until I get it paid. All the rest of the money goes into a general envelope, and if I have a little extra money then I buy something. If I don't have any money I just don't buy any clothes for that time, or nothing extra. I like it that way. I always know where I am.

By and large, such women prefer to make their purchases with cash out of the can than by the more indirect route of charge accounts, because "that way I always know where I am." Many working class housewives do not like time payments; they prefer cash purchases. They display a considerable preference for the idea of "paying cash for whatever we buy," that is coupled with an equally strong abhorrence of installment plans. This attitude seems to stem from many sources: for one, they tend to suspect a bit of financial treachery is usually involved in "time payments." They imagine that the financial manipulations and arrangements which make "time payments" possible are beyond their comprehension; they expect that their ignorance will be recognized, and they will be "taken" in such transactions. The whole idea of paying interest outrages them. They equate "interest" with old-fashioned concepts of usury.

This only summarizes the *attitudes* toward cash payments as opposed to installment plans. Their *behavior* can be summarized in quite a different way: in our study sample, on the day we interviewed them, about two-thirds of the working class respondents were in some kind of installment-planned debt (other than their house mortgage). The typical debtor was paying $32 a month for some installment-planned pleasure. The desire to "pay cash" had fallen victim to a more urgent desire for the benefits of some modern appliance.

The perpetual shock of these women at the interest charges on their long-term purchases is illustrated in the following stories:

We have the house on a pay-as-you-go plan, and we pay around $50 a month. But about half of that is for interest, and I am trying awfully hard to get that amount down first before I buy much else. You know, when I made my first payment on the house I went to the bank and I put down $50. When I came home and looked in the little book I almost fainted. The bank woman had only credited me with $21, and I didn't know what it was all about. My cousin was there when it happened and she explained to me that we had to pay more on interest at the first than on the mortgage, but that the more and the faster we paid off on the house the less interest we would have to pay. So I've been trying awfully hard to get to the point where more than half of our money was going on the house instead of interest.

When I bought my washer and dryer they were having a sale and the man said that if he could write it up as a charge he could get more credit on the store contest. So I let him write it up that way. But we went ahead and paid cash in 30 days so we would not have to pay any interest charges. I nearly fell over when they told me that I would have had to pay a whole $70 in interest if I had not paid for it in cash.

The tellers of these two stories added their own special "amens" at the end, which sharply point up their attitude toward these experiences:

We're certainly going to try to pay cash for a car when we get one. I've learned now how much interest there is on those things if you don't pay cash right off.

You can be sure that we don't have any installments now. I hate the interest you have to pay on them, and they tell me that the interest rates just keep going up and up.

Some of these women have learned "the hard way" that there are other hidden dangers in "time payments," as when a family is led to unrealistically over-extend itself in making the initial purchase. What has happened in such cases is very simple: the periodic payments have seemed so invitingly low, perhaps only in contrast to the cash price involved in outright purchase, that they have bought cars, houses, or household appliances only to discover later that they had gotten in "over their heads" financially. The image which these women now carry around in their minds of bill collectors or repossessors standing threateningly at their doors has frightened them into espousing policies of extreme conservatism.

I'll never again buy anything I can't afford to pay cash for right at the beginning. When we were living in that other house we were always on edge over whether we were going to meet the payments each month—but now that we've moved here we're so much happier because we're not always worrying. I don't ever want to see another bill collector standing at my door, not ever again.

Occasionally a working class wife will express the belief that cash payments are unwise "in the beginning"—although her ultimate allegiance to cash is unshaken. Such women are manifesting no less skepticism of the merchandising world; they just see the principal danger in another direction. They believe that the "cash buyers" are the fall girls for merchants who don't want to back up their merchandise or properly service it.

> I usually pay cash. I do not really like time payments, except in the beginning. I think you get better service if you have time payments. If you pay cash, you are stuck. The store people figure they have sold it and that's that. If you still owe them some money, though, they generally try to keep you satisfied. Sometimes you need service on things—but if you've paid cash, they forget about you and you don't get any service.
>
> I always have things delivered COD, even if I am going to go ahead and pay cash—which I usually do. If anything gets damaged in the delivery the stores will make it good for you if you haven't paid them yet. But they don't ever do anything for you if the things are already paid for.

These women display much the same attitude toward "rent" which they exhibit toward interest. They regard both kinds of monetary outlays as "money down the drain," just so much money taken out of their own pockets and put in somebody else's for no good cause or honest reason. To many, the "most important way in the long run" they can use their money is either saving it for a house of their own or spending it on the mortgage payments of one already contracted for. An important part of the logic in this choice is the freedom from rental payments.

> The best thing we can do in the long run is to buy ourselves a house, instead of paying someone else rent.
>
> Paying off on a house of your own, so you don't have to worry about moving, and you don't have to rent from somebody who can tell you to do this or that. Sometimes a landlord can make you so mad that you're fit to pull your own cork.
>
> Saving money for our home that we plan to get soon is the best thing we do with our money. You can't do a thing with a rent receipt.
>
> Paying off the house. It's a good feeling to know no one can raise your rent or make you move.

Of course, the general aversion to time payments does not extend to the problem of buying a house—they understand that the amount of cash they are ever likely to have available would never purchase them a house outright. When it comes to houses, the evil of rent seems greater than the evil of interest. These attitudes can be summarized best by this remark from one woman:

We're a cash family. We don't buy things that we can't pay cash for, unless it would be a house. We are saving up right now to make a down payment on a house.

It is probably fair to conclude that working class women essentially feel that if they cannot pay cash for something, they really cannot pay for it. It may not be going too far to imagine that they conceive of time payments as an almost immoral self-indulgence, they perhaps feel that an object which cannot be purchased outright is an unsafe, uncertain source of pleasure which might in the long run be denied them by someone else's whim. Much as they long for the security of a husband's or a child's love, so too do they long for the security of possessions which cannot be taken away. Finally, the financial difficulties of "keeping track" and "knowing where I am" are simultaneously reduced by cash transactions and greatly complicated by charge accounts or pay-as-you-go plans. The cash transaction is the easier, safer one.

However, the working class wife feels that she never comes out ahead, despite her allegiance to tin cans and cash. These women generally feel that they never manage to save as much as they would like, that for them every month is a not-so-new struggle to make ends meet. We can spot at least three sources of their difficulty: one is their tendency to "cheat" a little with their tin can games; another is their tendency to resort to time payments against their better judgment whenever their wants for some item become overwhelmingly great; and the third is a failure of will power when confronted with a "cute flower" which can be purchased on the spur of the moment (and contains the promise of brightening the day of either their children or themselevs) .

That the "tin can economy" is not necessarily economical in the long run is frequently admitted. (It still-in-all may be the best device for these women, given their habits of mind and will-power.)

Sometimes things come up and I'm not prepared for them, say like birthdays, weddings, showers, or pictures of the kids which I have taken for their birthdays. I get in a jam with my budget then. Something works out though. I'll take the money from one envelope and put it into another one. I usually come out pretty even, but I never get ahead.

It seems that there is never enough money to cover everything. It is always a struggle with it. It all depends on how my money comes in. I put away so much each month for the upcoming bills —but what I usually wind up doing is digging into the money I have set aside to pay one bill to pay another with it instead. Then I just have to hope I can put it back to pay the other bill before it comes due, I really get mad at myself. I guess that I really shouldn't ever buy anything if I can't pay cash for it—but I never

159

seem to get enough cash together to buy some of the things I want, and I'd just never have anything if I didn't go ahead and buy stuff on time.

In view of today's prices it is not very surprising that a woman with two children, trying to establish a home and furnish it, should find it difficult to save much money when her husband's income averages $360 a month or less. It would indeed be surprising if she did not resort to installment plan buying, despite an aversion to it. Where working class housewives are able to resist such a temptation, it is perhaps accomplished less through exercise of will power than in consequence of a generally pessimistic attitude toward the success of contemplated expenditures (as will be discussed shortly).

These women's efforts to "come out ahead" financially appear to be defeated more often by indiscretions at the $1 level than by failures of resolution in the $100 range. For many, a shopping expedition apparently is not complete until a knick-knack for the house, a ribbon for the hair, or a toy for the children has been unexpectedly purchased.

Everytime I go up to the shopping center I buy cute sox for the baby. They have a kind now with crocheting on top that are just real cute. They fascinate me. I cannot help buying more of them no matter how many pairs I already have. I must have 99 of them now. Then I always seem to buy some fruit glasses, the kind you drink from. They have all different designs and styles. I cannot resist them. I must have a million now, at least enough for twenty years. Then I buy fancy flower pots, too, and maybe some things for my hair like artificial flowers. I love to wear them.

Usually if I have a little money left over after I've paid all my bills I manage to buy a little something more—something I want a little bit of change in. I'll wander into the dimestores and come home with something that I had not planned on. I might buy some little plant, or maybe a toy for the children. Every time I get them in there they see something they want, and if I get something for one of them I've got to get something for the other and right away it runs into money. If the thing is not too expensive then I'll buy it for them—well, say a dollar apiece, or something like that.

Sometimes I spend what I have left over from my grocery money. Probably I will buy something for the little girl, maybe a little slip or shoes or fancy underpants. Sometimes I buy myself a book or a magazine. Anything very big I usually talk over with my husband first though.

I can tell you that it seems I'm always buying something for the kids on the spur of the moment. They have more clothes than they need as it is, but I seem to be always looking for more. I suppose I really wouldn't need a lot of the junky stuff that I buy— like when I'm in the dimestore and buy things because they seem to look cute. I just bought my little girl a real cute pair of sunglasses and they lasted only one-half an hour. It's things like that I'm always spending money foolishly over. But I don't do very much of that impulse kind of buying for myself.

Perhaps the pessimistic attitude of these women toward the goods of the marketplace is due in part to the results of their unfortunate proclivity toward the purchase of incidentals. In many ways, then, these women are not optimistically oriented toward spending and buying. In general, they lack confidence in their own buying skills and exhibit a distrust of the business community—which they see as being only too ready to take advantage of their own ineptitude. When they are asked whether they have ever bought anything that did not turn out as they had hoped, a large majority of them cited some specific complaint: a car had turned out to be a lemon, a vacuum cleaner came apart after the first time it was used, some bargain icebox didn't freeze as it should. The tenor of these complaints indicate their belief both that they have shown bad judgment in making the purchase and that they have been gulled by the merchant. (A much smaller percent of the middle class women seem dissatisfied with their purchases, and those who make complaints express the age-old feeling that "things just aren't being made as well today as they used to be— the workers just don't care.")

Working class women frequently feel that they have shown bad judgment by deciding to buy inexpensive furniture when more expensive furniture was called for, or by trying too hard to find a bargain, when after all, "you don't get something for nothing."

If I had it to do over, I'd get good bedroom furniture and cheap living room furniture. I did just the opposite and now I'm sorry. The bedroom doesn't get the wear and tear that the living room does. I should have gotten cheaper living room furniture until the children got older.

We bought some inexpensive furniture one time to save money. It didn't last a year. When you buy cheap stuff you have to turn right around and do it all over again.

They also believe that they have been "stuck" by both merchants and private parties often enough so that they have good reason now to express a wariness toward people with something to sell.

I don't like the deal we got on our furniture—when we buy

161

anything else it will be from another store. I'm going to look into the store's reputation a bit more next time.

I sold the car on an I.O.U. and now I can't get the fellow to pay it. That's the last time we'll do a thing like that.

Our old TV set was just no good at all. From the very beginning I felt we had gotten stuck.

We bought a sectional sofa from a private party. It's not going to last much longer. You really shouldn't buy anything except from a store that will stand back of what it sells. You can't get anything out of some person that sells you something if it turns out to be no good.

Working class women who felt that their sorties into the market were generally successful can be divided into two groups: those who apparently have experienced nothing but good fortune in the outcome of those activities, and those who practice so extreme a degree of conservatism in approaching the market that they have had few opportunities for dissatisfaction. Representative of this latter group are often residents of oldfashioned urban neighborhoods who claim that "we never gamble, we just buy what we need," or "we have to squeeze every nickel—we don't have money to throw around, so we're always pretty careful." Otherwise, most working class women who express confidence and pleasure over their purchasing skills and results are those who live in the newer suburban neighborhoods. (In our study sample, while only 20% of those in older neighborhoods found no dissatisfaction in their purchases, almost half (48%) of those in the newer areas were of such mind.)

We might speculate from this fact that the occupants of the newly-built working class suburbia are fundamentally more optimistic and self-confident people in their economic behavior. This venturesome commitment of having acquired a mortgage on a new house is likely a direct manifestation of this basic optimism. A general positive orientation toward acquisition of modern goods is also shown in these comparisons between the appliance possessions of those in old neighborhoods and those in new houses: in this study sample, 74% of those in new areas own automatic washers, while only 31% in the old neighborhoods do. The distribution of automatic dryers favors new suburbanites in equal measure, 41% to 17%. (These comparisons have been made only between women in both residential locations who are of upper working class social status, in order to rule out wide differences in monetary wherewithal.) Of course, suburbanites spend more money for their housing than do the urbanites ($75 as compared with $60 per month), but this difference is not as wide as might be expected from the quality of their housing. The rental bills for working class women in the city sometimes appear to be exorbitant when compared with value received.

Undoubtedly a large measure of the hesitancy felt by working class women toward large purchases is a product of their essential fear that the future will not treat them more fortunately than has the present, and may even threaten them with financial disaster. Their longing to save money for a rainy day frequently ladens them with feelings of guilt over their "spend-thrift" behavior.

Many working class women exhibit extremely narrow horizons in their choices of shopping places. In comparison with middle class women, they are very provincial shoppers. The working class wife confines most of her shopping expeditions to those neighborhood stores where experience has taught her that she will neither be "taken" nor "ignored" by the storekeeper and salespeople. She prefers to make her big ticket purchases through "connections," such as relatives or long-time friends who run businesses themselves or else have "connections" with people who do. Partly this reliance upon relatives or friends for help in making big ticket purchases has a real "bargain" or "discount" as its object. Equally, however, such reliance is a means of avoiding the unknown in stores or salespeople, where the outcome of the purchasing venture can be viewed much less optimistically. The working class wife's preference for a personalized world and her discomfort with the impersonal influence her shopping as they do the other aspects of her life.

A comparison between the shopping habits of middle class women and working class women shows the provinciality of the latter. Fewer working than middle class women classify themselves as "regular shoppers" in the central business districts. This is not simply an aversion to downtown; they also shop less often than do middle class women in the new super-shopping centers which rim most cities. Instead, their favorite shopping habitat appears to be the establishments along the business string streets which run through most working class areas.

The attributes of the string street stores which attract working class women and the characteristics of the areas which repel them are illustrated in these remarks:

> I go downtown very seldom for things. It is too tiring for one thing, and when I do go downtown I avoid any of those small type shops. In those smaller stores they have all those salesladies who tell you that something looks good or that "this is wonderful" and try to make you feel that you can't walk out without buying. They make you feel awful if you say you don't like something they have told you is nice. And they would certainly think it was terrible if you told them that you didn't have enough money to

buy something. In the larger stores downtown you can usually look around for yourself until you find the price range you can afford.

I like to shop here in our neighborhood. We keep pretty much to the level we can afford when we buy at the neighborhood stores. They are all mill people around here and the neighborhood stores cater to us by having things that are in our price range. They are not the most expensive, but they wear.

I try to buy at little places I know—where they will make things good for you and they won't be snotty. I may pay more sometimes by not looking around for bargains, but the stores I know are good and if anything goes wrong they will take it back. I get personal attention and service because they know me. For example, I buy meat from a butcher I know—the meat isn't any cheaper there, but he always gives me choice cuts. He has better meats and I feel that I get a better deal there than if I went scouting around all over.

Whenever I'm buying furniture I go to this one store in the neighborhood. I got my chest of drawers there a while back because the salesfellow was so darn nice. Some salesmen act like they do not care if you buy or not—they just ignore you.

These women want personal attention, but only as long as the salespeople do not humiliate them over the inadequacies of either their pocketbooks or their taste. (This is not to deny the popularity of such large stores as Sears, or Polk Brothers, in Chicago, but much of the image-building such organizations do is directed toward convincing working class shoppers that even such a big store can be friendly, too.)

Not only do their dollars flow to the local and "known" in stores, but their dollars also follow the handclasp of friendship and the bloodbond of kinship. Working class women utilize the latter sources of retail acquaintanceship most particularly when they are on the lookout for a "sure thing" in the way of bargains or for a discount on a major purchase, such as a stove, a kitchen outfit, or an automobile.

We usually buy things where my husband knows the people who run the store. They will let him have things a little cheaper.

The place where my husband works gives you a discount on the "X-brand" kitchen set. You just go to the store and pick it out.

We sometimes go to a wholesale house with a friend of ours who is a dealer. I have been to (Chicago's biggest wholesale house) to look around, but I never buy anything from them. After we've decided there what we want, we go with this friend of ours to buy what we've decided on. An uncle of my husband's sent us to this man originally.

164

My brother works for an auto dealer. He is a mechanic there. We bought our car from them. We did not look other places for it. We didn't get a discount there, but they did give us some special hubcaps with big discs that my husband likes without charging us anything extra for them. They also gave us a radio for nothing. We bought our car there just because my brother worked there. That was all.

We get all of our appliances through my husband's grandfather who owns a hardware store. We get them on a discount through him. Then we got the automatic washer through the builder here who could get them special for us. We got our TV through a neighbor who works for the TV manufacturing firm.

Another popular channel for the working class buyer is provided by demonstration parties or home contact salesladies. These women greatly enjoy the opportunity to attend such social gatherings with their neighbors or friends. Similarly, they find the visit of a saleslady-friend a pleasant relief from the monotony of their routine. Of course, the pressure to buy placed upon them so amicably and pleasantly in such situations is often irresistible.

I only buy "A-brand" cosmetics because I have a girl friend who sells it. She comes right to my house and we have a nice afternoon together every time she comes. I like the cosmetics she sells, too.

Whenever the "A-brand" people come around they are always able to sell me more things than I can really use. I like everything of theirs, and I buy the powder, the lipstick, and all the things I use from them. All their things are excellent. But I always wind up buying some extra little cream.

There's the "S-people." They always sell me a lot of things. Every time I go to one of their demonstrations I go too deep into them. Well, you know how you go and see all the stuff and some-how they sell it to you. The other day I went to a lingerie party. I didn't really have any money then and their things were all too high-priced. So I just bought silk pants for my little girl. A couple of pairs. I didn't buy anything for myself, though.

The working class housewife likes to buy nationally advertised brands. In the absence of a personal recommendation from close friends or relatives, she believes in relying upon nationally advertised name-brand merchandise. In name-brand purchases she feels the se-curity of doing what millions of her sister Americans are doing. She has an abiding faith that name-brands are good names, or else the brand could not have stayed in business so long and have become advertised so widely. Hence, she finds in name-brand purchases the greatest degree of certainty that she will not get "gypped."

> I have a tendency to go toward name-brands. I think they stand behind their things better. For instance, I would never get a TV set that was an unknown brand. I would be afraid I was wasting money. I always get my ideas about what brands and styles to buy from the big ads in newspapers and magazines.
> I don't trust off brands. Too many of them might not be good. I want the people who sell me something to back up the brand.
> I generally stick to one brand of food. I buy good food, like the "D" brand or "L" brand. And I also stick to brands in cosmetics—like "M" for pancake and "C" for cologne. I stick to the brands I'm used to and know about their reputation.
> I always buy "M" things because I saw about them in an ad when it first came out in the True Story magazine. I have used it for four years. Shampoos I get from magazine ads too. I've been using "D" for years. I first saw about it in an ad in True Story. They have one in there all the time now. It's a good company.

She also relies heavily upon word-of-mouth recommendations before making major purchases. She frequently buys television sets "like my brother-in-law has" because "his had worked real well for a long time," or she may settle for a "W" brand washer-dryer after an "aunt and uncle recommendad the "W" one—I saw it in their house and I knew what I wanted then." She reasons that "if the brand is good and you know others who have used it," you can in all confidence purchase an identical twin.

Working class women rely upon advertisements and pictures in the mass media to educate them about the latest ideas in home decoration or appliances, as well as to inform them about the brands which are national names. Thus they remedy their deficiencies in social contact or the narrowness of their shopping horizons. They can review the contents of the national media without stirring from the sanctuary of their own living rooms or kitchens.

> I like to look at the colored pictures and ads in magazines. I get an awful lot of ideas from there.
> I decided to buy a "G" air-conditioner after seeing their ad in a magazine. I'm always looking at the ads for ideas about new things that are out on the market. As far as I'm concerned magazines do a lot for me with their advertising.
> Sometimes you see something in the magazines you would like to have—maybe something you have never seen before. I don't

order from the magazines, but when you see that they have it in the stores you know about it already.

They can use their media-acquired knowledge of a product to provide them with defense against the assault of deceitfulness of salespeople. Finally, they may use print advertising to make their actual shopping operation more pleasant and expeditious, and to eliminate the need for time-consuming on-the-spot evaluation and decision-making.

I try to make up my mind about what I want to buy from the magazines or the newspaper ads—or maybe from something I've seen in somebody else's house. I don't want to have to do a lot of shopping around—not with the kids along. You can't take a lot of time looking things over when you've got to keep an eye out for them. Usually I am in kind of a hurry when I go to the store.

The kind of advertising which finally motivates the woman into making a purchase is more often the flier from one of her favorite stores. These contain the specific price information which is of vital importance to her; they provide the immediate impetus for her to go out and act upon the half-formulated ideas which have been occupying her mind. These fliers let her know when she can make a safe purchase by buying the nationally advertised name-brand from a trusted, local distributor at a price within her reach. For this woman, there can hardly be a more favorable configuration of circumstances to move her past her fundamental pessimism and into a positive frame of mind toward making a purchase, than when she has available a nationally advertised name-brand, a trusted merchandiser, a neighborhood store, and a price within her reach. All that is lacking is a relative, promising a discount. All this providing, of course, that the tin can is full and the cash is on hand.

CHAPTER X

PRIORITIES AND PREFERENCES

The working class wife, in her role as the family purchasing agent, goes to the grocery store at least once a week on a major shopping expedition, and maybe two or three times more on minor errands. She shops for clothes at least two or three times a month, and usually not for herself alone, but for her children and husband as well. She is in charge of furnishing the family's home and deciding which appliances are needed, and when. She tries to spend less than her husband earns so that the family can get something "saved up for a rainy day" or for a house of its own. When performing as family treasurer and purchasing agent, this working class wife tries to act according to certain conscious priorities and preferences, which she feels ought to give her management of the family's money.

In this chapter, we look into these "oughts" to which working class women pay verbal allegiance. Now, we do not believe that these women always behave in accord with the priorities and preferences expressed in interview situations. Behavior in a department store is usually less rational than what is contemplated from the distance of a living room sofa. Nevertheless, we suggest that these consciously held "oughts" reflect important motivations which guide, in one way or another, the economic behavior of these women.

When we speak of "priorities and preferences in consuming decisions" we refer to the order of importance assigned to various kinds of expenditures by working class women. These women, like those of higher (and lower) status, are always faced with the problem of "not enough money to go around" for all the things they imagine they would like. They are continually having to decide whether to buy an extra-good cut of meat and forget about a new apron, or vice versa; whether to buy a new TV set next or put the money into the bedroom curtains.

Sometimes the decisions are of even wider significance: with just so much money at her disposal, should the wife argue with her husband that they ought to spend a larger amount for a better apartment, even if this meant spending less on his car or cutting down on their movie-and-beer evenings? These are examples of the issues or problems in consuming priorities and preferences faced by working class housewives. There is first the priority point of whether money should be directed more toward food or housing (or in whatever major areas of consumption), and secondarily, there is the preference problem of what to "shoot for" in the way of housing, or food, given the financial limits.

In the previous chapter, when discussing the context for consuming decisions, we pointed out the anxieties felt by working class women over potential economic catastrophe, and indicated that particular consuming decisions frequently reflected the presence of this basic anxiety. We pointed out the dilemma in which these women continually find themselves. They don't like to buy more than they can pay cash for, yet their wants are greater than their wherewithal, so they find themselves continually plunging into the installment-planned existence without ever feeling comfortably at ease in the debt pool. In this chapter we will see which kinds of purchases apparently contribute the most toward allaying the deprivation anxieties of working class women, and hence precipitate the uncomfortable, yet satisfying, plunge.

In many ways, it is an academic question to ask what order of priorities a working class woman gives to food or housing or clothing as an avenue for expenditure. Neither these women nor middle class women directly confront themselves with the issue of whether they should spend more for the one than the other; it is resolved for them and reflected through the substance of a month's or a year's many and trifling decisions to spend a dollar here for food, that might have been spent there for a car, and so forth. If the record of these purchasing decisions could be studied, the pattern of priorities could be determined in their actual operation. Needless to say, such a study is not practically feasible.

Still in all, we feel that some notion about the relative importance attached to food, as compared with housing, versus vacations, etc., as a direction in which money should be spent would be useful in understanding the consumption priorities assumed by the working class women. In order to investigate this issue, we devised a special experiment for our study sample. To a large number of these working class women, and a comparable group from the middle class, we posed a hypothetical question of this order: "How would you like to spend $5,000 a year, if that were your annual income?" A list of twelve possible avenues for expenditure was provided and the women were asked to signify whatever amount (out of the hypothetical total) they would choose to spend in each of these directions. The budget items listed were a conventional collection, including food, housing, automobile, clothing, furniture, appliances, health, vacations, recreation, gifts and charity, savings and insurance. The question of managing an annual budget of $5,000 amounted to a fairly realistic issue for most working class women; but it provided a fantasy (nightmare variety) experience

169

to many middle class women. ("My heavens," said one in horror, "no family could possibly live on this amount of money.") So, in order to tap additional reservoirs of purchasing motivation, a second hypothetical question, asking: "What changes would you make if you had $2,000 more available?" was inserted. This presented the working class women with a fantasy challenge, and the middle class women with a realistic problem.

From both groups of women the results to this experiment can be interpreted as reflecting wishful thinking toward the use of $5,000, rather than as a measure of any likely or realistic employment of the sum on their part. Almost none of the women in either class had ever had experience in budgeting a year's money, so they were forced to approach the problem of being a budgetary architect as if it were "sheer guesswork" or "a riot—I really don't know what I'm doing, but I'll try." The height of wishful thinking was represented in the response of one of our working class women, when she remarked as she proceeded through the task:

> I really hate to spend very much on food, so I'll just put down $400 . . . and the auto is more important to my husband than to me, so I won't spend much there . . . but I'd like to spend about $500 on recreation, as it is we just go to a show now and then . . . then I'd buy a deep freeze . . . that leaves me with $2,000, which I can put into savings.

The results of this imaginary budget experiment can be summarized in the following five points:

1. The working class women gave first priority at the realistic $5,000 a year level to the idea of spending money for food. This changed, however, when they were placed at the fantasy level of $7,000 a year. There they advocated spending only $5 more a year for food than at the lower level, and devoted the extra $1,995 to other causes. Thus, we can hypothesize that whatever other anxieties these women experience with regard to economic deprivation, hunger fear is not dominantly among them. If it were, these working class wives might have displayed the classic compensation reaction: for one, they would have "over-eaten" in these imaginary times of plenty. Also, they would have chosen to devote a larger share of their money to food than the middle class women did. Instead, they were willing and satisfied to spend less at both the $5,000 and $7,000 marks—apparently, because other deprivation anxieties were crying louder for nourishment, than was food.

It would appear, then, that in current day American society, hunger fear and food deprivation anxieties are confined to the very lowest status levels. The average working class woman has been

170

elevated into an every day standard of living which is considerably above the subsistence level, far enough above, in fact, to have freed her from this classic anxiety of the underprivileged; or, if she is not totally freed, at least the anxiety is no longer of much functional relevance in her daily life. This impression is heightened when one considers that the $1,200 this sample of working class women felt they should spend for food out of an available $5,000 is absolutely less than the $1,400 which (by self-report) they really do spend out of an income that averages only $4,300 a year.

The conclusion is inescapable that working class women reject a picture of themselves as self-indulgent with respect to food; they reject food as an item worthy of lavish expenditure. What they show instead is a basic concern over meeting minimal nutritive requirements (with a few desserts thrown in), but the idea of spending for (and consuming) food above and beyond this level is a goal they do not consciously admit.

2. A second order of priority for working class women is their housing. At both budgetary levels, those in our sample felt they ought to devote approximately 20% of their available resources to rent or mortgage payments. This is on the low side of the estimates made by budget experts—who claim that a family should spend between 20% and 25% of its annual income for housing. It is low compared also to the middle class woman's desire to spend 26% of her hypothetical income for housing. This would indicate that working class women are concerned, primarily, with maintaining a "decency level" of housing, but are not anxious about either its luxuriousness or the envy which it might arouse. "A home of our own" is probably a more exciting housing dream to the working class women than are quarters of great sumptuousness, perhaps because the former is a realistic possibility (either already outlined, or something for "next year"), while the latter is only a "never-never-land" proposition.

3. For working class women, the equipment inside their homes— in the way of appliances and furniture—takes on a higher order of priority, than does achieving an exterior appearance of above average beauty. On $5,000 a year, working class women would like to spend 35% more of it for appliances and furniture than would middle class women; and on $7,000 a year, they would outspend the middle class by 110%! Working class women apparently can put up with "plain" exteriors if the interior of their home is well-applianced and nicely furnished. Middle class women care more for appearances; for them a labor-saving appliance saves nothing if "face" is sacrificed in order to afford its purchase.

4. Another item of high theoretical priority with working class women is *savings*. They would like to follow a 10% savings plan if

their incomes were $5,000, but they would try to increase to a 13% quota for savings if they had $7,000 available in a year. In each case, this is about 40% more than middle class women believed they could or would assign to savings. This result from the imaginary budget experiment coincides with our discussion in the previous chapter on the importance of saving against a rainy day. It indicates again an anxiety over potential catastrophes which could wipe out the family's hard won gains in its standard of living if there were not a cash reserve on hand.

In their desire to save money directly through savings, instead of providing future security through insurance, these working class women are quite unlike middle class women. Both groups feel they should put the same amount of money into a pool of savings or insurance—but the middle class women choose insurance as the wiser way, while working class women do not seem to acquire any real feelings of security through insurance. It seems too distant and abstract a way of providing for the future to appeal to them. They think they ought to have some (about 5% of $5,000) but beyond a minimal amount, no more seems necessary. To the contrary, middle class women seem to feel that insurance is something "you can never get enough of."

5. Working class women, by and large, place low priority on recreations and vacations as things on which to spend money. In this way, they are very similar to middle class women. Neither group, taken as a whole, could be called conscious advocates of a hedonistic "live only for today" approach toward the use of money. Of course, each class group contains a small number of women who are exceptions to this rule. There can be no question, however, that to the overwhelming majority of working class women the idea of spending money for recreation is much less attractive than spending on furniture or appliances, and trying to save for these or other things which constitute material well being.

In making out their imaginary budgets, working class women seem to betray a particular longing for the "new" and the secure, rather than an increase in the number and expensiveness of monetary gratifications and pleasures. They want to spend a reasonable amount for respectably attractive clothing, but no more nor no less than middle class women. Even at the fantasy level of $7,000 a year, they do not express an above average desire for the ephemeral appearance of glamor and well-being granted by expensive clothing. It is the more solid symbols of modernity and well-being, such as appliances, furniture, and an automobile, which exercise the greatest attraction upon working class women.

* * * * * * *

Within this framework of major priorities, working class women exhibit preferences for particular ways to spend their food money, their housing money, or appliance and furniture money. It will be seen that these preferences reflect at a more direct level some of the major concerns indicated above.

The end result sought by working class women in the area of food purchase and preparation is provision of their families with enough fresh, vitamin-laden food to meet nutritional standards of good health. Working class women are very much like the majority of American women in their allegiance to the notions that the best food is "fresh" food, and that the good housewife and mother makes sure everyone in her family gets the right amount of vitamins.

The working class wife is not usually greatly concerned with serving a wide variety of dishes, nor does she believe that high priced, expensive foods are necessarily worth the difference in taste or food value. She usually feels that a good, medium price standard in food will guarantee her family as tasty and healthy meal as it needs. In these attitudes, the working class woman is very much like her middle class housewife-sister. Indeed, if the actual grocery store behavior and stove-top practices demonstrated by these groups of women accord with their verbal advocacies, it would be difficult to distinguish working class women from middle class women in this respect.

What can be said of working class women's attitudes toward food purchases and consumption, in distinction to those of middle class women, is that the working class woman is more single-mindedly concerned with pleasing herself and her family than with following the dictates of dietary experts or heeding the advice or hints of culinary artists. Working class women are not as vitamin-conscious or as variety-minded as some middle class women appear to be. (A minority of middle class women seem bent on being veritable Clementine Paddlefords, but most middle class women agree with one of their number who said: "We love plain foods. No burgundy sauces for us. Roast beef is our favorite. I never read the menus in magazines or cook any fancy dishes. I just make sure the food isn't boring.") The typical working class wife might not even go so far as to utter the last sentence above. She is not too often worried about whether her meals are getting boring, as long as she knows her husband's and her children's food fancies are being appeased. She can be content to continually serve them their "favorites," as long as these foods remain in favor.

Working class women don't want to count the calories so rigorously or calculate the vitamins so determinedly that their meals become a treatment instead of a treat. Not that they believe that every meal must be a taste delight; they do feel, however, that the family's

173

appetite should be stimulated fairly often with those special dishes that are the family's favorites. They know their families go for just plain American cooking—and are happily relieved by this belief, since most of them are not entranced with the notion of creative cookery. On the other hand, they show some resistance to foods that are easy to prepare if they fear that the result would diminish their family's meal time pleasure. It is their viewpoint that: "It's not so important that food is easy to prepare—if you know your husband likes something, you fix it and never mind if it takes longer than just frying any old thing in a hurry." After all, working class women generally do not feel secure enough in their husbands' affections to risk incurring husbandly wrath with carelessly or thoughtlessly prepared meals. The fear among working class women is too great that: "If I didn't give him what he wanted, my husband would go out and eat in a restaurant." Among these women there are many practitioners of the food philosophy that the way to a man's heart is through his stomach.

When it comes to spending money for their housing, what working class women want most is "a home of our own." This does not make them too different from middle class women, who almost certainly also want to own their housing. Where the differences between the two groups appear is in the meaning of home ownership and the kind of homes sought.

In some ways, it appears that there is no prouder woman on the American scene than the working class wife whose husband has recently purchased a suburban home for her. Such a wife is firmly convinced that the act of purchasing such a home is both the "way of spending our money which has given us the most pleasure" in the short run, and promises also to be "most important in the long run." Her delighted pleasure is in sharp contrast to the discomfort felt by her working class sisters who still live in rented city houses or apartments. For this latter woman, any money saved toward a newer, more pleasant home of her own, is the money which takes on the most "long run importance." Working class women almost invariably feel that "for a family living in an apartment, nothing could be more important than moving into a house of its own."

What is it that a "home of our own" means to working class women? It seems to be a compound of many notions and motives. Perhaps most importantly it represents freedom from domination or intimidation by landlords, freedom from the possibility of tyrannical impositions by others over oneself. A working class woman is apt to feel when she's in a rented unit that she can't pound a nail here or there, at whim. For this woman, a home of her own gives her the "good feeling that comes from knowing no one can raise your rent or make you move"—at least not so long as you keep up the mortgage payments.

A home of one's own also dramatically signals long strides on the way toward stability, away from the brink of financial chaos. To working class women, a satisfying sense of release from marginal economic status is naturally induced by their ownership of so vital a factor in their daily lives as their homes. And, this is brought home to them every month when they see their mortgage payments solidifying their hold on their houses—for they can remember a time when they couldn't do anything with a rent receipt except regret it as representing one more instance of "money down the drain."

The housing goal of working class women, the kind of home of their own they want, can be summarized in these words: a modern, comfortable, safe, soundly-built, inexpensive, unostentatious, cozy home, where the family can be close and happy together.

Above all, a working class woman wants an up-to-date house with a modernized up-to-the-minute kitchen. In the first place, nothing in the way of an older house could so sharply symbolize a family's arrival into a 1950's middle-American level of housing respectability. Secondly, among the charter of freedoms sought by the working class housewife, the freedom from domestic slavery (as provided by a well-applianced kitchen) ranks high on the list. This will become clearer in the next section when we discuss the working class wife's appliance enthusiasms.

Of course, she wants this up-to-date house in a good neighborhood —by which she means an ordinary, friendly neighborhood where she and her family can feel socially comfortable, and not be "outclassed." As was reported in the previous chapter, the typical working class woman, contrary to some literary impressions, is not thirsting after residence in fashionable or wealthy neighborhoods. She is really more concerned about living at a decent remove from slums, "crumbs," or "a den of thieves."

The social comfort of living in an inexpensive, unostentatious, cozy home, built for close and happy family life, fits into the housing dreams of the working class woman. Housing extras like plenty of room for entertaining or distinctive architecture or more than one bathroom are not a part of this woman's housing vision, as they frequently are for middle class women. Even the middle class ideal of a "house with plenty of different rooms where each person in the family has a place to call his own and can have privacy when he wants it" does not appeal very strongly to the working class woman. Perhaps these women do not feel quite close enough to their children and husbands as it is—so we should not expect them to willingly provide these other members of their families with opportunities to barricade themselves away in private cubicles.

Finally, working class women exhibit a peculiar concern with the safety factor in a house's construction. Here their insecurity and pre-occupation with lurking disaster manifests itself as time and again they specify that any house they'd want to buy should be "made well," "should be built of good wood so that it will last for a long time," should be "a sturdy house," with a "strong foundation." Middle class women seem to take these qualities for granted, or at least they do not feel called upon to verbally insist on them as do working class women.

This concern with housing safety reaches its height when working class women seek to assure themselves that there are a minimal number of dangers for children in either the location or design of a house. Comments like the following illustrate the working class mother's concern over a home's safety rating:

> I want to be away from heavy traffic so I don't have to worry about the children.
>
> I don't want to have anything around the house which would be dangerous for little children.
>
> I wouldn't want a two story house. You've got to look out for your children, and when they're upstairs there is so much danger of them falling out a window or down the steps.

In essence, a working class wife wants a home "where the kids can mess it up" and where the "whole family can have fun together," without worrying about resultant damage to either house or people.

When we look inside these women's minds to see what they want inside their houses, we find them most devoted to the idea of appli-ance-rich, modernized kitchens for themselves, and "real cute bed-rooms" for their children. These are the rooms working class women are most notably concerned with having fixed exactly to please.

It is not surprising that they should want the kitchen fixed to order, since the kitchen is the focal point of the working class wife's existence. It is the room in which she spends most of her time—either through choice or the force of destiny. It may serve as a social center for the family, as well as amounting to a reception center for casual visits from relatives and friends. It is only natural that the working class wife invests more emotion in having that room as attractive as possible.

> I love to bake, and if I'm working in the kitchen and neighbors drop in, I like the kitchen to look nice enough so that we can sit there and chat over coffee.

176

In my home, we spend more time there—the kitchen is more informal. It's the most important room because we spend so much time there. It should be comfortable with nice comfortable chairs where people could sit and feel comfortable for a while.

I have always spent a good deal of time in the kitchen. I like to cook and bake, and if I have a nice stove, a freezer, large cupboard areas, and easy-to-clean linoleum—well, a kitchen like that could be the heart of my home.

The kitchen is the main room in the house as far as a woman is concerned. It's the one she's in mostly. I'd like to have mine remodeled and fixed up modern, with everything handy.

These working class women envision a kitchen completely modernized and filled with appliances—automatic dishwashers, clotheswashers, and clothes-driers, refrigerators with huge freezing compartments—all placed in such a way as to make their kitchen work handier and more pleasant. Middle class women are not too much less desirous of having this kind of kitchen, but there is this difference in their motivation: middle class women want such a kitchen in order "to make it as easy as possible to get through with the work" and out of the kitchen. Working class women on the contrary, do not anticipate that they will ever accomplish so easy an escape from the kitchen. Nor are they quite that eager to escape.

As far as most working class women are concerned, if their kitchens could be made attractive enough, they would be happy to make these kitchens the heart of the home. After all, the kitchen is a nice safe place to be. And, if the working class woman reigns anyplace, it is certainly in the kitchen that she is queen.

The strong interest which a working class mother displays in her childrens' bedrooms centers around the idea of making these rooms veritable little dream castles for the kiddies.

I'd fix it up real cute. I'd get bunkbeds, a toy chest, a chest of drawers and a big closet, with nursery rhymes on it and a picture of Christ, of course. I'd get them a little radio all of their own, and if I could I'd get them a portable TV all of their own.

This doesn't mean that working class women necessarily ignore their children's own whims in the matter. A goodly number are quite indulgent, feeling they ought "to let the boys have their room the way they want it—it's usually in an uproar—but they enjoy having it that way."

It appears that one motivation operating in these women's enthusiasm for fixing up their children's bedrooms attractively and invitingly

177

flows from the worry felt over the children's safety. Of course, they also hope to win grateful love.

I'd like for the children to have separate rooms so they could bring their friends over here—maybe even have them stay overnight—and that way the children wouldn't be away from home very much of the time.

To working class mothers, a child away from home is a child ever-presently exposed to danger.

Working class women are of two minds over what a "fixed-to-please" living room would be like. Most want the living room cozy and nice because that's where the whole family gathers to spend its spare time and watch television. But for some, the living room is regarded as the public announcement of a family's decency and economic competence. They feel that "when company comes they'll usually sit in the front room, so you like to be proud of it." (These are not the kitchen-centered variety of working class housewives.) These appearance-conscious women are a distinct minority among working class wives, and in their attitudes toward the living room they are much more nearly spiritual sisters to middle class women.

The young working class mothers in our sample are mostly in the "cozy and nice" frame of mind. They feel that as long as their young children are in a destructive temper, they can perfectly well postpone any dreams of living room grandeur until a later stage in their lives.

The living room is where a family like ours spends its spare time, so I'd like it cozy and comfortable—but I woudn't want to spend a lot on it yet because the children would scratch up anything very expensive.

Eventually, I would like my living room to be a real beauty—but that's going to wait until my kids are older. I ordered some French Provincial furniture a while back. It was really beautiful. But after I thought about it a while, I realized how I would have to keep after my children all the time to stay away from it. Then I cancelled the order. They are more important than furniture, and the house is as much theirs as ours. I can buy it later, but I'd just make us all uncomfortable now.

While young mothers, working class wives are inclined to aim only for a living room where there "isn't anything fancy—just comfortable furniture and enough room so that everyone can relax and enjoy himself." It is primarily older working class women who turn to living room beautification as a point for pride.

All down the line—when it comes to appliances, furnishing, and decorating their homes—working class women express a different order of enthusiasms and preferences than do middle class women. It is labor saving devices and the "new home pleasures" which have captured the interest of working class housewifes, while aesthetic luxuries are more sought after by middle class women.

For example, when we asked our sample of women from both groups to name the "new products" which appealed to them most, working class women confined their attention almost exclusively to labor-saving devices, particularly automatic washers and dryers, or to the all-American home pleasure of a TV set (in this instance, color TV). Middle class women, on the other hand, concentrated their focus on the aesthetic appeal of "beautifully designed modern furniture," "these elegant synthetic furs," "those trim-looking new cars," and if they mentioned more utilitarian items, they talked about such things which could beautify their kitchens—such as built-in refrigerators, table-top ranges, and wall ovens—rather than ones which simply reduce the work load.

Working class women readily acknowledge that their interest in these "new things" is a direct product of their desire to save time and ease the work load.

Any time-saving device is for me—they're fabulous.

Time savers are what I like most. They're all a great boon to the busy housewife.

I like gadgets to use around the house—I can hardly get enough of them.

I really dream about the new kitchens that make your work easier.

I like the labor-saving devices mostly.

The height of enthusiasm was expressed by one working class woman in our sample who said:

I have so much wash to do and so little time to do it in that you could take away my bed—but just don't leave me without that automatic washing machine.

It's a pretty sure thing that if a working class woman doesn't have an automatic washing machine or dryer, if she doesn't have an electric skillet, rotisserie, steamdry iron, coffee maker, automatic floor polisher, roll-away vacuum and what not, it's not for lack of wanting them. It's because she believes she "can't afford them yet—until they've flooded the market, and the price comes down to my range."

The working class homemaker tends even to judge objects of furniture or items of clothing for their labor-saving properties before deciding whether she wants them or not. Unlike the middle class woman, she doesn't look first at their aesthetic qualities. She likes the new "miracle" fabrics because they spare lots of ironing time. New

179

furniture styles and ideas are favorably regarded if they meet the same test: "I like that new, modern furniture—it's so easy to clean." When a working class woman says she wants a wall-to-wall carpet, she's apt to explain this preference by remarking that "floors are hard to keep clean without a carpet which covers the whole thing," or, "all you have to do when you have wall-to-wall carpets is to give them a light sweeping every now and then." Cake mixes, frozen foods, and all the "instants" are welcomed insofar as they save cooking and baking time, unless the family just "can't stand the taste." Working class women are inclined to scoff at, and pay a never-mind to, any imagined deficiencies in the taste appeal of these foods—at best, far more so than are middle class women.

With all these items, middle class women are apt to make their judgments according to "taste." Some reject the miracle fabrics as "ugly—they aren't rich looking like fabrics used to be." Some like the beautiful modern furniture, while others dislike it as too cold and austere. A middle class woman's first thought in buying a wall-to-wall carpet is not for its labor-saving properties, but rather for its appearance of luxury and whether "its color provides the proper background for the rest of your furnishings."

Of course, working class women are not opposed to the idea of beautifying their homes. They simply feel they are not in the economic brackets where such concerns can possibly be at the forefront. Meanwhile, they want more things rather than better things—and they want to get more done with less energy. They also want to have more fun right at home while getting that more done.

Television is the greatest of all the new home pleasures as far as the working class wife is concerned. With these women, the temperature pleasures of air-conditioned summers and centrally heated winters, and the ear-tingling pleasure of a hi-fi set are as nothing compared with the eye-catching and worry relieving pleasure of the television set. In one of our inquiries, one-third of the working class respondents named the television set as their favorite household object. Even those who didn't assign it first place acknowledged, along with those who did, that life without their TV sets would take on a completely different flavor.

If you took my TV set away, I'd be lost. We could do without most things, but not our TV.

The television set gives us the most enjoyment. It's entertainment for the whole family.

The TV is my main source of relaxation and enjoyment. I don't know what I'd do for amusement without it.

Thus, TV is the working class housewife's tranquilizer. (Next to the TV as the favorite household object is the homemaker's great energy saver, her automatic washer.)

Here again we see the contrast between the middle class and working class women. The most valued possessions for a good portion of the middle class women are those which appeal to aesthetic sensitivities: "a sterling tea set that is a family heirloom," or "all my Hummel figurines," or "this coffee table—the wood is so beautifully grained," or "my period furniture." It is a rare working class wife who has time or has developed a taste for this kind of home pleasure.

In their imaginary budgets, working class women assigned a much larger amount to the automobile category than did their middle class counterparts. This willingness to make a heavy outlay on an automobile is apparently a concession on the wife's part to her husband's happiness. Most working class women take no part in choosing the family's car. They usually feel that the automobile is, properly speaking, the husband's department.

Of course, working class women enjoy owning an automobile—and they enjoy it more if the husband doesn't drive it away to work all the time and leave them stranded out in the far parts of suburbia. They like to be able to use it themselves. It is true that a good third of these young working class wives have not yet learned how to drive a car, but for those who do know how, it provides them with a sense of freedom from the neighborhood scene or from reliance upon other people for their transportation needs. Still in all, working class women almost invariably feel that the major pleasure in automobile ownership is their husbands', and acknowledge that much of their own pleasure is a basking in the husbands' happiness. As one said, "That's what Joe likes most and I'm tickled for him."

The working class wife is by no means sure that her husband has displayed the wisdom of a Solomon when purchasing the family chariot. In fact, when these wives were asked to name the family's "unwisest purchase," it was most often one of the husband's automotive "lemons" which got the nod. ("We've done pretty badly with a couple of second-hand cars" and "one car my husband bought broke down on the way home from the lot" rang common critical themes.) This disappointment, however, does not seem to deter them from believing that a working class husband should be allowed to spend 10% of his annual income on the biggest play toy of them all.

As far as other play toys and play times go, the working class wife is more spartan. The young wife, in particular, is not vacation-minded nor recreation-oriented. She is not one to consciously advocate the philosophy of "have fun while it lasts . . . (since) you only live once." Maybe that point of view came earlier and will reappear later, but for the nonce, she prefers spending her money on the more solid

181

satisfactions of a kitchen refrigerator than on the fleeting pleasures of a night on the town.

Very rarely do young working class wives refer to a vacation or to a recreational experience as the most pleasurable expenditure of income. Perhaps their failure to make such mentions is due in part to the fact that they so rarely take major vacations or spend much money on week-to-week recreation. Surely, however, in equal measure it is due to the fact that they are at the particular stage in the family cycle where these other matters take precedence, no matter what the class level.

These young working class mothers generally are not interested in taking extensive vacation trips until their children are old enough to enjoy and benefit from the travel; for the present, they feel that young children as so much a nuisance on a trip that "the children don't enjoy it and neither do you." Usually, these women spend their vacations fixing up their houses or sitting at home with the children while the husbands go off to military camp, or on sporting expeditions. If the family travels at all on its vacation, the destination is most typically the home of some relative who lives no more than two states away, or an inexpensive resort in the fairly immediate vicinity of the home community.

There is some evidence to suggest that this denial of vacation pleasures while young creates a strong pent-up desire to brighten the years of later adulthood with lavish vacations. When we asked our working class sample: "What changes do you think there will be in your way of life when your children are grown?", the change they most fervently hoped for was the introduction of travel adventures.

Our social life will be different then—we'll definitely travel. I've always wanted to travel, but I never had the opportunity to do very much of it. Now we are concentrating more on bringing up the baby properly.

Then we'll be free financially to do a few things that we can't do now. Maybe it's just a pretty daydream, but I think I would like to travel a lot more and see the world."

Meanwhile, and while waiting for this hopefully travel-studded future, the working class housewife sees the world through her television set. This is her daily recreation, and it costs her more time than money. The television set serves many functions for the working class housewife. It keeps her husband home more frequently at night. It keeps her children quiet and docile during the day, and it brings many vicarious thrills into her living room (by spiriting her away in fantasy to strange new places). It is no wonder that the working class homemaker says that the television set would be the last thing placed on the auction block if economic difficulties were to befall her. After all, the less money available to these women for outside recreation, the more time they must spend at home attending the shows on their television sets.

And thus, we get back to the matter of priorities and preferences. Some of the ones we have discussed here are obviously pretty daydreams seldom realized in actual behavior by the working class housewife. We know how universally unsuccessful these women are at putting into practice the self-denial they urge upon themselves when they speak of saving 13% of their incomes for a rainy day. On the other hand, we saw television sets in 94% of their houses and automatic washers in 50% of them. Maybe it's only the saving that is the daydream, and it is those priorities and preferences which lead to spending that get acted upon by these working class women.

CHAPTER XI

BLUE COLLAR AESTHETICS

In the previous chapter we noted how the aesthetic qualities and "tastefulness" of goods were important values and goals in the consumption behavior of the middle class women. In contrast, these did not seem crucial factors in the judgments made by working class women in their priorities and preferences for houses, kitchen equipment, autos or favorite household items. The question naturally arises as to whether working class women exhibit any distinctive or characteristic tastes or aesthetic ideals, and if so, what are these like and of what relevance are they when working class women find themselves in the market place?

Our concern with this issue led us to conduct some specific investigations into the tastes and style preferences of our study sample of young working class housewives. The methods and results of this study will be discussed later in the chapter. To the conclusions from this investigation, we are able to add insights gained in other research concentrating upon the tastes and buying preferences demonstrated by contrasting groups of working class and middle class women with respect to apparel and home furnishings. From these various sources, we have sought to construct some fundamental notions about the "taste" of working class women—notions which could explain or characterize their choices in a wide range of consumption areas beyond even apparel, housing, furnishings, and food.

It has proved particularly difficult to develop basic notions about the working class housewife's tastes and aesthetic ideals because these women do not readily nor easily articulate their tastes as do their middle class counterparts. More broadly, they speak of preferences for "modern" things, by which they vaguely signify anything up-to-date. They do not specifically designate those designs known by industrial designers or architects as "modern." Middle class women use the term much more accurately. They are able, for instance, to differentiate "modern" from "contemporary" in furniture. Perhaps it is partially because the middle class women use the term in a much narrower sense (more properly, aesthetically) that they are not so universally in favor of modern design. All down the line, middle class women are more conscious of the names of styles and designs and, hence, they are better able to communicate the exact nature of their tastes.

It would appear that the heightened middle class consciousness of style names is a function of their greater concern with these matters. Taste simply does not seem to matter as much to working class women. The tastes they express do not seem to represent a well thought out individual approach to the problem of arranging the aesthetic stimuli in their daily lives toward some specific goal. Working class women tend to like something or dislike it without relating these preferences to general principles of what they like or dislike. About the only principle they themselves recognize is that some of their aesthetic tastes are aimed to conform with their general estimate of what they can afford, or their conception of themselves as plain and simple people. The other fundamental notions or principles which are developed and outlined here were conceived by the authors, acting as social scientists, and analysing the working class women's superficial claims about their tastes to discover underlying implications.

The tastes most commonly mentioned by working class women reflect an amorphous, ill-defined pursuit after "the current." Anything which these women can label "modern" is more popular than anything which they feel is "old-fashioned." For them, the newer things on the market almost invariably seem to be more attractive than the older things. Working class women seem to find the new models, whether in automatic washing machines, living room curtains or automobiles, better and more beautiful than last year's editions. Perhaps it is simply that they automatically accept the proposition that American business is continually trying to improve the attractiveness of its products. They automatically assume that a new model wouldn't come off the assembly line unless it surpassed its predecessor both in efficiency and beauty. Middle class women probably accept the same general proposition about American business, but reserve to themselves the right of judging whether or not business has been successful in this goal.

Things modern and up-to-date apparently appeal to the working class women on several levels of emotion. In the first place, *the modern* signifies the whole world of better things which go along with middle-status economic life in America. To working class women, the beauty of current furniture or clothes flows as much from this statement of stable economic status which ownership of them confers, as from any perceived aesthetic qualities.

Secondly, the new look in furniture, clothing, houses, and automobiles provides a break in the monotony of the *look* to which these women have become accustomed. Earlier in the book, when the daily lives and the social horizons of these women were discussed, it was pointed out that they feel that daily life is monotonous. Also, it was indicated that the range of their social and visual experiences is narrow. In this light, we can see how new and modern looking things, things to look at temporarily, take the working class housewife out of her rut. They give her new visual fantasies to enjoy, if not realities to brighten up and beautify her daily existence. It seems only natural that to women who are fatigued with the "old" look, from looking at it so much, any "new" look seems more attractive. All of this is to say that working class housewives' taste for modern design is not alone a product of its aesthetic appeal to them. It is, as well, a by-product of their quest for middle-level social and economic status and relief from monotony in their daily lives.

Finally, the working class housewife's preference for modern bespeaks her flight from domestic slavery. An automatic washing machine becomes an object of beauty to these women when it promises to deliver them from the bondage of the more laborious, now old-fashioned, methods. According to this standard, the most glamorous washing machine is that with the highest washday work capacity. By the same token, a large two-story house—requiring as it does more upkeep labor—is less attractive than a smaller one-story home which promises more time for its leisurely enjoyment.

The tastes of middle class women, whether they be for modern or early American, for expensive ostentation or quietly elegant simplicity, are not so obviously dictated by a search on their part for a "new" look, or for release from household drudgery, or by a quest for symbols of economic solidity. At a secondary level their tastes may, indeed, be a product of fascination with other climes and times (as attempts to widen the horizons beyond the present), or they may be a byproduct of thirst for social advancement (with its imagined requirement of either ostentation or elegance in appearance). Regardless of the motives involved, however, the tastes expressed by middle class women are almost always given a more precise formulation; the enthusiasms are more individual; they do not necessarily go along with the trend of the times.

Now let us look at the evidence from some of our experimental investigations into middle class and working class taste. In these we will learn of the specific manifestations of the general principles mentioned above, and we will also learn of other aspects, so far unmentioned, regarding the problem of clarifying the working class woman's aesthetic goals.

Our study sample of working class women and a contrast group from the middle class were asked a series of open-ended questions of the sort: "What ideas do you have about furnishing a house? What styles in furniture do you like best?" or "What special qualities about a home are most important to you? What should a house be like, as far as your family is concerned?" The answers to these questions were evaluated and added to the evidence provided by responses to a series of picture preference tests. In these tests the women were presented with line drawings of houses, lamps, sofas, and dresses. They were asked to specify their two favorites out of ten alternatives in each category.

Line drawings were employed in this experiment instead of color photographs so that the details of material or fabric could not influence the choices. Our objective involved looking into more basic aspects of taste than color or texture preferences. We hoped to isolate out attraction to the simple, as contrasted with the decorative or the elaborate, preference for the plain versus the prettified, or for the grand as against the merely glamorized. These experiments were concluded by asking each respondent for a defense or rationalization of the indicated choice.

The housing tastes of working class women can be summarized in three words, uttered by one of their number: "modern—yet homey." By and large, these women did not betray any overwhelming yearnings for housing grandeur. They were content to daydream within the limits of their purses. Even when offered a fantasy situation they did not seek to overstep themselves for the fun of the game. Their stated preferences for inexpensive or medium-priced houses were apparently dictated by a realistic assessment of their financial status.

> The houses I picked fit my purse. Some of the others are much too big for us to think about.
> Those houses I chose look more economical for our family. They're more in my bracket. A lot of the others would involve too much money.
> I picked the biggest ones we could afford with our bracket of income. The others are too distinctive—and to tell you the truth, I like ours better than any of these.

In our sample of working class women, 62% were willing to settle for houses they might reasonably expect to be able to afford. For young working class housewives, the charm and advantages of an inexpensive and unostentatious house is that a family can relax more easily and feel more genuinely at home in such quarters. An expensive looking house is vaguely frightening to these women. They are afraid both for their physical safety and their social comfort in such homes.

> I want things nice and homey, that look lived-in, like a family home. Some of the houses you showed me are too big and old-fashioned and sprawled out. They're too ornate.
> I like those that aren't too fancy so that you couldn't feel com-

187

fortable in them. The ones I chose are just plain homes, but still they are nice.

I want things nice and homey. I do not want a castle that I am afraid to sleep inside of.

Above all, a house should be homey, not a show place without any comforts for people. I want a relaxing place where the residents feel at home.

In evaluating these responses, it should be remembered that definitions of a "homey" place, of a "family-type" home depend on the definer's expectations and previous experiences. The very houses which working class housewives described as ornate or too fancy were happily characterized by higher status, middle class women as being "large and homey-looking" or "a nice, livable family home." The "plain" and "relaxing" homes of working class women seem insufferably small and cramped to middle class women.

In the working class women's attempts to avoid daydreaming about houses beyond their income bracket, in their denial of interest in a housing level they cannot afford, we see how the aesthetic goals of these women are generally limited by their economic resources (as self-estimated). In a sense, these women thus block out a wide range of aesthetic expressions or tastes from consideration, on the grounds that such are too fancy for them to get entangled with. Working class women look for economic security and signs of medium level economic respectability in the exterior appearance of their homes. If the houses give that, they are content.

Whenever a working class woman has acquired a modern suburban home, far removed from the slums of her fears, she is a happy woman. Her visions of housing beauty have been quite well satisfied, at least for the moment. The working class women in our sample who were living in modest, but pleasant homes in the newly built suburbs of their communities, frequently gave active expression to this satisfaction by choosing the house pictures in our test which looked most like their own dwellings.

I like all the ones there that look like ours.

That looks something like the house we might build ourselves.

That looks almost like our house on the outside—and I think ours is very nice.

This one I've picked is just like mine.

I like four or five of these houses really. They are fairly average like the ones along Ada Street here where we live.

The homey look of modern and attractive (but inexpensive) houses like their own is the look in *American Home* that spells *House*

Beautiful to suburban working class women. These houses provide the best possible proof of social and economic affiliation with the secure, middle majority of American women.

This working class preference for "modern" homes over the "traditional" or "old-fashioned" in architecture or houses applies at all price levels. Given houses of both types from which to choose (at three economic levels) the working class housewives chose the modern over the traditional by a three-to-one margin. Middle class women, in contrast, showed a slight preference for the traditional style. The working class women apparently are more attracted to modern homes on several scores beyond the virtues of homeyness and inexpensiveness already mentioned. They regard such houses as safe, more convenient, less trouble to keep clean, and not as physically fatiguing to navigate around in. In short, a "modern" house is merely the largest of labor saving devices in the mind of a working class housewife.

An upstairs (in one of the older houses) can mean "just that much more house to keep clean—and I don't like keeping house that much anyway." It is also regarded as a strain upon both the woman's leg muscles and her heart.

> None of this climbing steps for me. I want my house all on one floor.
> I don't like two stories and lots of steps. I'd like a basement, but I sure don't care much about an upstairs.
> A house with a lot of steps in it is taboo with me. I don't want a house where I can't even go to the restroom without running up to the second floor.

Furthermore, an upstairs is regarded as uneconomical. "It is harder to heat in the winter time." These are the practical, everyday fears which working class women express about the older style, two-story house.

Their rejection of the old-fashioned in houses revealed several kinds of irrational fears as well. Occasionally a working class woman equates an old-fashioned house with a "haunted" house (.e., "that one looks sort of spooky like"), as if she feared the ghosts of occupants past. Or she may fear for her children's safety in two-storied houses, where a careless child might fall out a second-story window or down the flight of stairs joining the floors. Many a working class woman doesn't like two-story houses "because I want to be on the same floor as my children at all times."

These fears about a house which stands two stories above ground are not paralleled by fears over a house which burrows into Mother Earth with a basement. The most frequently heard complaint about

189

the modern one-floor ranch houses is their lack of a basement—with the working class women who reject a second floor simultaneously expressing desire for a basement. In this superficially contradictory attitude (after all, children can fall down stairs to a basement, and there is some climbing involved in getting back and forth from the first floor to the basement) there is a hint of the old "storm cellar" psychology. ("A place to go when the cyclones blow.") Above and beyond a basement's value as a place of retreat from windy chaos, the working class woman may find there a psychological storage vault in which to hoard "chestnuts for the cold winter ahead."

We must not conclude, however, that a modern house is an unmixed blessing to the working class wife, particularly if the architecture gets too glassily modern. Then she no longer regards it as amounting to much of a storm cellar. Such houses, she is apt to feel, are a "bit extreme—they don't look very solid." After all, a working class housewife doesn't want to have her house blowing away with the first strong breeze—because she hopes that her housing purchase is going to be able to last her a lifetime if need be. Neither does she want her house going out of style at the next shift of architectural winds; her biggest fear of extreme modern architecture in houses is that "they're faddy— they'd get dated looking and you couldn't live in them a long time." If the working class housewife's greatest goal in external appearances, housing-wise, is an up-to-date looking structure, one of her fears is that sometimes the up-to-date look gets "dated" sooner than she'd like.

The working class women's goals for the internal appearance of their homes are very similar to those for the exterior. Their taste in home furnishings runs toward the unostentatious, the comfortable, the sturdy, and the latest mass market styles. For the typical young woman of this class, a basic consideration, beyond price, which she applies to a piece of furniture is this: can it take a beating and be comfortable for a long time to come? If it looks comfortable, if it looks sturdy, and if it looks reasonably attractive (from an up-to-date viewpoint), a bed or sofa or chair will likely capture her.

These notions about the working class tastes in furniture derive from both conversational discussion and controlled experiments with picture preferences. For example, when our sample of working class women were asked to choose among pictures of ten living room sofas, they registered strong preferences for those which we had characterized as comfortable, as contemporary, or sectional (as contrasted with period).

Unlike the middle class women, this sample of working class women completely rejected sofas of antique, traditional, or old-fashioned vintage. For the most part, they used as excuses for their dislike the accusations that these sofas were too "fussy, "elegant," "fancy," and

190

"overly expensive," or else they looked too "cold" and "austere," too "flimsy" and insubstantial.

> It doesn't look sturdy enough.
> That's the old-fashioned, uncomfortable kind.
> That's not my type, it looks too fussy.
> I suppose it's beautiful, but it doesn't belong in a home where there are children.
> It's too fancy and curly to fit into my home.
> They're old-fashioned, that's what.

It is clear that these women generally look for comfort and utility in sofas more than for beauty or ostentatious display.

A sofa must be comfortable enough for a nap, they feel. No formal elegance or stiff-backed chairs for these working class women. Thin, wooden-armed sofas (even of modern design) are also unpopular with them, since these do not provide comfort, in a psychological sense.

> I don't like those that are small and cramped-looking—you couldn't stretch out on them without banging your head.
> That's cold looking, like a porch glider. You couldn't relax on that comfortably, and it looks like they've got wooden arms.
> I don't like anything with wooden or thin arms. I want arms that are upholstered. Pillow arms is what I like. I also like a higher back for comfort.

In general, the bulkier and softer looking the sofa or chair, the more comfortable it appears to be to a working class woman, and thus the more desirable it is for her to have. Middle class women, on the other hand, are by no means so comfort-conscious. To many of them, bulk in furniture—rather than connoting either comfort or solidity—implies a borax cheapness in construction; in fact, the bulkier the sofa, the more its sturdiness was held in suspicion by middle class housewives.

Yet, middle class women are not as concerned with their furniture's qualities of rugged sturdiness as are the working class women. This seems to be a quality the former take for granted, as if it were an automatic characteristic of the higher priced furniture they buy. The working class housewife cannot so blithely assume that a sofa she buys—at her price level—will stand up under the beating it's going to take from her youngsters, the rough treatment from husbands and older sons who can't be counted on to "handle it with care." In a very real sense, then, this sturdiness of construction is the ultimate standard of a "good furniture bargain for the working class woman. She says: "I want something that will last. If it looks stout and won't fall down, I think it's a good buy in furniture."

191

These women see the sectional sofa as the answer to their prayers for sofas which are comfortable, utilitarian, and up-to-date. Where middle class women frequently find the sectional sofas ungainly in appearance, the working class housewife finds them a great gain over the old one-piece models.

I like sofas big and roomy. Those sectionals can seat a lot of people if you need to.

I like sectional myself. You can change your room around better and the whole family can sit together on it.

Sectionals are so good because they can be used in more different places. The other kind can't be used as well because they are all in one piece. I think now that they have sectionals, the others will slowly go out of fashion.

I like modern, or sectional. The next sofa I get will be a sectional. The girl next door has one and everytime I go over she has it changed around. Each way seems to look better than the last.

The striking preference for sectional sofas demonstrated by these working class women cannot be explained alone by the fact that they seat more people. It appears that it has another advantage: these women see a sectional as the wave of the future in living room decor.

We can note this attitude in some of the quotations given above: other sofas are expected to "slowly go out of fashion" and the words "sectional" and "modern" become practically interchangeable, if not synonymous. The idea of a sectional couch was so frequently placed in juxtaposition with the word "modern" that it became obvious that many working class women would not consider any living room truly up-to-date if it were lacking a sectional sofa.

I like a sectional couch. I guess I just like a modern house filled with modern things. The old sofas are too out-moded.

Apparently, the most adequate and succinct definition of working class housewives' taste in living room sofas is this: comfortable, modern, and hence sectional.

This equation of sectional with modern, and the working class woman's enchantment with both ideas, illustrates again how these women tend to define any style as modern, so long as it is the latest thing on the market. This holds no matter what its aesthetic content or intent. Of course, among the middle class cognoscenti the latest thing is Dunbar– (or McCobb or Herman Miller) inspired modern, and not the sectional sofa. These designers' products are not yet on the mass market, however, and what little the working class woman knows of them has caused her to reject them as "too cold and unfriendly looking.'"

Thus, for the working class woman, furniture beauty is found in the newest things on the mass market; she wants her furniture to have an up-to-date appearance. She feels that dated-looking furniture, more than inexpensive-looking furniture, speaks negatively of her financial status. She is apt to think of traditional or period furniture as dated-looking, even though it never becomes dated in the eyes of higher status women.

Another aspect of modern furniture which appeals to the young working class woman is its labor saving qualities. She is especially grateful for the modern, washable fabrics used in furniture upholstery, and she likes the "sleek lines of this new furniture because it's easier to polish and clean than all that gingerbread used to be." Here, though, these women find themselves at cross purposes. At one and the same time they want bulkier sofas for comfort and durability, sleeker sofas for upkeep ease. They try to strike a happy medium by advocating "this new thinner furniture you can get under to clean—but it should be strong, not quite so bulky." In short, it appears that when a working class housewife says: "I like the simple clean lines—they can be used anywhere," part of the reason she likes these modern lines is because they are easy to clean.

We can conclude this discussion of the working class housewife's sofa preferences by noting that her ideal might well be a sectional sofa-bed. We already know why she likes the sectional: it's the latest thing, it can be juggled around in more different ways to break the monotony of her living room's appearance, and it provides enlarged seating capacity in front of the television set. The sofa-bed adds one more utilitarian advantage:

> I like those sofas that look like they might have beds in them, so they could be used as an extra bed if necessary. The sofa I picked out looks like one of them. Most of the others don't look like they could open up that way.

The working class homemaker's sofa motto appears to be: "the more people a sofa can seat the merrier, and the more it can bed the better."

The choices on a lamp preference test made by our study sample of working class women are additionally instructive in revealing their tastes and conflicting motivations of these women with respect to their aesthetic experience. The table lamps they were shown represented all conceivable combinations of clean-lined and decorative, modern style and pure borax, traditional and wall-pulley, period and contemporary. In their response to this experimental test of their taste, the working class women once again demonstrated high favor for furniture (lamps, in this case) which they can define as modern or

193

up-to-date ideas. At the same time, they revealed some contradictory well-springs of desire for the highly decorative kind of minor object which "pretties up" the house, and we learned that these women are not always up-to-date about what the "latest thing on the market" is —even at their price level.

In the matter of lamp choices, working class women most frequently selected those which they felt were simple, plain, and modern. They chose these lamps on two grounds: either they felt that this style harmonized and conformed with their overall style of living, or they welcomed the simple, clean lines as labor savers.

I like those that are more practical—not so fancy.

The ones I picked are real plain. I like that.

They're sorta' simple, and more durable.

They're just plain and modern. They're lamps that you can match with anything.

They're modern and simple in design, nothing fancy about them. They've got plain shades and plain bases. They are very nice.

They're plain and easy to clean. You wouldn't have to spend so much time dusting them.

However, a sizable minority of these women—twice the middle class proportion—went to the opposite extreme and chose the hyper-decorative, super-borax lamps as the ones they would "love to have" in their homes. One of these working class housewives perhaps spoke for all when she explained her predeliction with these words: "I've always liked these figurine lamps. Yet I really think I usually like plain things better. I know that doesn't make sense, but that seems to be the way I feel." The contradictory facets of working class tastes given voice by this woman were given visual expression by several of the women we interviewed. They simultaneously chose a clean-lined lamp in the test situation, while prominently displaying a borax blackamoor lamp in their living rooms.

We cannot really speak of working class women as a group who inescapably prefer decorative lamps, though more may choose them in a test and at the furniture store than do middle class housewives. After all, the majority of our sample expressed distaste, on the conscious level, for such lamps. For every working class homemaker who said, "I just love that figurine type of lamp," there were four who said, "I wouldn't want that at all, it's too elaborate." For every one of them who said, "I've always wanted a planter lamp, it would look so nice in a picture window," there were two who exclaimed, "Planters—oh heavens, no—they look so old-fashioned," or, "Planters are too much of a bother—you've always having to water them." A few working class women like a taffeta-shaded lamp because it has "this feminine-looking ruffle that I think is pretty" and a small number like a William-and-Mary clock antique because "any television fan would like a clock lamp to watch for the different programs with." Nevertheless, the more common judgments placed by young working class homemakers upon these lamps charged them with being outmoded: "They belong back in the 18th century," or "They're just dust catchers," or "They're too extravagant and wouldn't look right with the rest of my furnishings."

The lamps chosen least frequently by these women were those in the wall-pulley style. They are regarded as strange or extreme by those who have noticed them in a store window, but not in a home; other women simply could not imagine how they were to be used, and so did not want them. All were inclined to believe they must be expensive, yet the authors know that both Sears and Wards have begun to feature them, at mass market prices, in their latest catalogs. In this way, we learned how far behind the times working class women can be in receiving news of the latest things on the market. Inasmuch as hardly any working class women are yet aware of this wall-pulley lamp's status as an up-to-date idea, almost none have discovered a taste for it. How long it takes for ideas to catch on with these women is a moot question—and it may be that this particular idea is one which never will.

Essentially, the lamps preferred by these working class housewives are those which they feel will fit in most appropriately with their families' social and economic status. An inexpensive, modern lamp seems to be regarded as the ideal. For these women, it signifies—through its "up-to-dateness"—and absence of pretentiousness—the on-going, economic security (however modest) of its owner. Such a lamp informs the world that its housewife-owner is neither dated in her ideas nor deficient in pecuniary resources. It announces her position as a reasonably comfortable member of the middle majority of American women. More indirectly, such a lamp would help a working class woman achieve this status by reducing her domestic work load. After all, a sleek, modern lamp is "easier to keep clean than the ones with all those necks, curlicues, and ruffles."

We have now observed our study sample of working class women professing a taste for the modern, unostentatious, comfortable and easy-to-clean in lamps and sofas. These two items represent the range of household furnishings rather well, in that one of them is highly expensive and an important feature of the interior decor, while the other is relatively inexpensive and (theoretically) more subject to whim in its purchase. We can say that our working class women displayed marked sensibility at the sofa level, and even generally withstood temptations toward "fancifulness" at the lamp level.

When working class women discuss their tastes in furniture without being confined to the choices in a home furnishings taste test, their free expressions are in agreement with these test results. The appeal, and some of the motivations behind their preference for modern furniture, can be seen in the following statements made by young working class wives:

I like modern things—plain, everyday things, not too modern, just conventional. I'd like them all through the house. They're easier to take care of. I'd also like to paint the walls and take this paper off. I think I'd like everything modern and up-to-date.

I think that modern is more economical than period or Victorian furniture. I don't care for antiques at all. I just want plain, ordinary furniture, nothing elaborate. I'd furnish the whole house in modern.

I'd like to furnish mine with all new and modern furniture. Not the most expensive, but real nice. I'd like one of the modern curved sofas. They dress the house up. Then a nice rug is important and good comfortable chairs.

I'd like modern furniture for the type and location of my house. My taste wouldn't vary from room to room. I'd like the whole house furnished the same. It doesn't seem right to have one room laughing at the other.

When a working class woman says she likes "plain things—I don't go for fancy stuff," she is not thereby announcing any lack of desire for an attractive living room; she is only avoiding daydreams over lavish ostentation, which she knows she can never afford.

Finally, the concern over a relaxed, homelike atmosphere she exhibits in her tastes for the size and external appearance of her home is mirrored again in the working class woman's desire for a comfortable furnishing of its interior which invites family "togetherness."

When you have children you get something that will wear good. I like things to be comfortable so you can sit in them and not worry about getting them dirty. I'm just crazy about colonial really—but it's too expensive, and it really isn't practical, so I won't get it. It just wouldn't be right for this house.

I like furniture because it is comfortable and not because it is stylish. When I go into a house where everything is ultra-modern I get a cold-looking feeling—particularly from iron legs and things like that. They look like they are there for looks and not comfort. I like furniture that is homey and inviting—you can get that in modern kinds as long as it isn't ultra-modern.

The living room furniture would have to be sturdy. I'd like to decorate it more or less in a plain fashion. I love for my house to look nice and comfortable, with nothing fancy about it. I'll just get the best I can afford for the price. Something comfortable and something sturdy that the kids can't hurt. The main thing is that it should be homey-like.

It seems safe to conclude that a working class housewife's ideally furnished house would include "modern, yet homey" dining room tables and bedroom dressers, as well as living room sofas and end table lamps.

Working class women also like the plain, simple, all-American standard in foods and clothing, according to the results of our taste tests. They selected the simple dresses over the fancy dresses by a three-to-one margin when asked to choose their two favorite costumes from among ten shown. In fact, dress for dress, their selections almost exactly paralleled those registered by the middle class housewives. In their choices both groups of women seem to be under the influence of the current swing toward the "casual" mode in clothing. This finding conforms with the results of a study done by Social Research, Inc. for the *Chicago Tribune** on the apparel attitudes of Chicagoland women. There it was observed that women of all ages, all classes, and all conditions of housing, whether suburban or city apartment, were devotees of the casual note in clothing for any and all occasions, except the most formal.

Among the party dresses shown our sample of women, the most popular was the least fancy one. With the working class women, the great popularity of this dress reflected a definition of it as being a "party dress, yet not too fancy."

It's dressy, yet not too dressy.
It's sort of a dress up dress with the wide skirt and neckline. But still, it's a little plainer than the others.
It's not so flashy-looking as some of the other party dresses.
It's all right if you're going to get dressed up and go somewhere special. It doesn't have too much fancy trim.

And among the street and meeting dresses shown, the most popular were those which the working class housewife saw as having the greatest simplicity, and hence the greatest versatility.

It's plain. You can dress it up or down. You can wear it formally or informally.
It's a more basic outfit. It can be worn by a woman anywhere.

**Chicagoland Women and Their Clothing,* September, 1957.

It's simple in design. It has good lines. You could change accessories with it to make complete-looking ensembles.

On the other hand, all the dresses, whether street or party, which were on the fancy end of the continuum were condemned on that very account by most of the young working class housewives.

I don't like all the frou-frous. Simplicity is always my choice.
It's too fancy. I wouldn't be caught wearing anything with too many frills and bows.
It's too cheap looking—with all that decoration. I don't like fussy things on the side.
It looks like a dress you couldn't wear anyplace but a party, and I don't go to too many parties.

In short, the working class woman's ideas about dresses seem to be dictated by many of the same considerations which direct her toward the "new but ordinary" in furniture: her way of life allows her no chance or reason to be expensive or fancy, and in fact she tends to fear the implications or consequences of such tastes and behavior.

Yet, we know that the working class women are often among the fanciest, frilliest, and fussiest dressers on any given occasion. We know that their conscious, superego-directed apparel goals are sometimes betrayed; that a fancy dress somehow gets into their closets and gets worn to a party. If working class women reject such clothing in a hypothetical taste test, it is partially because they are aware of the strictures placed by style experts against too much frilliness in clothing; and because they too share in the general feminine intelligence which upholds the advantages of simple, versatile clothing. Secondly, these women—and some of higher status, as well—always imagine (in self-defense) that any clothing they like is "not too fancy." Our Chicago study* showed that the overwhelming majority of women at all class levels believe they dress "less fancily" than the average woman. Since this is obviously impossible, we are driven to the conclusion that women try to believe "the dresses are frillier on the other side of the room." The typical working class woman probably fancies she's trying to be on the underplayed side of the fashion parade, but doesn't always succeed.

As we mentioned in the last chapter, young working class homemakers are very much like most other American housewives in their lack of enthusiasm for fancy and exotic cooking. They too claim that their tastes in food and cooking run to the plain and simple:

Ibid.

I specialize in nothing except just plain cooking. Once in a while we try something new, but my family prefers just plain American-style cooking.

My family likes meat and potatoes. Nothing fancy or exotic. Just regular meals. That's what my husband and the boys like.

My family likes plain cooking. They don't like things all fancied up. For instance, I usually fix pork chops fried and smothered in milk. So I tried apple slices to jazz it up and the family said, 'we liked it better the other way.'

I cook just plain American food. No special dishes, except maybe once in a while spaghetti or baked beans. We like just what the average family eats.

Here again, we have an instance where the working class woman is not a devotee of the latest thing or the up-to-date, i.e., the gourmet cuisines favored by the taste-minded Upper Bohemians and Exurbanites, because word of this trend has not yet reached her.

These references to the working class housewife's tastes in food and apparel were introduced to further illustrate the pattern of their aesthetic goals in all consumption areas. For in these things, as well as in homes and their furnishings, the working class women consciously and conscientiously attribute to themselves a preference for the plain and simple, the modern and up-to-date (as they know it), the in-all-ways all-American way.

These verbalized preferences are not always realized in the actual behavior of these working class women. We know that these women do not always, or even usually, buy dresses or sofas or lamps that middle class observers would consider plain or simple. Our interviewers noted many artificial flowers adorning working class mantle pieces,* they observed in these homes a large number of lamps upheld by nude blackamoors (which most certainly require frequent and loving application of the dust rag), and they reported the presence of super-fancy ashtrays. From market studies we are acquainted with some facts about their actual purchasing behavior, which indicate that they are a prime market for the bizarre and gaudy in drapery fabrics and chair upholsteries. Obviously, the whole story of the aesthetic considerations which enter into a working class housewife's market place choices is not told in her conscious proclamations about her tastes.

Let us briefly examine some of the discrepancies between the work-

---

*There are changes through time, of course, in what is fashionable. Recently, top-flight stores have been marketing high priced, highly realistic artificial flowers for middle class mantle pieces. The ones noted in these working class homes were not of this order.

ing class woman's proclamations of taste and the middle class judgments about her display of the same.

It is in the field of apparel that the divergence is most marked. Middle class people believe that young working class women, when they dress for street or party, are inclined toward cheap glamorization; this is the very opposite to the impression which these women claimed to seek (in their expressions on the taste test). Part of this impression is probably created by the working class woman's fascination with the mass produced, marked down, machine made copies of Paris fashions. This behavior is well known to merchandisers and manufacturers.

We can surmise that the working class housewife buys such clothes partly because she wants to be up-to-date in dress, as well as in kitchen appliances and sectional living room sofas. She does not see her copies as being overly fancy, because she compares them with the originals printed in the newspapers and is able to tell herself that since hers are less expensive, they are less exotic than what she thinks other women are wearing. She knows that she's ever so slightly behind the times compared to the real devotees of high fashion, so she does not realize the extent to which she is ahead of her middle class counterparts. Finally, from the *Chicago Tribune* apparel study* we learned that the working class woman is not generally as conservative in dress as the middle class woman, partially because she addresses her efforts to a different audience. Where the middle class woman carefully dresses to conform with rather rigid social expectations about what is right and proper on any given occasion, the working class woman dresses more to please her secret fantasies over "what makes me look my best." Thus, while the middle class woman is sometimes afraid to follow the new mode until she's sure of its widespread acceptance, the working class woman is afraid not to—and indeed may welcome it as the "new hope."

This contrast in the apparel behavior of these two classes of women provides the middle class women with the chance to scorn the lower class group as slaves to cheap glamor. Yet, in the final analysis, it is not necessarily the basic design of the garments themselves which give their working class wearers this reputation. As much of taste goes into fabric and color selection as design choice, and it is entirely probable that in many cases it is these aspects which give the garment the appearance of elegant simplicity or cheap imitation.

Secondly, the accessories worn with a dress can also greatly enhance or detract from its appearance. It is frequently her choice of accessories which gives the working class woman her dime store look, even when she's wearing the same basic dress as an upper middle class woman

Op. cit.

who has achieved the Saks-Bonwit chic. Inexpensive ornamentation, if not worn with flair, makes its wearer look "prettied up"; expensive ornamentation can either look ostentatious or sophisticated.

Thirdly, the use of makeup, the care and styling given the hair, the presence or absence of the well-scrubbed look, all contribute their share to a woman's attractiveness. We find that working class women, when considering ways and means of improving their personal appear-arance seem singularly attracted to the beauty market's latest promises of glamour. They experiment with these, hoping that whatever defects in appearance nature gave them will be overcome. Middle class women try to avoid succumbing to this temptation, they tend to suspect these glamorous promises, and content themselves with trying for "the natural look," not necessarily, the "newest." It may be in this area alone that the working class woman departs more from the standard of simplicity than does the middle class woman. Unfortunately, this departure casts its halo of artificial over-decoration on her entire appearance.

In furniture, much the same story can be told. The working class woman's decorative touches are obviously inexpensive, as far as the middle class woman is concerned—so that the former is accused of a taste for a prettied-up home. The silver-threads-among the-gold in the fabric of a working class woman's draperies or slip covers seem to sparkle like tinsel, while the more expensive ones in the middle class home give off the duller sheen of genuine silk. Hence, the identical ideas when applied by the working class woman on more limited economic resources are called "cheap and flashy." There are probably as many floral emblems in the rugs and upholstery of middle class homes as in those of the working class; in the middle class homes they have been combined in such a way as to merit a judgment of "tasteful in a feminine way," but when found in working class homes, the clash of patterns frequently gives rise to the accusation of "tasteless over-decoration."

In short, even where there's no more measurable decoration in the working class homemaker's living room, middle class observers are apt to find more, or judge what's there as being in poor taste. Partly this seems to be a result of the working class woman's lack of training or intellectual resources (not to mention economic) for the business of planning and coordinating whole rooms filled with many diverse items. The end of her efforts tends therefore toward either an over-matched monotony or a helter-skelter "mess"—at least as judged by middle class eyes.

Simplicity in home furnishings or anything else is a hard row to hoe. The inexpensive, plain and simple approach can, and often does, produce a particularly painful end product, shedding an aura of poverty rather than good taste. It is probably only expensive simplicity which strikes the connoiseur as exquisite beauty. Since the latter approach is beyond the means of the working class homemaker, she must attempt some relief from stark simplicity. So she tries a touch here and a touch there, and believes she's kept it simple, modern, and homey. After all, she knows her touches are plainly not ostentatious and expensive. It's these touches, however, which are classed as false glamorization and cheap prettification by middle class onlookers.

The extreme in glamorization or prettification represented by blackamoor table lamps or bespangled street dresses are abhorred as violently by the majority of working class women as they are by all middle class women. There is, however, a minority of young working class housewives who exhibit a fatal fascination with them—so, it must be admitted that if there is a market today for these and items akin, it is certainly concentrated among this group of women. Whether or not the number of them with such yearnings is diminishing over the years is a moot point which we cannot answer here.

Let us conclude with this note. Recent studies on American taste levels seem to indicate a growing preference for simple and clean lines in many product areas, and incidentally among the several social classes. Advertising undoubtedly plays a part in this change in taste— it is an educator, if you will. We have pointed out before that working class women are extremely conscious of national advertising and tend to read much of it with care. It is possibly as a result of such exposure that they indicate a strong conscious preference for the plain and simple. They know that there is where their taste should lie, at least the advertising they see tells them so. Not all of their possessions conform to this ideal, of course. The general indication is that the working class housewife's taste levels are still in the process of change— and will continue to change in conformity with what the advertisers suggest to her is correct.

Part III

STRATEGY IN MARKETING AND ADVERTISING

CHAPTER XII

REACHING THE WORKINGMAN'S WIFE

The goals toward which consumers strive in their advertising response, purchasing behavior and use patterns are complex and variegated. We have suggested through our discussion of the working class housewife, that what she does in connection with purchase and use is complexly determined by the kind of woman she is and the world in which she lives. Based on the more detailed examination of consuming style in the previous three chapters, it is now possible to form some conclusions about the goals which persistently guide the working class housewife in her day-to-day consuming behavior, and suggest how these goals are related to effective advertising and marketing strategy. In Chapter X, several particular product areas were examined. Here, however, we will be concerned with those goals which operate broadly in many product areas and which have some relevance for her purchasing behavior in almost all areas, whether the particular relevance be to the nature of the product itself, to the brand image, or to the symbolic context which the advertising provides for product and brand.

It seems worthwhile to consider five basic goals which activate the consumer behavior of the working class housewife. These are: the search for social, economic and physical security; the drive for a "common man" level of recognition and respectability; the desire for support and affection from the people important to her; the effort to escape a heavy burden of household labors; and the urge to decorate, to "pretty up" her world. Out of such striving, and the inevitable compromises which must be made as they conflict, derive the everyday purchasing decisions which ring cash registers in the supermarket, the department store, the drug store.

Much of what the working class housewife does is directed toward securing herself and her family from real or potential threats to their well being. This is one of her most deeply rooted motives, and one which operates steadily to guide her actions. It is also a chronic concern, stemming as it does from deep laid preoccupations and experience in growing up. In the analysis of these women's personality structures we discussed their ongoing preoccupation with calamitous events. Their pessimistic view of the world as a place of ever-present danger is reflected in their fear of a depression-ridden future. For example, they express this fear when they speak of what they expect from the next ten years. They show very little confidence in their husbands' future earning abilities. In fact, they generally believe that "things probably won't ever get much better with him"—and that, if there is any change at all from the *status quo*, (and there is always the possibility that fate will intervene) things will get worse.

The expectation that things will not get particularly better for them is, of course, very much a reflection of their lack of mobility. Most working class women do not expect their lives to change markedly, nor in many ways do they particularly want them to. Thus, while they may hope for many things in the future, and be planning for various improvements in their standard of living, such hopes and plans are constantly subject to their underlying anxieties and pessimism.

The feelings of working class mothers about their children tend to reflect the same kind of outlook. They show, for example, a great reticence to leave the children in the care of baby-sitters. They express fears of living in two-story houses (the children might fall down the stairs or out a second-story window). These mothers engage in many activities (and purchase many products in connection with these) to protect their children against such dangers.

On a more economic level, these women, when discussing their consumption habits and fiscal policies, show a strong desire to save their money against the inevitable "rainy days" of the future. Not for them the philosophy of "live only for today"—since "you can't take it with you." Instead, they admonish themselves to be cautious, thrifty, and impervious to the temptations of immediate fun and frivolity. They show no particular interest in spending large amounts of money for recreation or vacations. Although such expenditures, they recognize, might relieve the monotony of their daily routines, they still would rather save their money and thus assure themselves that monotony will not be supplanted by misery.

An outside observer may often feel that working class women do not manage their expenditures in ways best calculated to save against a rainy day. We should not be deceived by their action, however, into believing that it is because their values sanction the short term view, or that they are incurable optimists. Rather, they often sacrifice long term goals because of monetary impulse, or some stronger value. Their earnest hope is to save, and a good many of them do succeed.

Such strong desires to save as much money as possible, coupled with some pretty grave doubts about their own abilities to handle debts, causes them to feel exceptionally uncomfortable when they do purchase goods or pleasures on installment plans. To them, cash payments offer the double advantage of helping them keep track of where they are financially, and of keeping them at a safe remove from the

206

clutches of usurers, and money lenders. Ideally, they would even like to pay cash for their houses. In this instance, however, their drives for housing security and freedom from a landlord's whims tend to overcome their passions against long-term debt.

However, despite these conscious resolutions regarding debt and overspending, these women are perpetually finding themselves right back at the brink, as it were. Some "want" (perhaps a washer-dryer combination) becomes too strong and overcomes all the good resolutions of thrift. Since the cash is probably not in the tin can, other methods of purchase must be sought.

Actually, working class women are rarely able to feel themselves as fully removed from danger as they might like. This is partially because their worries and imaginings are so great that no actions of their own—or of others—are likely to render them completely and satisfactorily secure. On the other hand, the plain fact of often having no more than $360-a-month available to them plays a significant part in preventing the attainment of economic and physical security. Their incomes, sometimes, are not adequate for such goals, particularly if other desires for the good life, in terms of nice houses, neat clothes, good quality foods, and a decent complement of appliances, are to be satisfied.

Working class women's responses to advertising are clearly influenced by their uncertainty, unsureness, and suspicion of the world around them, and their corresponding needs for reassurance about themselves in relation to this world and their needs for encouragement in the hope that things will go well for them. Advertising can and does address working class women in terms of these needs and concerns. Its role is to communicate to these people, then, an image of the gratifying world, a world in which products fit functionally into the drive for a stable and secure life, and in which products are shown to fit constructively and effectively into the daily activities of the housewife working to maintain a family in a secure and stable way.

In doing this, the advertiser must take into account the fact that he is addressing a market which is also the primary object of many local merchants who use methods which, although they may result in sales, also leave the working class consumer feeling that she has been taken advantage of, and that she must be on her guard because people who sell to her cannot be trusted.

Thus, unfavorable experiences with, and attitudes toward, those who sell to them often leave the working class women uneasy and cautious in their consuming behavior. The advertiser needs to be careful in his advertising that he counteracts, rather than unwittingly furthers, this kind of suspicion and distrust.

The search for the "good buy" represents one of the main solutions which these women apply to the problem posed by their desire for goods and services coupled with their tendency to distrust those who provide them. Very often the national brand serves them as a symbol of the good buy. Thus, they believe that a brand which is well advertised is probably a good bet because it means that a solidly established company stands behind it. The advertiser who succeeds in presenting a strong image of his product, as a well known and popular national brand, has an advantage with these people. They will see his brand as trustworthy in a market which they believe is full of uncertain values.

Although these women are concerned with spending their money in economical ways, they are afraid of the cheap buy. They like to feel that their money is well spent rather than that they "went for a bargain" which tomorrow may turn out not to have been such a bargain. Thus, although they are susceptible to the appeal of economy they very definitely need assurance that the economy is not only in the purchase price, but in the long term value of the object. (It is also true that these women sometimes buy things which they do not believe are good values, because they feel pressed by economic circumstances. Purchases made in this way do not contribute to a long term brand loyalty. As such women become more securely established, they seek to avoid these kinds of purchases.)

In these women the drive for security also involves a strong element of physical concern. They want to feel that the products they buy are safe, that they will not prove harmful to themselves, and most particularly to their children. With a product for which this issue is relevant, the advertiser does well to communicate in his advertising a feeling of confidence and safety about the product and its operation. This does not mean, however, that safety should be a central, explicit theme in advertising. Often by raising the issue in such a conscious way, the advertiser will merely reinforce fears and anxiety. It may be better to communicate safety by the overall feeling of security and confidence, which the advertisement communicates, than by making safety a central copy theme.

Also, the interest of these women in the physical security of their families means that they will show particular interest in products and brands which facilitate their families' health and well-being. This is true whether it be a disinfectant that protects the babies from germs, a mattress which insures the children's sound sleep, or food that builds good strong bones and muscles.

The strivings connected with the goal of security *per se* are rather negative ones. One saves for the rainy day when that is possible; but, given the working class wife's image of a rainy day, a rather high rate of saving would be necessary to make her really feel secure.

A more positive goal for these women is that of maintaining and enhancing the family's status within the "common man" level of her society. To the extent that this goal is achieved, much is done to allay the anxieties connected with insecurity. The working class wife strives to maintain the family's status as modern, respectable, and comfortable. It was noted earlier that these women are powerfully motivated to stay away from the "slums." They do not want to live in the very best neighborhoods, but they do seek a plain, ordinary, comfortable way of life that signalizes mass market respectability and they want to have neighbors like themselves—decent, hard-working people who don't "put on airs."

The houses they aspire to are appropriate to these neighborhoods. They want a house which is comfortable and in good shape, with enough room for the family; but they do not want to feel awed by it, or feel that it out-ranks them in status. They seek something that is good for the average person, a home in which they can feel that they are participating in what modern life offers to the modern woman.

As with houses, so with furnishings, we find working class wives do not covet the elaborate, ornamental, or rich. Rather, they say, they will be quite happy with simple, cleanlined modern (though not extreme) furniture. They want things that are sturdy enough to withstand the assaults of their children, yet attractive enough to provide a pleasant introduction to their homes whenever neighbors or relatives come to call. They want furniture that will be in harmony with their modest, modern houses. They are tired of dated things, of furnishings and accessories which make them look as if they have not been able to afford something new for a long time.

In clothes and foods these women again pay avid lip service to the good, simple American standard. They emphasize that their taste in both these categories runs to the plain and unadorned. They do not care, they say, for frills and frou-frous in clothing, and they certainly do not get excited over exotic or gourmet cooking. They and their families like good, plain American food and they see absolutely no reason to "pour 50% of a family's income down its stomach"—or, for that matter, "to wear it all on our backs."

They are happiest when buying brand name merchandise. Such products give them the "feel" of economic security, of getting a well known product that the store or manufacturer will "stand behind." Also, the purchases of such products confer upon these women the social security of having done the same thing as millions of other Americans. It confirms them in their own private feelings of being acceptably in the midst of the common man level.

The greatest obstacle to accomplishment of this standard of modernity and decency is the working class wife's eagerness to avoid living on the installment plan—her desire "not to buy anything we can't pay cash for." Apparently, she has not yet accepted the mid-twentieth century American concept that it is frequently inevitable for people in her economic circumstance to live to the limit of income, particularly if they strive to feel far removed from its limitations.

A much smaller obstacle, but still an obstacle, is the fact that many of them are driven to make spur of the moment palliative purchases. The little "gifts for the children" or "doo-dads" for the house only serve to keep the tin can emptier and thus to delay the ultimate purchase of larger, more satisfying contributions to the desired appearance of modernity and respectability.

Thus, the search for security is most fully expressed in the way working class families strive to achieve and maintain a common man status. These women want to be regarded as part of the large middle "core culture" of the country, and much of their consuming behavior is oriented toward achieving that goal. As working class people, they know that they are always in danger of being socially downgraded, by other people or by circumstances. They want to include themselves in the common man group rather than be regarded as "low average"; but as has been pointed out, their personalities and social circumstances often make this difficult.

Advertising can and does facilitate this self-identification by the readers as part of the common man group. It does this by relating its product and brand to the good life, to the culture of the average man.

These people want to enjoy the reward of participating in the core culture and living up to its values and standards. Advertising offers them the products which both enable them to live up to these standards (by making their homes cleaner, healthier, and the like), and which are in themselves rewards for living up to these standards. To the extent that these women give up some of the less responsible, more impulsive possibilities of lower class life in order to define themselves as within the respectable common man group, they feel that they have earned the material rewards which go with that life.

The material possessions which these people accumulate serve them as a symbol of their being in the common man group. They serve to indicate that the family is as well off as other Americans. Advertising must present products and brands as part of the "well stocked larder" which goes with the average man's status. It does this as much by implication as directly, particularly to the extent that it presents products and brands as part of the context of the average woman's living and consuming, as a to-be-expected item in the good life.

Since these women are in the process of building and solidifying their identification with the common man level, advertising plays a strong educational role. Advertising both communicates the fact that an object is an expected part of an expected common man life and, in addition, teaches these women how to use the object in that context. This educational function is often recognized by women when they discuss advertisements. They will point out that they learn from advertising how to use products and how to fit them in with ongoing experience. It should be remembered that the *ability to consume* is as important as is the desire to consume. Often working class women are uncertain about what to do with a particular product and how to fit it in with their lives. Advertising communicates this as much as it communicates the desirability of the object. Thus, the woman who has never had a coffee table and has not grown up in a home with a coffee table, needs as much to learn how it is used and how one behaves with a coffee table, as she needs to be encouraged to want it.

Thus, the setting in which a product or a brand is advertised has heightened importance. This setting has the function of making this object seem desirable, and of giving the woman a sense of how she might use the product and how she might relate it to her own situation.

It is important in all of this, that the advertising not set too high standards nor give the woman the feeling that the object is beyond her ability to handle comfortably. Since many of these women are quite uncertain of their own competence as participants in the core culture, they need a good deal of reassurance from advertising that the object is within their reach socially and psychologically, as well as economically.

Another striving relates to these concerns about common man status, often playing in with it, sometimes conflicting with it. This is the working class wife's need to constantly secure herself in the affections of others, to reassure herself that her husband and her children love her, and that other significant persons do, too.

As was pointed out in the discussion of their personality and social world, these women tend to feel relatively little security in the affections of their husbands, their children, or the world of people at large. They appear to direct a good deal of energy toward ensuring their hold on the affections and love of these others. Since in many ways they tend to try to buy this affection, the concern often manifests itself in their purchasing behavior.

They show a good deal of indulgence in handling their husbands. To the men go the responsibility for the purchase of the family automobile. This is the man's department. These wives are even relatively happy to have their husbands indulge themselves in whimful purchases, as long as this does not seriously imperil the family economy. When it comes to the husband's clothes, they frequently acknowledge that this is a function of their own department. Many a

211

working class wife is sure that her husband would never have anything new to wear if the purchases were left to him. As a result, she takes matters into her own hands, and certainly within limits, sees to it that the husband shows a relatively presentable figure to the world.

Most of the other family expenditures are definitely in the wives' department. Even here, however, they display their concern over their husbands' attitudes toward them by carefully checking "on anything over $10.00." They do not want to run the risk of making their husbands even momentarily angry over some $25.00 mistake.

The fact that as mothers they indulge their children a great deal has already been discussed. Their concern is shown again by such statements as: "I never come home from the store without something for the kids." The children are the most readily and enjoyably prettified objects on their horizon and when they "take something home for the kids" they score on two counts: they actually are doing something for the children (thus assuring their affection), and they add a little something to relieve the monotony of their own environment. These women are never prouder of themselves than when they can claim:

> . . . 90 per cent of all we spend goes on our children . . . I go in town to get something for myself and get something for the kids instead.

or,

> I make sure they have plenty of clothes and toys and are well fed . . . we'd do without, if necessary, so the kids could have what they want and need.

With the world of friends, neighbors, and relatives, working class women are fond of playing the "kind lady" role. The thought of a reduced income brings, among other pains, such worries as "I'll have to make my heart a little smaller," or, "I'll have to stop giving to other people—and I really love to give." The thought of later adulthood—child-free and work-free as it will be—inspires in them a desire to do social work or to help out in a hospital. When asked how much of their money goes to gifts, many reply, "If I ever figured it all out, I'd probably be shocked."

There can be no question that "doing for others"—whether it be their own families or their friends—is a major motivation for the working class woman. It is the best way they know of relating to other people. A more varied emotional or intellectual exchange is difficult, given their personal resources.

This urgent drive to display affection for the other people frequently places them in conflictful situations. It is the same old bugaboo. After too many gift cakes have been baked for relatives and neighbors, and too many baubles have been bought for the children, they find that the money being saved in the tin can against the purchase of a new appliance has just disappeared. As a result, cakes must continue being baked in the same old-fashioned, labor-and-time-consuming oven. The desire to give is at odds with the urge to save and modernize.

Her sensitivity to the people in her life, her desire to avoid their criticism and rejection, and to win their love, influences product and brand choice in many ways, and plays a large role in her response to advertising and sales appeals. Advertising which is people oriented is much more meaningful to her. Advertising that communicates a highly technical, impersonal, or objective atmosphere is not as meaningful. The latter leaves it up to the woman herself to work out the relationship between what is advertised and her own interpersonal world. As will be discussed below, labor-saving devices achieve much more importance when the housewife feels that they can help her to be a better mother and wife; that is, aid her in caring for and pleasing the people in her life.

Sometimes, too, it is not so much the direct relationship between the people in her life and the product that is important in her response to advertising. It may simply be that advertising which shows people, and shows them pleased with themselves and each other, strikes a responsive chord. Thus, pictures of babies will have a special attention-getting value for working class women, over and above any direct relationship between the product and her role as a mother. Because she thinks of people as the only really important matter in the world, she attends more to advertising which has a human feeling and she is more inclined to ignore it when it lacks this.

Just because she strives so assiduously to realize these goals, the working class wife has an arduous job, and she seeks ways of freeing herself from the unending round of household chores. She tends to describe her daily life as "monotonous—just monotonous." Each day seems filled with the thousands of little tasks connected with feeding a family, keeping the house and clothes clean, maintaining the family's health and (completely) mothering the children. Whenever she can delegate any of these tasks (except, of course, tending the children) to a machine, she is pleased.

As a result, working class women tend to regard their labor saving devices (the washer-dryer combination, the automatic floor polisher, the automatic cake mixer, the vacuum cleaner) as the most valuable objects in their homes. If they do not already have these labor saving devices, the contemplation of such purchases fills their waking hours with the brightest daydreams. Typically, working class women, unlike the middle class women, choose a modern, labor saving appliance over an eye-appealing piece of furniture as the thing most necessary to their daily happiness.

These women are so "escape-from-work" oriented that anything they can label as "labor saving" takes on an added appeal. Such diverse items as sofas, lamps, and rugs are assessed on this criterion rather than judged on the basis of their aesthetic appeal. Wall-to-wall carpeting's greatest value for them often lies in the fact that it eases their floor cleaning work. Even a simple, clean lined lamp offers such secondary values. It is easier to dust than a fancy lamp. A second floor in the home is an added handicap to keeping up with the chores.

In actual fact, these women are probably not as eager to get rid of their household labors as they say. It must be remembered that their families can interpret all these chores as labors of live, and reward the women accordingly. The idea of a cake mix may entrance the woman insofar as she realizes how much time and effort it would save her. However, in the long run, the cake mix would lose its charm if she came to the conclusion that her family felt slighted by this reliance on the ready-prepared.

Thus, these women seek a delicate balance between being saved from unending chores, and having nothing to do and therefore without claim on their families for recognition and affection.

The housewife's goal of escaping from unending household labors, and more effectively mastering her job and its duties, is a familiar one to advertisers and a theme which has been effectively utilized in advertising for a long time. It may be worthwhile then to attend to some of the dangers involved in advertising concentration on this motivation rather than for us to elaborate on its obvious importance in purchasing behavior.

Certainly these women are very interested in labor saving possibilities, whether these be in the simple easy-to-clean lines of a piece of furniture, or in some particular product which makes housework easier to do. They think of their jobs as housewives as both difficult and very time consuming. They are always on the lookout for things which can help them do their jobs and lessen the wear and tear on themselves.

At the same time, the housewife's being hard pressed is felt to be a symbol of her worthiness and of her love for her family. Therefore, advertising which places too great emphasis on easing the housewife's burdens runs the risk of being reacted to negatively because it seems to detract from her personal importance. These women need to be busy keeping house—both because they need to feel they are doing something worthwhile and because they have few psychic resources for occupying themselves in ways other than as housekeeper for the family. There is a neat balance, then, between saving enough labor to make the job tolerable and saving so much that she could not occupy her time and would feel lazy or uneasy or bored.

These women have an extremely personal conception of their homemaking role. While the solidly established middle class woman may be very happy to have a machine wash the dishes, these women feel that using their own hands to wash the husband's and children's dishes has some value in and of itself. It is a sign of her love for them and of the personal care she takes for their well being, even though she may complain that the task is an onerous one.

Thus, at the same time that advertising offers these women a chance to do their housework with less effort, and to feel themselves less pressed and burdened down, it must also communicate to them a sense of their worth, the sense of being important and essential to their families. The saving of labor must somehow be compensated for by something which is worthwhile, something being done for the family. The implication that with this product the housewife will have more time to idly enjoy herself is probably best avoided. (The housewife who wants idle time is quite capable of discovering this possibility herself.)

Finally, the working class wife is very much in the market for "pretty" things. Apart from the more serious goals discussed above, these women often find themselves yielding to the impulse to pretty-up their lives in little ways. We know that they feel a good deal of pressure in their lives, and are inclined to see life as rather hard and uncertain. It is not surprising, then, that they covet the little things that make life seem more pleasant, nicer, prettier. They like to have their environments a little more pleasant, a little more stimulating.

More often than they would like to admit, working class women find themselves bringing home some pretty trifle (fancy flowered glasses or a highly decorated ashtray) from shopping expeditions which originally had more worthwhile purposes. The evidence for such indiscretions is found as often in the interviewers' descriptions of the homes as in the women's confessions.

As we have reported, these women do not like to think of themselves as women who are given to buying fancy objects. They really prefer not to think of themselves as purchasers of fancy little incidentals, either. Perhaps they succeed in keeping their day-to-day expenditures on food and their heavy outlays on furniture and clothing under sterling control. Undeniably, however, they go soft at the sight of "baubles." It may well be that the effort required to approximate victory in the major battles of the market place saps their energies to the point that a series of defeats in the minor skirmishes marks their paths through the neighborhood five-and-dime stores.

215

They are, in effect, caught in a cross fire between warring tastes for practicality and novelty, for propriety and prettiness.

It is when they are confronted with something cute for the children that their control over the urge to buy and prettify most readily breaks down. Under these circumstances their desire to stand well in their children's affections apparently conspires with their ever-present urge to pretty up their environment.

They find ready justification for this indulgent behavior on behalf of "the kids." It is certainly less selfish to buy something for the children than to buy something for themselves. The world, so they apparently reason, can never criticize a mother for a prettily dressed child. On the other hand, the world might find a prettified living room in bad taste, or what is worse, accuse its possessor of a shamefully uneconomic use of her husband's income.

Given these propensities for pretty things, advertising probably gets a better reception when it communicates something of this prettied-up atmosphere, when it is not simply factual and practical in its presentation of the product and the brand. These women show a strong preference for advertisements in colors, for example, because they find the colors themselves stimulating and gratifying.

Overall, if a product can be made to fit in with the woman's more serious strivings for common man status and at the same time prove emotionally stimulating and gratifying, its appeal will be very strong.

For example, while these women are "appliance hungry" and want their kitchens to be the most modern and efficient possible, we have seen that they also like to spruce up the kitchen with artificial flowers, spots of color, etc. Since she spends a good deal of her day in the kitchen, the housewife likes it to seem homey and cozy. It would seem worthwhile in advertising items for the kitchen, then, to portray them in a setting which involves some of these more emotionally satisfying images. This would be particularly true of appliances and other articles of kitchen hardware which are in themselves fairly impersonal and work oriented.

In connection with their urge to improve, the educational role of advertising plays a part. These women are, often more or less, consciously aware that their desires in the direction of pretty-ing up conflict with their strivings for common man status. This is true, not only because of the money that may go into such purchase, but also because of the lower class image which may attach to some of the pretty objects they yearn for. Advertising which enables them to bring these two desires in line with each other by presenting the "prettier" solutions to their serious problems of maintaining a well-run, respectable home will certainly prove doubly attractive.

BIBLIOGRAPHY

ALLEN, FREDERICK LEWIS. *The Big Change.* New York: Harper and Bros., 1952.

BAKKE, E. WIGHT. *Citizens Without Work: A Study of the Effects of Unemployment Upon the Workers' Social Relations and Practices.* New Haven: Yale University Press, 1940.

————. *The Unemployed Worker: A Study of the Task of Making a Living Without a Job.* New Haven: Yale University Press, 1940.

DAVIS, ALLISON. *Social Class and Influences Upon Learning.* Cambridge: Harvard University Press, 1948.

———— AND HAVIGHURST, ROBERT J. *Father of the Man.* Boston: Houghton, Mifflin Co., 1947.

————, GARDNER, B. B. AND GARDNER, M. R. *Deep South.* Chicago: University of Chicago Press, 1941.

———— AND DOLLARD, JOHN. *Children of Bondage.* Washington, D. C.: American Council on Education, 1940.

————. "American Status Systems and the Socialization of the Child," *Am. Soc. Rev.* 6 (1941), 345-46.

————. "Child Training and Social Class," in Barker, R. G. et al.; *Child Behavior and Development.* New York: McGraw-Hill, 1943.

————. "The Motivation of the Underprivileged Worker," in Whyte, W. F. (ed.), *Industry and Society.* New Pork: McGraw-Hill, 1946.

————. "Socialization and Adolescent Personality," in Newcomb, T. M. and Hartley, E. (eds.), *Readings In Social Psychology.* New York: Henry Holt and Co., 1947.

DOLLARD, JOHN. *Caste and Class in a Southern Town.* New York: Harper and Bros., 1949.

DOTSON, FLOYD. "Patterns of Voluntary Association Among Urban Working Class Families," *Am. Soc. Rev.* 16 (1951), 687-93.

FLESCH, RUDOLPH. *The Art of Plain Talk.* New York: Harper and Bros., 1946.

GALBRAITH, JOHN. *The Affluent Society.* Boston: Houghton, Mifflin, 1958.

HENRY, WILLIAM E. *The Analysis of Fantasy: The Thematic Apperception Technique In Study of Personality.* New York: John Wiley and Sons, 1956.

HESS, ROBERT D. AND HANDEL, GERALD. *Family Worlds.* Chicago: University of Chicago Press, 1959.

HOGGART, RICHARD. *The Uses of Literacy.* London: Chatto and Windus, 1957.

HOLLINGSHEAD, AUGUST B. *Elmtown's Youth.* New York: John Wiley and Sons, 1949.

———— AND REDLICH, FREDERICH C. *Social Class and Mental Illness.* New York: John Wiley and Sons, 1958.

KAHL, J. A. *The American Class Structure.* New York: Rinehart and Co., 1957.

LYND, ROBERT S. AND LYND HELEN M. *Middletown: A Study In Contemporary American Culture.* New York: Harcourt, Brace, 1929.

——, *Middletown In Transition.* New York: Harcourt, Brace, 1937.

MARTINEAU, PIERRE. "Social Classes and Spending Behavior," *The Journal of Marketing,* 23 (Oct., 1958).

RAINWATER, LEE. "A Study of Personality Differences between Middle and Lower Class Adolescents: The Szondi Test in Culture-Personality Research," *Gen. Psych. Mono.* 54 (1956), 3-86.

REUSCH, JERGEN B. AND LOEB, MARTIN. *Chronic Disease and Psychological Invalidism.* Berkeley, Calif.: University of California Press, 1951.

SCHATZMAN, LEONARD AND STRAUSS, ANSELM L. "Social Class and Modes of Communication," *Am. J. Soc.,* LX (Jan., 1955).

SEARS, R. R., MACCOBY, E. E., AND LEVIN, H. *Patterns of Child Rearing.* Evanston, Ill.: Row, Peterson and Co., 1957.

SPINLEY, B. M. *The Deprived and the Privileged.* London: Routledge and Kegan Paul, Ltd., 1953.

TRUE STORY WOMEN'S GROUP. *The New America.* New York: Macfadden Publications, 1957.

UNITED STATES SAVINGS AND LOAN LEAGUE. *Savings and Loan Fact Book,* 1958.

WARNER, W. LLOYD, HAVIGHURST, ROBERT J. AND LOEB, MARTIN. *Who Shall Be Educated?* New York: Harper & Bros., 1944.

——, ET AL. *Democracy in Jonesville.* New York: Harper & Bros., 1949.

——, MEEKER, M., AND EELLS, K. *Social Class in America.* Chicago: Science Research Associates, 1949.

—— AND HENRY, WILLIAM E. "The Radio Daytime Serial: A Symbolic Analysis," *Gen. Psych. Mono.* 37 (1948), 3-71.

—— AND ABEGGLEN, J. *Big Business Leaders in America.* New York: Harper and Bros., 1955.

——. *American Life—Dream and Reality.* Chicago: University of Chicago Press, 1953.

——. *The Yankee City Series.* All published in New Haven, Conn., by the Yale University Press. Vol. I., (with Paul S. Lunt), *Social Life of a Modern Community,* 1941, Vol. II, (with Paul S. Lunt), *Status Systems of a Modern Community,* 1942. Vol. III (with Leo Srole), *Social Systems of American Ethnic Groups,* 1945. Vol. IV, (with J. O. Low), *The Social System of the Modern Factory,* 1947. Vol. V, *The Living and the Dead,* 1959.

METHODOLOGICAL APPENDIX

As mentioned in the Introduction and Chapter I, the analysis presented in this book of the working class wife and her world stems from research studies conducted over several years, in several different areas, and for a variety of practical purposes conceived by their sponsors. It has not been possible, then, to describe one single research design as responsible for all that has been said in this book. However, our analyses have relied fairly heavily on a large study undertaken for Macfadden Publications, Inc., which was completed in 1958. We outline below some of the major aspects of the methodology and sample of that study as an example of the way in which socio-psychological studies of this type have been conducted. We hope that this appendix will be of interest both to researchers who want to know what we did and how we did it, and to other readers who would to know a little more about how "motivation research" is done.

THE SAMPLE

The findings in this study are based on interviews with 480 readers of the Family Behavior Group magazines and 120 middle class women. This total of 600 interviews was gathered in four cities: Chicago, Louisville, Trenton, and Tacoma, providing a wide geographic spread and populations with quite different characteristics. From each of these four cities 150 interviews were collected, 120 from the FBG readers and 30 from middle class women. We adopted this sample design in order to clarify and more fully illustrate the attitudes and customs of working class women.

It was known from Social Research, Inc. studies of the FBG readers that they are typically wives of wage-earners or blue collar workers. They are most frequently classified as members of the working class by social scientists. Their status as working class housewives is best illustrated by this fact about them: more than four-fifths—81% to be exact—of their husbands are craftsmen, factory operatives, or service workers. In short, they are married to men with "blue collar" occupations.

In the light of this knowledge about the social status of FBG women, we decided that the contrast women should be selected to represent a distinctly different way of life. To accomplish this goal, we did not need "society women" or even "extremely prosperous women." We felt that we could achieve a suitable contrast by interviewing women who lived in residential areas which were "above average" in status, and who occupied houses of equally "above average" character.

By interviewing women in such areas and houses, we obtained a contrast sample in which some women are no higher in status than the lower middle class; while others are clearly part of the upper middle class world of "organization wives." The exact procedures followed in choosing the middle class group, as well as a statement of its social character, will be presented later in this section.

We interviewed FBG readers and middle class women in four different cities, representing four different sections of the country, in order to rule out the possibility of purely local biases in the character of either group. Trenton is a heavily industrialized community; the readers who live there are most frequently wives of steel workers or shipyard employees. Far more than half of them are Catholic in religious preference, and a large percentage are second-generation Americans. The middle class women from Trenton are also quite frequently Catholic, though more often Irish or Bavarian in descent rather than Italian or Hungarian. At the opposite extreme, geographically and ethnically, is Tacoma. Tacoma is also an industrial city, but the biggest employer there is the Army. A considerable number of the working class women interviewed in Tacoma are wives of service men. Some of the husbands are enlisted men or draftees and the families are only stationed in Tacoma for the "duration," rather than being permanently resident there. On the other hand, many of the husbands are career non-commissioned officers and some are career officers. Both types of families are as much residents "of Tacoma" as any other place. The ethnic and religious tone of our Tacoma sample is less marked than that of any other community—but to the extent that we have sampled in long-time-Pacific-Northwest-households, the trend there runs to Scandinavians and Lutherans.

In Louisville, still another pattern prevails. There, a striking post-war influx of industry (auto assembly plants, General Electric's new Appliance Park establishment, etc.) has brought into Louisville a large number of folk, only recently urbanized, from downstate Kentucky and Tennessee or from the hill country of Southern Indiana. Many of these "immigrants" have bought homes in the burgeoning working class suburbs of Louisville—at $25 down and $69 a month "forever." Many of the FBG readers interviewed there are of such families—and they are "old American" to the core. Usually, they are Baptist or members of evangelical sects.

In Chicago, all our interviewing of working class women was done on the Southwest Side. The husbands work in a wide range of industries—railroading, steelmaking, farm machinery, auto assembly, or meat packing. They represent a variety of ethnic backgrounds—Polish, Italian, Irish, Hungarian, Belgian, German and Slovak. Of course, in every city, many of the FBG women were of no discernible "ethnic background" and many were not married to factory employees, but to truck drivers, bread salesmen, shipping clerks, or carpenters.

The middle class women in every city represented the overall population trends for their cities. Some of their husbands were office workers in the same industrial establishments where husbands of working class women were employed at more manual labor. For example, in Tacoma several middle class women are the wives of Army captains or majors, while most of the working class husbands were corporals or sergeants.

One other kind of contrast was sought by our sample design: this time a contrast within each of the two principal groups. We wanted to learn whether there might be any discernible differences between inhabitants of newly-built houses in post-war suburbs and those of older houses located in the long built-up and solidly packed central city areas. We inquired into a possible variation between these two groups in the belief that fundamental differences in the psychology of spending—particularly the "optimism" or "liberality" component —might appear. Therefore, we sought to obtain half of our working class women and half of our middle class women from the newer residential areas in each city.

These, then, were the general considerations and principal procedures we followed in designing the sample for this study of the consumption style of FBG readers: we compared the working class readers with a group from a distinctly higher social level; we sampled both groups in four different cities whose populations exhibit marked variance in ethnic and religious tone, and we concentrated on securing interviews with both types of women in new suburban residential areas as well as in older city center neighborhoods.

Special procedures used for obtaining a representative sample of FBG readers in the four cities.

In order to "cover the waterfront" of FBG readers we decided that it would be necessary to interview readers of all four magazines. We also wanted to interview both subscribers and newsstand purchasers. It was necessary to interview newsstand purchasers of two magazines—*True Experience* and *True Love Stories*—if we were to interview any readers of these magazines at all, since they are circulated to the public only through newsstands.

The Macfadden company provided us with the names of all subscribers to *True Story* and *True Romance* who lived in the four cities and their suburbs. (In Chicago, we interviewed subscribers from the Southwest section of the city and two Southwest suburbs, Oak Lawn and Blue Island, and hence were provided with the names of subscribers from those areas only.) The publisher collected for us a list of newsstand purchasers of all four magazines. This list was assembled by inserting a coupon in one issue of each magazine, offering a free copy of some later issue of that magazine to any woman who sent in the coupon.

With the publisher's help, we drew up a quota to guide us toward a representative sample of subscribers and newsstand purchasers, as well as a representative sample of the total Family Behavior Group readership. The quotas which we thus established are listed below.

22.0% *True Story*: Subscribers.
31.2% *True Story*: Newsstand purchasers.

5.2% *True Romance*: Subscribers.
10.4% *True Romance*: Newsstand purchasers.

15.6% *True Experience*: Newsstand purchasers.
15.6% *True Love Stories*: Newsstand purchasers.

These quotas were all met, and then some, inasmuch as two-thirds of the women we interviewed proved to read two or more of these magazines, and hence could be placed in two or more of these categories. Of course, it was impossible to contact and secure interviews with a goodly portion of the women whose names were given us by the publisher. Some had moved without leaving forwarding addresses, others were sick. However, only 10% of the readers whom we found at home and well refused to be interviewed.

We arbitrarily ruled that only married housewives between the ages of 20 and 44 would be interviewed. Approximately five out of every eight (62%) are in this age bracket; another 24% are less than 20 years old, while 14% are older than 45. The age groups which we carved out for study include those women who are "most active in the marketplace." Most of these young women are between 22 and 35 years of age. They are in the process of rearing small children, establishing their families, and furnishing their houses. Though these women do not necessarily have the largest amount of "disposable income" at their command, they necessary have to dispose of the largest share of their incomes. The housewives who are between 35 and 44 are also of considerable interest to advertisers and are getting their "second wind," so to speak. They are replacing their early furniture and appliances with new and better quality pieces. Many families find that these purchases serve them for the rest of their lives.

Women over 45 were excluded from this sample because the typical working class family's living standard goes into decline after this age. The husbands begin to lose physical vigor and are unable to earn as much money. Illness and, sometimes, death begin to take their toll of the family's financial balance sheet. (Of course, this financial decline after 45 is only an average tendency for this social level—many older families in which the husband has been able to continue on the job, and thus reap the benefits of seniority, have more "discretionary income" at their disposal than at any earlier point in their lives.)

One other consideration is pertinent to this discussion. The middle class families experience a somewhat contrary pattern in the relationship between chronological age and their standard of living. For most middle class families, adulthood provides them with one continual upward progression in living standard as the husbands advance up their respective corporate hierarchies or increasingly acquire "reputations" within their professions. Thus, the income of many middle class families is very similar to that of working class families up to the age of 35 or even 40. Thereafter, the gap between the two progressively widens in favor of the middle class families. Identical as the income level of these young middle class families may be with that of their age mates in the working class, the manner in which they choose to spend it appears to be as different at this age as at later points in their lives. By contrasting young working class women with young middle class women, we obtained enlightening evidence on basic differences in the "spending philosophies" of the two social types.

With respect to the intended sample division into "old urbanite" women and "new suburbanite" women, we were able to accomplish a 60-40 split among the readers, and a 50-50 division among the middle class contrast women.

Special procedures used for obtaining an adequate sample of contrast women.

The principal goal in our use of a middle class group was to interview women from a completely different social level. We decided that we could not acquire a different enough sample—with any solid assurance of its being different—if we sent our interviewers to neighborhoods which might be designated "ordinary lower middle class" in social tone. Previous research on social life in cities has shown that such areas generally contain working class families, perhaps in proportions as high as 30%. In consequence of these understandings and goals, we determined to gather most of our middle class interviews from neighborhoods which could be characterized as "above middle class average."

We identified the location of such neighborhoods in the four communities by use of census block statistics and real estate advertisements in the newspapers. Previous research has shown that a residential block with "above middle class average" status can be located from census statistics in this way: the value of a city's "average house" as reported by the census is doubled to obtain the median value of "above average" housing. Those residential blocks in the city for which median housing values approximate this "doubled average" figure can then be labeled, with a high degree of accuracy, as "above middle class average." When there are several such blocks adjacent to one another, it is generally safe to assume that these blocks taken together constitute a "better than average" middle class kind of neighborhood. This procedure cannot indicate the whereabouts of "new suburban" housing with above average status. In order to locate these, it is necessary to refer to the real estate advertisements in local newspapers. A recently built housing development where the typical house sells for three times the 1950 housing average usually turns out to be "better than" middle class average in social tone.

Having identified the areas in each of the four cities where "above middle class average" housing—both new and old—could be found, we chose fifteen new blocks and fifteen old blocks in each city and charged our interviewers to recruit a contrast woman from each of these blocks. The interviewers were instructed to start at the northeast corner of the assigned block and knock on each door until they were able to secure an interview with a young married woman in the 20-44 age category. In this way, we obtained our 120 interviews from middle class women—thirty from each city, sixty living in older urban neighborhoods, and sixty residing in new suburban residential areas. The social class distribution of middle class women we obtained from this method of selection was 36% "upper" middle and 64% "lower" middle.

The one similarity between the contrast women and working class wives which we expected to obtain from our sampling procedure was similarity in chronological age. We fell somewhat short of this goal: the median age of the FBG reader is 30, while that of the middle class women in the sample is 35. Any contrary effects of this five year age differential are somewhat vitiated by this fact: the middle class women generally did not marry until three or four years later in their careers than did working class women, and as large a percentage of them still have young children—not yet of school age—living in their homes. Thus, the middle class women and the somewhat younger working class women in our sample are at practically the same stage in family creation and household establishment.

SOCIAL CLASS PLACEMENT

A major concern throughout this report is with the social class identity of the respondents in our study. This interest in social classification is of particular relevance in the present study, inasmuch as we are concerned with characterizing the consumption style and motivations of a certain group of American women.

The method employed in this study to place respondents into social class categories is a modification and expansion of the procedure known as the Index of Status Characteristics. A full account of this procedure, popularly called the "Warner I.S.C.", is contained in the book, *Social Class in America*, written by W. Lloyd Warner and associates. The modification of the procedure employed here was first tried in the University of Chicago's Study of Adult Life in Kansas City, and has since been used extensively at Social Research, Inc. (This method has been tentatively entitled the Coleman Index of Urban Status—I.U.S.)

The I.S.C. procedure for class placement relied on information about a respondent's occupation and source of income, the quality of his housing, and the social reputation of his residential neighborhood to produce an estimate of social class status. The I.U.S. goes beyond these facts, and in addition, assesses information about the educational background of both husband and wife and the family's religious preference, formal social affiliations, and friendship choices. The I.U.S., then, rates a respondent on six status characteristics:

household head's occupation, reputation of neighborhood, quality of housing, educational background of husband and wife (two separate ratings), and associational behavior (formal club and religious memberships and informal friendships).

For each of these six status characteristics there is a seven-step scale, along which individuals are rated. The top point on the scale— a rating of "1"—implies upper-class-like behavior in that particular status characteristic, while the lowest point on the scale (or a rating of "7") signifies lowest-lower-class-like behavior. This scaling principle can best be illustrated by referring to the occupation scale. Whenever an individual is an executive of a large company and his salary is above $25,000 a year, he is given a "1" rating on the occupation scale, because research has shown that the majority of such executives are in the upper class socially as well as economically. On the other hand, whenever an individual is an unskilled worker, a ditch-digger, or common laborer, he is assigned a "7" rating on the occupation scale, because research has shown that most of these individuals are in the lowest class socially. In the middle reaches of the occupation scale a "4" rating signifies lower-than-middle-class-like occupation behavior —and is given to department store clerks, office bookkeepers, highly skilled technical workers, railroad conductors and plant foremen. Also near the middle on the occupation scale are carpenters, mechanics, electricians, and plumbers—men generally regarded as having "average working class occupation" and therefore assigned a "5" rating on the occupation scale. The same principle in rating was applied to each of the other scales. A "5" rating on any one of them implies average-working-class behavior with respect to that variable, whether it be neighborhood, housing, educational background, or club membership.

The final class placement of a respondent was made after the total score was added up from these six separate ratings. In adding up this total score the occupation rating and the associational behavior rating were weighted doubly, though each of the other ratings were only counted in once.

By employing this Index of Urban Status procedure in placing our respondents, we were able to "socially locate" the contrast women in either the upper middle class (36%) or the lower middle class (64%). Every now and then in our report we have separated off the higher-status 36% of the middle class cases from the others in order to compare the working class women with only those middle class women of clearly superior status. In such instances, we have labeled the contrast women appropriately, calling them "above average middle class women."

ANALYSIS OF THE INTERVIEW

The data and conclusions which have been presented on their daily lives, patterns of social interaction, and consumption goals result from the FBG readers' answers to seventy different questions. The information we needed for this survey was of greater scope than could possibly be encompassed within a single interview. As a result we were forced to gather a less-than-complete picture of the life of each individual whom we interviewed. We were only able to sample a few goals, attitudes, and habit patterns from each of our respondents. We developed three different interview plans—employing alternate forms within two of these three main interview schedules.

The main bulk of each interview was devoted to conversational type questions which probed into the respondents' (whether FBG readers or contrast women) social behavior and personal attitudes. The first interview guide relied almost exclusively upon these conversational questions to explore the personal lives, the "social world," and some consumption habits of the respondents. Included in this interview were some projective-type questions which were used in personality diagnosis, as explained below.

In the second guide, the emphasis shifted toward more objective measurement of attitudes about various social forms and institutions. In this guide conversational questions were interspersed with multiple choice objective questions—although each of these multiple choice questions became a conversational question once the choice had been made, as we tried to ascertain what rationale lay behind each choice.

The third guide also combined objective questions with conversational questions, emphasizing this time the respondents' goals and taste in consumption. In both the second and third interview schedules, there were projective questions, some TAT pictures, and some sentence completions.

The use of alternate forms on each main guide was dictated by the necessity of keeping interviewing time per respondent to less than two hours. Consequently, such questions as "What do you do on your vacations?" or "How do you celebrate the various holidays?"—which were regarded as less important than "Describe your daily routine"—were given to only half as many respondents. Whereas, we asked 200 women about their daily routines, we asked only 100 about either their holidays or vacations.

The data and the conclusions were drawn from several different questions and these questions were usually located in two or more guides. In consequence, we can say that all of the major conclusions about the study sample—such as their social life, their attitudes toward religion, their relationships with husband, children, and other people, etc., are based on material gathered from at least 320 of them, and usually from all 480 working class women in our sample. This procedure of drawing from several different questions, located on two or more interview guides, for the conclusions with respect to any given topic was as much an inevitable by-product of our research methods as it was the result of a deliberately conceived plan.

Let us illustrate the procedure described in the preceding paragraph by taking the section on the relationship to children as a case in point.

226

We expected that most of our material from the first interview guide which could be relevant to this problem would come out of the first four questions, where the women had been asked to describe their daily routines (including a sub-question on "What do your children do?"), their typical weekends, and the effect of the seasonal cycle on these habits. Into the second guide, we had inserted an objective question about theories of child-rearing, as well as a question on the division of parental responsibility for child-rearing. In the third guide we placed a question asking the respondent to tell about her family, including a probe on "what the children are like."

Indeed, from each of these questions we elicited much valuable information on the mother's relationship to her children, and the dynamic center of her interaction with them. For example, the central importance of the children in the working class mother's life emerged very clearly in the role which she assigned them while reciting her daily routine. So, too, did her choice of happiness and morality as the goal for child-rearing reveal how her deeply felt indulgence toward them was mixed with a fear that her children might not turn out as well (or as "good") as she might wish.

Our conclusions about the working class women's attitudes toward their children were not based solely on these questions. Actually, a number of our most useful insights emerged as by-products from other questions. Throughout the questions on participation in formal social institutions—clubs and churches—or recreational experiences, we found the FBG readers citing a desire to devote primary attention to their children as the reason why they found no time or available energy for these other pursuits. We observed them caught in the ambivalent situation on feeling "tied down" by their children, yet being so deeply involved in their children's well-being and fearing the effect of any disinvolvement, that they could not possibly escape being "tied down."

Quite incidentally we learned and confirmed ideas about the working class woman's means of dealing with her children, through gifts rather than goals, from replies to a question on the "expenditures which give you the most pleasure." The contrast women on the other hand, and in answer to another question, very rarely gave expression to this kind of purchasing pleasure. Instead, these women cited as the money "most beneficially spent in the long run" that which was saved for their children's educations or spent on so-called "worthwhile" experiences for the children. This lack of interest by the working class mothers over the nature of the experiences which their children received from the wider world, was also reflected in their rejection of "near a school with nice children" as an important consideration in choice of neighborhoods.

Also, we learned about these women's concern over their children's happiness from their answers to many questions on consumption habits and tastes. Time and again, the asnwers of working class women revealed that an ever-present issue in their purchasing behavior was the

227

sub-conscious question: "How will this affect my children's attitudes toward me?"

This is probably sufficient illustration for our point: that the data and conclusions in each main section were drawn from several different questions—some of which were directly calculated to elicit the pertinent information, and others of which gave it to us co-incidentally.

In many instances, where questions from two or three different guides were relevant to a single issue, the questions on the earlier guides were "pilot-type" and were used to develop hypotheses for later tests. The questions on the subsequent guides were phrased to specifically test these hypotheses. This was particularly true in the case of the multiple-choice objective questions in the second major guide. For example, after we had read the FBG reader's descriptions of their "typical" days, we concluded that their husbands' occupations were of relatively little interest to them, or else that their husbands did not discuss "the job" with them. In the light of these findings, we hypothesized that they would not feel that a wife's role in her husband's career involved much more than doing a good job of housecleaning or simply being a respectable wife. We deliberately constructed the alternate choices to the objective questions, "How do you think a wife can be the biggest help to her husband in his work?" in such a way as to test this hypothesis. The results bore out our tentative estimate of the situation.

The objective question on "the kind of people with whom you most enjoy spending your time" was also built on the basis of some assumptions developed from answers received in the first interview guide. After scanning the descriptions our working class respondents gave to the question, "What people do you see most frequently?" we concluded that an unusual number of them had given an answer which said in effect, "We are clannish people and mostly it's relatives that we visit." We felt that a quantitative question could provide us with a simple index to some of the more complicated patterns which emerged from the open-ended inquiry into people-preferences. Actually, by following a method of question analysis called "content analysis" (which will be discussed briefly later) we were able to conclude that relatives, on the whole, were more frequently preferred by working class women than by middle class women—but a large measure of time consuming interpretive judgment enters into this method. By allowing the respondents to describe or characterize themselves, however, we pass the interpretation over to the respondents and reduced our own task to the more quantitative and objective one of counting their answer choices. In this case, the more objective method merely confirmed the hypotheses.

Almost invariably we attached an open-ended type question to these multiple-choice objective questions. This was done for two reasons. In the first place, we felt that the job of choice-making was rendered less difficult for the respondents if they were allowed to modify any choice they might make. For example, most of the respondents found the idea of a wife "taking an interest in her husband's work" somewhat attractive, even though they felt that this was not her most important contribution to the husband's career. When we told the respondent that she "may not completely agree with any one of these choices, but choose one, and then tell us how you might change the statement to better express your point of view" we made it easier for her to select one maximally attractive response to the exclusion of other somewhat attractive responses: in short, we let her have her cake, and eat it too, or more accurately, we let her sample a bite from each cake as long as she would tell us which one she thought tasted better.

The second advantage of attaching an open-ended probe to a multiple-choice question is in the clarification of the rationale behind any choice made. The best illustration of this advantage appeared in the answers to the question on "which of several neighborhood considerations is most important?" A large number of respondents in both classes of respondents selected the "neighborhood where the more substantial kind of citizen lives" as their choice. The motivation for this choice and the definition of "substantial" appeared to vary greatly between the two groups of women. Whereas, the middle class women were really attracted by the notion of "substantial people who are well-educated and civic leaders . . . so that the schools will automatically have a fine type of youngster," the working class women generally qualified their endorsement by saying, "as long as substantial doesn't just mean wealthy people—if it means just ordinary, decent people then I'd like that, because I don't want to live next to a den of thieves, but I don't want to try to keep up with the Joneses either."

In this instance, as well as in many others, the responses to multiple-choice questions cannot be adequately interpreted without knowledge of the motivation behind the choice and the definition given by the respondents to the words with which they are registering agreement.

In our analysis of the answers given to open-ended or conversational-type questions we followed the "content analysis" procedure. According to the rules of the procedure, the analyst tries to categorize the answers given to any particular question. Admittedly, this effort involves considerable interpretation, but the analyst is aware of this and strives to categorize in accord with the "facts" rather than any "wish to prove his hypothesis." An example or two will illustrate this procedure.

The analyst initially reads through a sampling of answers given to a particular question, such as "how your weekends generally go," in order to ascertain the important themes which are relevant to his study. In this case, we readily observed that many readers felt "weekend is no different from the weekday—all monotonous." Another segment of readers felt that the weekend was perhaps busier, both because the husband was home and required additional attention and because Sunday was given over to relative visiting. Meanwhile, several middle class women reported that the weekend was time for "relaxation" and "for the whole family to do something together."

Several ways to categorize the answers suggested themselves then: do the respondents feel that the weekends are "the same" or "different" from the weekdays? Do the respondents feel that the weekends are "busier" or a "time for relaxation?" Do the respondents describe the weekends as a period for interaction with relatives (i.e., the extended clan), or is it a period for "family togetherness" (meaning only the immediate family of parents and children)? Of course, not all answers fell into one of these either-or categories. Some of them did not even touch on these concerns, or an ambivalent attitude was manifest.

After these answers have been categorized we can ascertain two things about a study group: the dominant trend in its responses to a given question or issue, and the strength of these approaches in comparison with other groups. In this case, we learned that the dominant trend for the working class women was to feel that the weekends are "the same as their weekdays," while the contrast women were more apt to feel that they were "different." Of course, there were women in each group who felt that the weekends were "different." One such difference, noted more frequently by the working class women than by the middle class women, was related to the amount of relative visiting which occurred during the weekends.

Another question which was submitted to this method of content analysis was the one on "What ways of using your money you feel will be the most important to you in the long run?" The most common responses were focused on such answers as: "saving money for a rainy day," "saving up money for down payment on a house," "saving money for the children's education," "any money spent providing the children with worthwhile experiences," "money spent on labor-saving appliances put into our homes." The answers actually given by our respondents were not always this neatly stated, so that an element of judgment was required to determine which answer was being given, and which was the dominant theme in the response.

The working class women were more often placed in the category of "saving for a rainy day" than in any other. However, slightly less than a majority were so categorized. Still in all, this proportion was much greater for working class women than for the middle class women, so that the former can be readily characterized as more deeply concerned over this use of their money than are the latter women. We interpreted this concern as growing out of, and reflecting, their preoccupation with the hazardous course of life. The consistency of the answers, as they appeared in question after question, contributed to the total outline of our interpretation; in fact, an interpretation is usually built upon a coincidence of conclusions simultaneously reached from a variety of separate sources.

There is one area, touched upon only tangentially in this study, where the methods of qualitative, motivational research were particularly relevant or useful. This is the area of the actual spending habits of our respondents.

The classical methods of budget research require observation of the purchasing behavior and careful record-keeping through a period of time. We were neither equipped nor prepared to engage in this kind of research. We attempted to learn whatever we could about our respondents' expenditure patterns by asking them to list their expenses for a single month (the one previous to that in which the interview occurred). Apparently, we learned more about the inadequacy of their recollection than about their actual expenses. We certainly discovered that the majority of women are able to readily specify only their housing payments and food costs for any given period of time. We learned that a large percentage of middle class women enjoy denying any knowledge of "where their money goes" while a correspondingly large proportion of working class women feel that they ought to have some idea about how their money has been spent—muddle-headed as these ideas might, in fact, be. Thus, we were able to utilize the answers to a question, even though the specific, factual goals planned for the question were not attained.

After we had learned that obtaining an actual record of expense patterns was beyond the ability of our techniques, we settled upon a projection procedure as the most helpful way of understanding the respondents' attitudes toward distributing their incomes. In the third guide, we asked our respondents to "imagine how they might spend $5,000 in a year"—if they had it, spreading it over twelve important "budget items." The imaginary income of $5,000 a year was chosen because such an income is fairly typical for FBG readers (the real average seems to be $4,500). Interestingly enough, when these imaginary expenditures were averaged the amounts women felt they would like to spend on each item came quite close to actual behavior reported in the classical budget studies. The imaginary expense patterns of the middle class women were less in tune with "actual behavior" than were those of the FBG women, but this might be expected in view of the fact that they are more experienced in spending $5,000 a year than are the contrast women (whose husbands more often earn $8,000 or $10,000 per year). Perhaps research gets closer to the "truth" of an individual's behavior when it asks for "imaginary" samples of behavior rather than actual recollections!

Each interview contributed something toward every major point in the study—it either furnished suggestive data or contributed toward the "proving out" of hypotheses. Many times the most useful insights on any given issue emerged "accidentally," as it were, in the answers to questions which were more essentially directed toward other issues. Some questions on each interview piloted us towards hypotheses which were more directly tested in later guides.

231

SPECIAL METHODS FOR THE STUDY OF PERSONALITY

The principal non-interview procedure for the study of personality used in this research is known as the Thematic Apperception Technique. It consists in having the respondent tell stories to pictures which depict a variety of human and non-human situations. The depictions are ambiguous in nature, so that in making up stories the individual necessarily attributes actions, motives, and personal qualities which derive from his own personality. The materials for analysis consist not only of *what* is said but *how* it is said. Further, through acquaintance with many stories to the picture, the investigator is attuned to what is *customarily* said. In the light of this, each new story encountered requires the investigator also to attend to what might have been said but was left *unsaid*.

The technique was originally devised in 1935 by Professors Henry A. Murray and Christiana Morgan of Harvard University. Since that time, it has been used in hundreds of research studies by many investigators, and particularly has been intensively studied and developed by Professor William E. Henry and his students at the University of Chicago. In his recent volume, Professor Henry points out how the stories told are a complex product of the storyteller's personality, simultaneously tapping many facets:

> On the one hand, fantasy in storytelling derives from the less conscious and less structured aspects of the individual's personality. To these areas of personality, the rules of logic and propriety do not apply. On the other hand, the task set for the storyteller is one that requires him to organize his fantasy into a recognizable story form and to verbalize this story for the inspection of others. To this latter requirement, the rules of logic and propriety do apply *at least those particular rules of logic and propriety that the subject has found applicable to his own life.* Thus, interpretation of thematic apperception must take place within these overlapping frameworks: the more nearly private and less conscious motives and generalizations derived from past life experiences, and the public, socially determined, more nearly rational framework of convention.[1] [Italics added]

Considerable previous work, conducted by both Dr. Henry and by Social Research, Inc., has demonstrated the fruitfulness of studying groups as well as individuals with this method. The procedure is essentially very simple. It is first necessary that the sample studied be defined by some socially meaningful characteristic. In the present study, of course, the core sample consists of women who are predominantly working class in social status. To facilitate comparison, a

---

1 Henry, William E. *The Analysis of Fantasy: The Thematic Apperception Technique in the Study of Personality.* New York: John Wiley and Sons, 1956.

smaller contrast sample of women who are of white collar and upper middle class status was also studied.

All the stories to a card are read and examined for their communalities. These are noted, and they then serve as hypotheses to be corrected, corroborated, or expanded in the light of the stories to succeeding cards. This procedure is repeated for all the stories to all the cards, and for each group.

While every story differs at least slightly from every other, as any human datum is in some sense unique, broad gauge similarities do emerge and are the foundation for generalized statements concerning the personality of the group as a whole. While any particular woman may differ from a particular asserted characteristic of the group as a whole, the personality of the group is described in the statements about them. The logic is identical with that of drawing a line through a set of points plotted on a graph. Such a line describes the central tendency of the phenomenon, even though all of the points do not fall exactly on the line.

In the present study, stories were obtained to 32 different cards. Of these, seven were used in the pilot study, and the remainder in the larger study. The cards were selected from three published series and from two unpublished series. The selection is designed to meet these requirements:

(1) *Degree and kind of ambiguity.* It is desirable to include pictures which range from relatively familiar to quite unfamiliar situations. Another dimension of ambiguity is that in some pictures the sex and approximate age of the depicted figures is quite clear, whereas in others these attributes are unclear.

(2) *Sampling of depicted situations.* The cards should include a range of human situations and relationships. Thus, there should be cards which have only one person; cards which have two persons of the same sex; cards with two persons of opposite sex; cards showing a group of persons. There should be cards showing an older and younger person together, and cards which depict contemporaries. In addition, it is desirable to have at least one card in which no people at all are visible.

Despite the wide range of data necessary in the study, it was impossible, of course, to administer 25 cards to any one person. Our procedure was to administer three cards to each woman interviewed, these being introduced approximately midway in the interview. The order of administration within each set of three cards was varied from woman to woman so that no single card was always presented in the same position.

The pictures used in the research, with a description of each, are listed below, identified by the series to which each belongs and the number it bears in the series.

233

THEMATIC APPERCEPTION TEST (HARVARD SERIES)

Card No.	*Description*
3BM	On the floor against a couch is the huddled form of a person with head bowed. An object, frequently seen as a revolver, is on the floor.
3GF	A young woman is standing with downcast head, her face covered with her right hand. Her left is stretched forward against a wooden door.
4	A woman is clutching the shoulders of a man whose face and body are averted as if he were trying to pull away from her.
5	A middle aged woman is standing on the threshold of a half-opened door looking into a room.
7GF	An older woman is sitting on a sofa close beside a girl, speaking or reading to her. The girl, who holds a doll in her lap, is looking away.
8GF	A young woman sits with her chin in her hand looking off into space.
9GF	A young woman with a magazine and a purse in her hand looks from behind a tree at another young woman in a party dress running along a beach.
10	A woman's head against a man's shoulder.
12F	The portrait of a young woman. An old woman with a shawl over her head in the background.
13MF	A young man is standing with downcast head buried in his arm. Behind him is the figure of a woman lying in bed.
18GF	A woman with her hands at the throat or shoulders of another person against a bannister at foot of a stairway.
19	A weird picture of cloud formations overhanging a snow-covered cabin in the country.
SRI variant of 13B	In the original, a little boy is sitting on the doorstep of a log cabin. Our artist drew a similar picture, substituting a little girl for the little boy.

MICHIGAN PICTURE TEST (UNIVERSITY OF MICHIGAN)

2	Two rural-looking children. Young boy is standing with straw hat in hand, looking at girl whose head is turned away.

8G   Young girl in pigtails sitting at a school desk, her face propped in her hand. A part of the child and desk in front of her are visible.

11B   A woman in apron on doorstep faces a policeman and young boy.

TAVISTOCK OBJECT RELATIONS TEST
(These are all shaded and silhouette)

A2   Two figures are outlined. Background is shaded.

AG   A group of figures is dimly outlined. Setting exceedingly vague.

B1   A figure on a staircase before an open door leading into a bedroom. Bed and dresser are visible.

BG   A group of figures visible in an arch of a wall. A single figure is visible in a second arch.

UNPUBLISHED PICTURES

From a series used by Dr. Theron Alexander of Florida State University:

   Two children with expressions of pleasure looking at something.

From a series used by Dr. Benjamin Wright of the University of Chicago:

   A group of four girls before a building. One seems to be pointing at another.

   A young woman seated on a bed very close to and looking up into the face of a man who is smiling down at her (from a publicity picture for the movie, *Claudia*).

   A girl or young woman whose skirt is being torn and pulled from one side by an older woman and from the other by a figure whose hand only is seen, as she appears to try to keep it down. (A *Life Magazine* picture of a French collaborator with the Nazis.)

The following pictures were used in the pilot study. All were from the Object Relations Test.

A1   A solitary figure is outlined against an indefinite background.

A3   Two persons together and one some distance away are dimly outlined.

B2   Two persons are silhouetted close together beneath a tree before a building.

B3   A man and woman close together in a lighted doorway, while a third person is evident in the shadows.

C1   A kitchen scene, with a figure dimly visible at the window.

C3   Three persons, two seated and one standing, in what appears to be a living room or library.

CG   A group of persons of indeterminate number apparently at the foot of a public building-type of staircase on which falls the shadow of a person.

In the pilot study, the stories to pictures provided the principal source of data for the description of personality. This was also true in the larger study. In the latter, however, several ancillary projective techniques were also utilized, providing expanded and corroborative material. These techniques were:

(1) *Draw-a-person.* A small group of women was asked to draw a person and then to draw a person of the opposite sex to the first. This technique has the advantage of being non-verbal and consequently provides a somewhat different type of corroborative material. The drawings were analyzed by a member of the Social Research, Inc. staff who had no other connection with this study.

(2) *Projective questions.* This is a type of question which invites the respondent to talk about imaginary persons or imaginary situations rather than directly about herself. Three of these were used; each one was presented to a different group of women, each consisting of 38 working class women and 12 middle class women. These questions are:

> Let's imagine for a minute that two women are talking who have been good friends a long time—and they can talk quite easily together, and often discuss their problems and difficulties. One woman tells the other that she has a problem with her husband. Imagine what this problem might be, how it came about, and what the other woman would offer in the way of advice.

> Imagine you are having a dream, and in this dream you meet someone whom you don't know and have never seen. He will ask you something, and you want to give a good answer. People do often dream about being asked questions, you know. I'll give you the question and you say simply whatever comes to your mind, and give as many different answers as possible. So, in this dream this person asks you "Who are you?" and you say . . . . (PROBE FOR AT LEAST THREE ANSWERS.)

> Imagine that a magician would change you into something. You would be allowed to select which form you wanted to take, but you could no longer be a human being. You would choose, though, what you wanted to be. What would you most want to be? Why would you choose that?

INDEX

Alexander, Dr. Theron, 235
Allen, Frederick Lewis, 17
American Home, 188

Bakke, E. Wright, xi
"blue collar," 15, 184 et seq.

Carter, Hugh, 68
"cash purchases," 156
Chicago, 219, 220, 221
Chicago Tribune, ix
  apparel study, 197-99
Chicago, University of, 232, 235
Church, attitude toward, 121 et seq.
Clubs and associations,
  attitude toward, 114 et seq.
Coleman Index of Urban Status
  (I. U. S.), 224
Consumer preferences, 173 et seq.
  appliances, 176
  automobile, 181
  carpet, 180
  food, 173-74
  furnishings, 176
  housing, 174
  labor-saving devices, 179
  television, 180, 182
Consuming style, 21
Consumption priorities, 169 et seq.
  food, 170-71
  furnishings, 171
  housing, 171
  insurance, 172
  recreation and vacations, 172, 181
  savings, 171

Decorator taste, 187 et seq.
  clothes, 197-98
  food, 198-99
  furnishings, 190-97
  housing, 187-89

"envelope" economy, 155

Family Behavior Group, 21, 57,
  219 et seq.
Flesch, Dr. Rudolph, x

Florida State University, 235
Food deprivation, 170
Friends, 103 et seq.
  attitudes of middle-class and working-
    class wives compared, 103-04
Furniture styles, 192

Galbraith, John K., 17
Gardner, Burleigh, B., 21
General Electric, 220
Glick, Paul C., 68
Griswold, Erwin, viii

Habit lag, ix
Harvard Series, 23, 232, 234
Henry, William E., 232
Hollingshead, August B., 19
House Beautiful, 189
Household Finance Corp., viii
House purchase,
  attitude toward, 158-59
Hunger fear, 170

Index of Status Characteristics,
  (I. S. C.), 224
Index of Urban Status, Coleman
  (I. U. S.), 224

Johnson, Arno H., viii, ix

Levy, Dr. Sidney J., 56
Louisville, 219, 220
Lower-status person, ix, 225

Macfadden Publications, viii, ix, 21
Macfadden Women's Group, x
Marriage, 67 et seq.
  attitudes of middle-class and
    working-class wives compared, 68
Martineau, Pierre, ix
Michigan, University of, Series, 23,
  234-35
Middle-status person, ix, 225
Motherhood, 88 et seq.
  attitudes of middle-class and
    working-class wives compared, 94, 102
Morgan, Christiana, 232

Murray, Henry A., 232

"name brands," 165

Object Relations Test, 235

Personality,
    working-class wife, 42 et seq.
P.T.A., attitude toward, 119

Redlich, Frederick C., 19

Sears, Roebuck & Co., vii, viii
Social Research, Inc., x, xi, 21, 56, 197,
    219, 232

Tacoma, 219, 220, 221
Tavistock Institute Series, 23, 235
Thermatic Apperception Test
    (TAT), 23, 226, 232
Thompson, J. Walter Co., viii
"time payments,"
    attitude toward, 156, 157

"tin can" economy, 155, 159
Trenton, 219, 220
True Experience, 221
True Love Stories, 221
True Romance, 221
True Story, 126 et seq., 221
"typical" day
    working-class wife, 26-33
    middle-class women, 33-35

Village Pump, The, 127
Vacations,
    working-class wife, 38-39
    middle-class women, 40

Warner, W. Lloyd, xi, 224
Weekend,
    working-class wife, 35-37
    middle-class women, 37
"white collar," 15, 37
Wright, Dr. Benjamin, 235